THE LOVELY REED

You must do this work with love or you fail.
You don't have to think, but you must love.
–John Muir, How to Keep Your Volkswagen Alive

The Lovely Reed

An Enthusiast's Guide to Building Bamboo Fly Rods

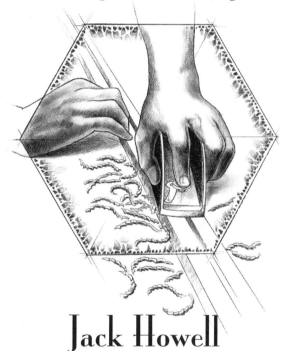

Jack Howell

Foreword by Glenn Brackett

PRUETT PUBLISHING COMPANY
BOULDER, COLORADO

Printed in the United States
10 9 8 7 6 5 4 3 2 1

Library of Congress Cataloging-in-Publication data

Howell, Jack.
  The lovely reed: an enthusiast's guide to building bamboo fly rods /
Jack Howell.
    cm.
    Includes bibliographical references and index.
    ISBN 0-87108-868-1 (hc)
    Fishing rods—Design and construction. 2. Bamboo. I. Title.
  SH452.H68   1998
  688.7'9124—dc21   97-51371
                                                                   CIP

Cover design by Jody Chapel and Kathleen McAffrey
Interior book design by Kathleen McAffrey, Starr Design
Book composition by Lyn Chaffee
Illustrations by Rod Walinchus
Photographs by Jack Howell
Cover illustration by Mark Bremmer

*My dad was a science teacher
who always said,
"If all else fails, read the instructions."
This book is for him.*

CONTENTS

FOREWORD

Jack Howell has honored me with the opportunity to cast the opening line about something we both share as very dear, the craft of bamboo rod making. It has long been known to those of us who share a passion for this art that no book will ever be written that fully expresses what the craft is all about. However, Howell has come as close as I feel one can, has tried to crack the impossible "lovely reed" nut, and has done well in the effort. The book lives up to all my expectations in title and text.

Much has been written, and more shall be written, about making bamboo fly rods. But in reading *The Lovely Reed* I was struck by the realization that virtually everything in print on the craft has been written by the hobbyist. With the days of the quality production rod shop gone, it's the hobbyist who keeps the craft alive today. This book honors the rod-building hobbyist and the traditions of the craft. From its simple, quiet beginnings, the craft exploded in a roaring, pre-graphite industry where every imaginable aspect of design and technique was put to the test. Now, once again the domain of the artisan, the craft has returned to its humble origins: a basement, a weekend, some hand tools, a hand-planed rod, a craftsman.

With careful handling of the means and methods of bamboo rod making as well as of the underlying myths, metaphors, and mysteries of the craft, Howell walks the weekend hobbyist through every step of the rod-making process with understanding and compassion, i.e.: Keep the bandaides near and an experienced fellow of the craft close at hand. He has sifted through information, refined it, and states clearly what is important, from rod-building tools, the workshop, skill and technique, to attitude. He has done his best to orchestrate a work that, I'm sure, will make you whistle and hum happily while you plane, plane away. This fine book has everything you need to begin and complete the task. It is an honest, honorable work that challenges and encourages you to complete the course, your first rod.

Man needs to do things connected to ritual, one reason so many of us are drawn to the angling life. Like the sport that inspires the craft, bamboo rod-making is rife with ritual. It demands, above all else, respect for its ritual and Howell teaches this well. He leads the reader to the ritual gradually, drawing on clear, meaningful language, research, and experience to help you make your first rod. Howell encourages participation and he inspires you to become part of a unique fellowship, where two hands remain the primary tools for creating something exquisite, something no machine can match. No matter how great one's enthusiasm or how sophisticated one's tools, the craftsman's hands are ultimately the deciding factor for turning bamboo into fly rod successfully. In this respect, there is a Zen-like quality to the craft. In some way, the discipline and ritual of the work touches deep inner chords, where one experiences an evolving rich self-meaning. Who knows, you might be guided by some universal rod-building force in the bamboo dust of the cosmos! For me, the physical work becomes soul work: making rods turns into making the soul sing, rods by rote becomes rods by inspiration. This is what soul work is—the essence of creativity, work that is inspired and spiritual. Howell keeps you true to the path, centered in practice.

Solace in the sawdust is a given. And without a doubt, you'll experience dark moments of frustration. Howell does himself credit here by admitting he has not got all the answers nor a foolproof method. Even this exceptionally thorough how-to manual cannot anticipate all the questions a reader will have, and Howell reassures us that for such questions the answers will come "by doing," through experience gained. In my beginning years of rod making, my mentor, Gary Howells (no relation to Jack), responded to my river of questions with, "Glenn. After you build your first one hundred rods, come ask me again." Here, Jack Howell encourages the less experienced rod makers in much the same way: forgive mistakes and imperfections, for they are necessary experience in the craft that no book can provide.

Whether or not you take up this craft, Howell's book will help you appreciate the passion and rewards that are part of it. There are no secrets, *just damn hard work,* and you'll find that there are many ways to "skin a cane." I am not a hand-plane rod craftsman. My experience lies with machining. So,

I'm out of water when it comes to hand-planing techniques. But after reading this book I was moved to want to try hand planing because I feel it keeps you in touch with the magic of the cane, the lovely reed, as no other approach can. I've seen very fine rods produced by the hundreds with primitive hand tools, jigs, etc., with speed that even my sophisticated machines can't match.

After learning to cultivate patience and experience, the next lesson in rod making is to understand that there are no absolutes. What works best is a simple approach; try to stay away from the elaborate or the unnecessary. Always remember that you are transforming something natural and unique into a fishin' pole, first and foremost. Perfection cannot be achieved with something natural. The condition you may be selecting for on one hand may be selecting against another on the other hand. What Chinese winds once moved and strengthened is now being moved and shaped by the hand in a redefined form—cane pole to cane rod. Nature's lovely reed lovingly modified for our needs.

Which brings me to the only point on which my opinion differs from Howell's, and that is that bamboo is less durable than graphite. Over my many years in this business I have seen first hand that bamboo is a more durable and forgiving material than any other I've worked with. Thin-walled graphite is more vulnerable than the solid make-up of bamboo. Once, I lost four rods (three graphite, one bamboo) in a boating accident, which put them all on the bottom of a river for two weeks. All four rods were recovered about 1/8-mile downstream. The bamboo survived intact, where only handles with reels remained of the graphites. For myself, I don't see a graphite rod outliving bamboo, and I make rods in all materials, so there is no partiality here.

Between the covers of this book I found a well-written presentation and the spirit of a man deeply in touch with his craft and with life. There has to be passion in rod making—that's what gives it character, history, and soul. I am grateful to Jack Howell for giving body and soul to our craft. He has bared his bamboo soul to share something special with us all. It reminds me of the same generous spirit that shines through Harry Middleton's *On the Spine of Time,* where the character Tewksbury speaks to the author at streamside:

> I'm allergic to synthetics of any kind, whether they be blended in my underwear or my fly rod. Dacron, polyester, nylon, all those things are a danger to my health, happiness, and peace of mind. . . . Cane is an honest material, reliable. It is loyal in the same sense that a fine leather jacket is loyal. Both improve with the elements and passing time.

While *The Lovely Reed* will not be the last word on this subject, I will venture to say that it has the substance to make it a classic in its own time. It deserves a place alongside those time-honored works we all love. The greatest compliment Jack Howell will receive will be to dog ear, finger print, and fill these pages with bamboo dust. I suggest you get two copies, one for the library, the other for the rod bench. This book will forever be a useful, important reference to the craft of bamboo rod building.

—Glenn Brackett

PREFACE

The idea for this book, or rather the determination to begin it, came in the spring of 1993. Dale Darling and I were sitting in Bob and Tony's Pizza in Estes Park, Colorado, after a day on the Thompson River, talking about books. One of the things Dale and I have in common is a fascination with books, language and writing, and along the way it came up that although I had an itch to write a book about bamboo rod building, I wasn't sure it was needed. After all, Wayne Cattanach's book had just been published, Claude Kreider's book had been reprinted recently, and there was always a chance that, as soon as I finished my book, Winchester Press would run off another ten thousand copies of the Garrison-Carmichael *A Master's Guide.* Who needed another book on rod building?

"That's not a realistic question," said Dale. "Who *needs* another book on fly tying, and how many are published each year? An enthusiast never has enough information."

True enough, and this is a book by an enthusiast for enthusiasts. My own ideas about bamboo rod building were sifted and compiled from all the books I could get my hands on as well as from dozens of conversations with rod builders. No one author or builder, regardless of how fine his rods were

or how willing he was to share, could tell me everything I wanted to know. Sure, there are a finite number of components and processes involved in building a rod, but leaving the matter there is like saying that all a batter has to do is hit the baseball. It's true, of course, but there's more to it than that.

There's another aspect to how-to books. One of my favorites is John Muir's *How to Keep Your Volkswagen Alive.* I've never owned a Volkswagen, but I picked the book up more or less by chance while browsing in a bookstore and immediately was hooked. In addition to dishing out plenty of hard information and sticking like glue to the theme that "anyone can do this," Muir's book exudes a sense of humor and calmness, and encourages an attitude of devotion in tackling even the grimiest tasks. It places great emphasis on paying attention to what you're doing, not just because things turn out better that way, but because what you're doing at the moment—say, scraping off a head gasket—is part of your life, and it would be a shame to waste it by hating it or doing it poorly. Working on Volkswagens was a meditation for Muir, partly because he liked working with his hands, but also because he believed in Volkswagens, in their simplicity and integrity, in what he regarded as their magic.

Bamboo rods have become this same sort of vehicle for me, and may, I hope, be the same for you. Building bamboo rods is an engrossing occupation for the hands, an escape for the mind, and, I am convinced, very big medicine on a trout stream. In this book I will present what I have found to be the best way to build a fly rod. However, since needs, resources, and tastes vary, I will try to present the rationale and theory for each facet of rod building in such a way that you can decide whether a method other than mine will better suit your needs. There's a lot of detail in this book because good rod making is a matter of details, though it's not brain surgery. The main idea is to enjoy making an item of fly-fishing tackle that will become yours in a way that nothing else could be. If it is my good fortune to convey a small part of my absorption in the delightful craft of building bamboo rods, my main intention will have been achieved. Best of luck to you.

A quick word about the photos in this book. Most of them are of me doing things, and I'm left-handed. Many of the operations, like straightening nodes or using a lathe, require no particular handedness. Other operations, like wrapping guides, seem best done left to right no matter which hand is dominant. However, I always hold a plane, knife, pencil, or hammer in my left hand, which may make some photos look odd. I thought about reversing the negatives for some of the photos but decided against adding another layer of complexity to an already complex project. I figure if I can deal with a right-handed camera you can deal with a few left-handed photos. Fair enough? Thanks.

ACKNOWLEDGMENTS

Bamboo rod makers are generally outstanding folks. My rod building was helped by the generosity and kindly interest of several makers who took time to answer questions, help solve problems, and volunteer ideas. That these gentlemen have become friends may go without saying, but I'll say it anyway as a partial excuse for shamelessly incorporating their ideas and advice into this book.

Thanks to Wayne Cattanach not only for rod-building advice but also for encouragement, bordering on insistence, that I write this book. And to Mike Clark, who never seemed to mind my hanging around his shop asking questions when he should have been working. And to Ed Hartzell, a dependable and gracious source of information and hospitality. Although I haven't bugged Joe Saracione much lately, he gave me some

great ideas. Daryll Whitehead I owe for just about everything—tapers, guides, advice, and encouragement foremost, but plenty else besides. Thanks also to Bob and Lee Widgren of Los Pinos Custom Rods, who were my first customers and have been unfailing in their support.

Special thanks to Ed and Daryll for their reading of the manuscript and for their many improvements, and to Jim Pruett for his enthusiastic willingness to back this project and his astonishing patience with a first-time author. Thanks to my Mom, Shirley Howell, for advice and encouragement, to my friends Sue Heineman and Barry LaPoint for helping with photos, and to Melissa, for letting me do whatever I wanted. Also to the folks at Goffe Photographic, and to the folks who waited patiently for their rods while I worked on this book.

Believe nothing, no matter where you read it or who said it—even if I have said it—unless it agrees with your own reason and your own common sense.

—Buddha

PART 1

THE BASICS OF
BAMBOO ROD BUILDING

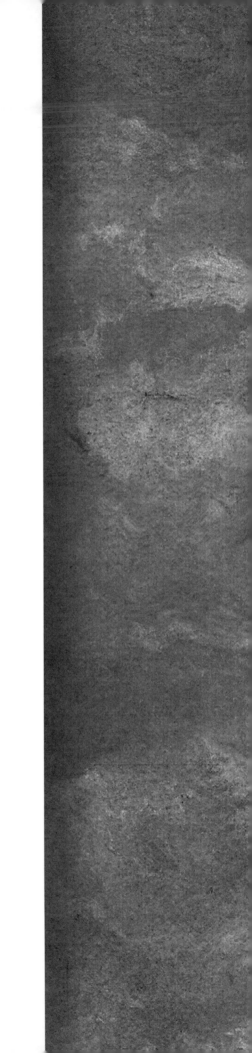

1. THE BAMBOO FLY ROD: QUALITIES AND CHARACTERISTICS

This book is intended to be encouraging to the would-be rod maker. Of course, if you already build rods, you are probably far beyond encouragement. If you are just getting started, you may find the occasional encouraging word helpful, but you most likely are already a member of the choir and don't need a sermon. So for the moment, let's assume you're not committed yet—either you're thinking about building rods or you've picked up this book out of curiosity. Although building bamboo rods isn't for everyone, it *is* a highly satisfying craft. I recommend it to anyone who likes to work with his or her hands and has an interest in fly fishing. Nothing the average fly fisherman can create possesses greater personality or greater intrinsic beauty, or evokes greater pride of ownership. Many people are proud of their possessions, but it should be evident that pride in something you have made with your own hands is different from the kind that, as Russell Chatham says, has to do with "firsthand acquaintanceship with the price sticker."

If you have never fished bamboo rods, you should give them a try. The bamboo rod feels heavy at first, and you're self-conscious about your casting, even though no one is watching. The people who use bamboo rods in the books are described as unhurried, styl-ish casters, so if someone sees you casting with a bamboo rod without the expected style you might feel like a fraud. You have no idea how long it will take to aquire the proper technique. A small fish splashes at your fly, and, preoccupied, you miss him.

After an hour or so, the heft of the rod feels good, and you've begun to sense the rod's rhythm and stopped trying to dictate it. You find that it's pretty hard to underpower a cast and that the rod loads easily, turning the line and leader over with very little effort. And with the line unrolling lazily, there's more time to mend in the air, even to have some fun.

The bamboo rod has surprising power, too. The soft, noodly feel you had expected is absent, and it occurs to you that you're casting every bit as far as you normally do with graphite. You don't feel handicapped in the distance department at all—in fact, you realize that you need bamboo's touch more than you ever needed graphite's power, and you feel a little smug to be in on the secret.

And then, the rod has a certain magnetism. It obviously was made by human hands—split, straightened, milled, glued, sanded, straightened again, and finished—so it's no surprise that it has a distinct personality. Maybe it doesn't happen on the first trip, but eventually you find yourself making a particularly difficult cast, hooking, playing, and landing a particularly large fish, and you're proud of the old rod, that it's still putting out at what would be well past middle age for a human. If you are frank with yourself about these things, you might admit that you are in love. And if you have the right kind of itch, it might occur to you that you could make something like this rod yourself.

Modern Bamboo Rods

Once considered by many to be relics of a fading past, made obsolete by fiberglass and carbon fiber, and used mainly by cranks or people with more money than sense, bamboo fly rods are enjoying a renaissance. In addition to the fine rods still being built by established makers, a new generation of builders has joined the craft. Today's rod maker benefits from several books, a newsletter, classes, conferences, even videos, all of which can, collectively, tell him what he needs to know to make a good rod.

Far from quaint anachronisms, bamboo rods today seem to be beneficiaries of a shift in the tone of fly fishing in recent years. Fly fishing has more or less kept a characteristic genteel, literary undertone, but the relentless march of technology and industry—not to mention population—has made just about every aspect of life, including fly fishing, less pastoral than it was fifty, twenty, even ten years ago. When the notion that technology might be the answer to everything became widespread, it had its effect even on our low-tech, contemplative sport when terms like "state of the art" and "improved" came to be applied to everything from high-power rods to landing nets. Technology made lots of promises. In some cases it delivered, and in graphite rods it delivered in spades. The TV dinner of fly fishing, they were and are lighter, more powerful, and cheaper than bamboo. What more could an angler want? Graphite rods fit snugly into the sporting-

technology marketing program that assumed faster was automatically better. Using a space-age fiber, who couldn't catch more and bigger fish? I recall a magazine advertisement from a leading rod manufacturer that closed a description of perfect stream conditions with, "You've got the right rod. The fish don't have a chance."

Now, I own one of this company's rods, and it's fine. Still, not only do the fish still have as much of a chance as they normally do, I'm not sure an advantage is what I want anyway. Some sportsmen repudiate technology precisely because of the advantages it grants. For instance, some bowhunters are abandoning the compound bow (a deadly weapon in good hands) for longbows and recurves, and others are even making self-bows from native woods.

The last thing I want to do is imply that using a bamboo rod places anyone at a disadvantage. If bamboo rods have a corollary in the pursuit of nonaquatic game, it would have to be the fine double shotgun. Both are guided (but not bound) in their design and construction by tradition; both went into an apparent decline because of the escalating costs of handwork and the availability of cheaper alternatives; and both, though often seen as somehow limiting (double guns in lacking a third shot, bamboo supposedly in lacking the ability to throw an entire fly line), are beautifully evolved and efficient hunting tools, often tailored to their users. Like good double guns, bamboo rods *feel* great; in addition to carrying all the aesthetic advantages of an object lovingly handcrafted from natural materials, they vividly transfer the sensations of the cast, the strike, and the fight.

I prefer bamboo to graphite for all but a few fishing situations, but I'd never attempt to convince anyone to try a bamboo rod with promises of more or bigger fish. Still, people are coming to bamboo all on their own. As you dig into the romance, mythology and literature of fly fishing, sooner or later you run into bamboo. Even anglers and authors who profess to fish nothing but graphite on practical grounds (graphite is better, bamboo is too expensive) leave the impression that bamboo rods are still wonderful. Even if they firmly believe that there's no practical reason for anyone to fish bamboo, they know that lots of good fishermen still do, and they know in their hearts that practicality is a weak defense for anything that has to do with fly fishing.

Besides, bamboo rods have a kind of magic. A lot of people might look askance at this, but I think fly fishers as a group come pretty close to accepting it intuitively. In prehistory, inept hunters starved. Period. Given this dearth of career options, the issue was not skill but worthiness. Hunters had to convince the universal spirit that they were deserving of taking life, and this was the focus of prehunt rituals, including the making of weapons. Perhaps the dim echoes of those beliefs awaken in some of us, along with the urge to hunt (catch-and-release notwithstanding, fishing is hunting). Perhaps that's one reason it's more satisfying to catch fish on flies one has tied oneself, and also why it's more satisfying to fish with a bamboo rod, particularly if it is self-made. Anything that contains at least forty hours of dedicated labor has got to be big medicine.

Ascribing the allure of bamboo rods to a refined atavism may seem far-fetched. I'd just observe that people find magic where they look for it, and bamboo rods have a pretty strong grip on some of us. Although it really does seem as if I've caught more fish with my own bamboo rods, that could be because I've fished more frequently since I started building them, and with greater attention and relish. That is magic enough.

Any serious argument about whether bamboo is better than graphite, however entertaining, is ultimately useless. Anglers vote with their checkbooks, and bamboo is, for whatever reason, making up some lost ground. What's more, a significant number of anglers who began with graphite or fiberglass are getting into bamboo. There are still plenty of folks who started on bamboo and never really fell for graphite, but the recent converts are the future of the craft.

In some respects, that future looks pretty bright. The cost of bamboo has risen, and the curing and handling it receives in China ranges from careless to abysmal, but I don't think the plant itself is inherently better or worse. Good cork is becoming scarce and expensive, but what natural material isn't? The bright part is that the best makers today are making the best rods that have ever been made. More people building rods, more people taking up rod making as a hobby and taking their time, a marketplace more demanding of cosmetic excellence, more information more freely shared, computer-based rod-design tools, and better adhesives all add up to better rods. If you want to learn how to build bamboo rods, these are the good old days.

Arundinaria amabilis: Some Facts About the Best Bamboo

Out of some thousand different varieties of bamboo in the world, none has been found that is better for the purpose of making fly rods than *Arundinaria amabilis,* called Tonkin cane by exporters and tea-stick bamboo by growers. This is a fascinating material, possessing extraordinary strength and elasticity for its weight. Like all the grasses in the bamboo family, the main plant above ground consists of a long hollow tube partitioned at intervals by internal membranes (*septa*) corresponding to external ridges or nodes, with leaf-bearing branches sprouting out of the nodes toward the top of the plant (see Fig. 1.1).

The plant is able to grow to great heights relative to its diameter because of this reinforced tubular structure and because the tube itself is made up of long, fantastically

Fig. 1.1. A split culm, showing the internal membrane, or diaphragm, and node. These internal septa give the plant its stiffness.

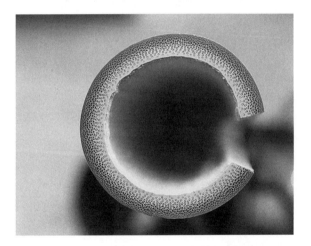

Fig. 1.2. The end of a decent culm in cross section. Notice the density of fibers toward the outside of the cane. That's the whole ball game, preserving those fibers.

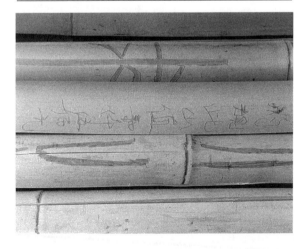

Figure 1.3. Grower marks—interesting, but more destructive than interesting.

tough cellulose fibers held together by lignin. These fibers are most dense just under the exterior rind or enamel and least dense at the inner surface of the tube (see Fig. 1.2). This is an ideal arrangement for split-bamboo fly rods, because the toughest fibers, which are on the outside of the tube, wind up on the outside of the fly rod as well. Having the greatest strength at the point farthest from the neutral axis of the rod is one reason bamboo makes better rods than solid wood, and why graphite and glass rods are fashioned as hollow tubes.

Tonkin cane comes not from the Gulf of Tonkin, as one might assume from the name, but rather from China's Guangdong (Kwangtung) Province, and a relatively small area at that, for the best Tonkin bamboo comes from between 1,500 and 2,000 feet above sea level. Its Latin name, *Arundinaria amabilis,* meaning "the lovely bamboo" or "the lovely reed," was given by Floyd A. McClure, an associate professor of botany at Lingan University in Hong Kong, who in 1931 traveled to the area where it is cultivated. The speed at which bamboo grows is nothing short of spectacular. Emerging from the ground at the diameter of the mature culm, the bamboo shoots (no pun intended) up to its full height in the space of a couple of months, becoming denser and stronger as it ages. After two to four years it is harvested, stripped clean of leaves, scoured with river sand, and dried in the sun. Readers interested in the life and many uses of bamboo may enjoy a fine article, "Bamboo, the Giant Grass," by Louis Marden in the October 1980 issue of *National Geographic.*

Cane for fly rods must survive a variety of hazards. Growers often mark culms with identifying characters that are interesting enough but that often are scratched into prime rod-making cane and can cover half the diameter of the culm (see Fig. 1.3). These marks usually are found on the biggest and best pieces because the growing area is farmed by sharecroppers and the marks are made to identify plot boundaries. Naturally, the marks go on the most prominent plants along the boundary. After harvest, warehouse workers straighten overly crooked culms by heating the entire circumference of a culm at a specific point and bending it until it is straight. Though portions of such a culm may be usable, the telltale brown spots and indentations left by such straightening must be avoided when building a rod.

Actually, most culms have at least a couple of spots rod makers need to avoid. Between harvesting, scouring, transporting, sorting, and everything else, many culms are scuffed and scratched seriously enough to damage the power fibers, and others are damaged in the shipping between the U.S. warehouse and the rod maker's door. Cane also is subject to spoilage by worms—the larvae of a certain beetle (or fly, I've read about both) that lays its eggs in the growing plant. Worm holes may sometimes be seen in the enamel or in the pithy inner surface of the tube, or they may be hidden under the enamel and revealed only when the cane is split or beveled. Not all cane with bug holes is unusable, but enough of it is to make worms a serious problem. If the holes are few, it may be possible to split the cane and cut around them.

The same caveats hold for leaf nodes, or the spots where the leaves emerge from the culm. These occur with greater frequency toward the top of the plant, so it is rare to have more than a couple in a culm. So, although leaf nodes may constitute an additional complication, avoiding them (and you must avoid them) shouldn't keep you from getting a rod out of a culm that has no other problems.

Curing and Storing Bamboo

When you receive your cane from the importer, some tubes may have a distinct greenish cast caused by insufficient curing in China. Heat-treating cane will overcome such deficiencies to some extent, but even so, further curing of green cane is advisable. The quickest way to achieve additional curing is to leave a manageable number of culms outside during hot, dry days, keeping them away from contact with the ground (a wooden deck works well), bringing them back inside when it rains (that's why I recommend a manageable number), and rotating them regularly to equalize exposure to the sun. Though hot, dry days are easily come by in Albuquerque, other parts of the country may not be so lucky. If you live in Seattle, it may be necessary to plan on curing greenish cane inside for a longer period of time. If the cane has been stored in a relatively dry place (an attic is ideal) for a year or so, or if it's all you have, I'd go ahead and use it even if it looks a little green. A pronounced green might show up on a light-colored rod, but heat-treating to a medium straw or light caramel color will toast out the offending color in all but the greenest cane, and heat-treating to a medium brown will take care of that.

Check Splitting

Bamboo splits very easily; almost every culm a rod builder receives will have splits from the drying process. If the culm does not have any splits in it, it is a good idea to put in a *check split,* a split in one side of the culm that starts at the butt and extends upward through at least two nodes. I extend the split through the entire culm, bottom to top, to decrease stress on the cane while it is drying in storage. Although it is true that a split started at the bottom of the culm will work its way through the entire length as the bamboo cures, most of the culms I have seen already have large splits in the middle or upper portion of the stick. Rather than assume that a drying split started at the butt will do its job before other cracks that do not align with it open up, I simply extend the existing crack

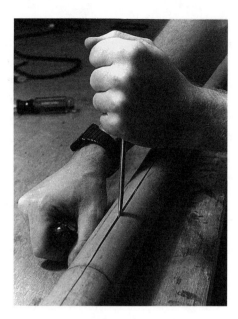

Figure 1.4. Extending a check split with rounded screwdrivers.

plished with a couple of screwdrivers with blades that have been smoothed and rounded a bit to avoid gouging or bruising the edges of the bamboo (see Fig. 1.4).

To create or extend a drying split with screwdrivers, insert the blade of one in the crack and twist. Push the second blade into the widened crack ahead of the first and twist. Withdraw the first tool and repeat, walking your way down the tube hand over hand. This process offers an opportunity to gauge the bamboo's quality and curing. Cane that splits with a loud, sharp, and resonant crack is well cured and probably quite strong, but cane that splits with a dull and spongy pop needs additional curing at the least and should be marked for particularly thorough testing in the future, before you try to make a rod from it.

(or the largest if there is more than one) the remaining distance to the ends in each direction. This sort of splitting is best accom-

2. GETTING STARTED: EQUIPMENT, TOOLS, AND MATERIALS

What does it take to build a bamboo fly rod from scratch? Because various people do things differently, there is more than one answer. A person who is willing to make most of his own equipment will find the process to involve a major time commitment, whereas a person who buys the same equipment will find it to involve a more or less serious financial commitment. In order to make this book as useful as possible to both readers, I will detail the construction of the necessary equipment in Part 2, and also include a list of sources for those who wish to purchase equipment. This seems the easiest way to include the most information without interrupting the discussion of actual rod building.

The method discussed in this book involves hand-planing six-sided rods using adjustable planing forms. There are other ways, of course. You might stumble across an old Herter's nonadjustable planing form and save some money, but at the expense of an astronomical increase in time. Or, you could buy a rod-building company complete with power milling machines and an expert staff. This book represents what I see as the best compromise and also points out other options as we go along.

But before we go on, let me devote a paragraph to explaining broadly how a rod is made, in case you're starting from square one. A bamboo rod is made from thin strips of bamboo that are split from a *culm*, a large (around 2 inches in diameter) tube of Tonkin cane that, as it arrives from the importer, may be 6 or 12 feet long. The culm (and therefore the strips) is segmented by nodes that must be straightened with heat and pressure before a strip can be planed. Straightened strips are planed into six tapered triangular strips, now called *splines*, that are glued together, enamel side out, to form the rod blank, which is fitted with ferrules, grip, reel seat, and guides, then varnished. Either as the culm or after preliminary beveling, the bamboo is heat-treated to drive out moisture and toughen the fibers.

The six-strip rod is not the only kind, but it *is* the most popular, at least partly because the equilateral triangular strips that constitute it require only one set of adjustable forms—with a 60-degree groove—to be made. If you are just beginning, this short introduction should furnish some context in which to place the tools and processes that follow.

Where were we? Right, getting started. Getting started takes *some* time, no matter how much money you are willing to spend, but you're not on a deadline. When you do something it stays done, and there's no reason building a rod can't spread over months or even years. Taking your time will only improve the quality of the final result, and besides, building bamboo rods is, for the vast majority of us, a hobby. Spending time doing something fascinating is the whole idea.

Rod building takes a modicum of space, probably not as much as you would expect. You will need a dry place in which to store bamboo (in 12-foot lengths if possible, but 6 feet is fine) and a solid waist-high workbench with about 70 inches of clear surface. If you intend to dip-varnish rods you will need a certain amount of vertical space, but you can get that in a couple of ways. Your rod-building activities should take place where dust and shavings, glue drippings, and the like will not be a problem. My own work is done almost exclusively in the margins of a two-car garage that actually holds two cars.

Money. Prospective rod builders always ask how much it costs, and the answer, again, depends on how you do things. Materials will cost some money, but you can start out with small amounts or get together with other builders on a wholesale purchase. Equipment can cost a bundle if you just up and buy it, but if you are patient, are marginally familiar with wood- and metalworking, own a few common hand and power tools, are used to figuring things out, and are an accomplished scrounger, getting started may cost you next to nothing. My friend Wayne Cattanach boasts that although it took him a year and a half to build his first rod, it only cost him sixty dollars.

You may be able to top that, but you need to know that Wayne is a resourceful, self-sufficient guy and a brilliant improviser with a lot of friends. He designed and built his own house from timber he felled himself, rebuilds motors when his cars start coughing, and, well, I could go on, but you get the idea. I would guess that the average person, lacking a class or another rod builder to sup-

ply access to equipment, could expect to spend at least four hundred dollars just to build forms, binder, and oven and to purchase the essential hand tools and materials. Not bad, actually, considering how much it costs to get into anything these days.

If you buy your forms, binder, and oven, you can double that four hundred dollars and probably triple it. Forms start at around three hundred dollars and go up to more than eight hundred. The last ad I saw for Garrison-style single-string binders offered them for three hundred dollars, though you might find some local guy willing to tackle the job for less. A single-string binder is pretty simple. I don't know anyone currently building ovens for sale, but the materials alone for an electric oven will probably run one hundred and fifty dollars or more, so if you can find an electrician or handyman to build one you should probably tack on a hundred dollars or so. Without too much of a stretch, that's eight hundred fifty dollars right there. Even if you intend to buy your stuff, at least read the information on building it. If it doesn't change your mind, it will at least give you a better idea of what you're looking for.

One thing that is really handy and can cost anywhere from a case of beer to thousands of dollars, depending on what you find and what you can afford, is a lathe. A metal lathe is best, but a wood lathe that has a hole all the way through the headstock and that will accept a three-jaw chuck will work. It is possible to do without a lathe, but the best thing if you can't own one is to look for one you can use. Some machine shops will let you buy time on their machines (after you sign an ironclad liability waiver), or you may have a friend who has a friend who owns a lathe, or a local high school or college may have a shop where you can sneak in after cultivating the goodwill of the teacher.

Apart from demands for time, space, and money, rod building requires a fair amount of patience and humility. You may be blessed with an easy path, but I'd have to say that just about every single task involved in building a bamboo rod kicked my butt initially. It doesn't matter what you know intellectually about rod building—it's your hands that know when to stop bending a node, when your plane is cutting smoothly, or when a rod section is hot enough to straighten. This knowledge *in your hands* takes time to develop, and you'll make some mistakes, including some apparently disastrous ones. Look at it this way. Rod making presents you with a wide range of opportunities. When you have a rod all but done and you burn up a tip trying to straighten the last little crook or twist, it can provoke a storm of self-reproach or it can provide a particularly vivid illustration of the virtue of patience. It's up to you.

Shop Safety: Some Important Considerations

Every book on building or fixing anything has the obligatory section on shop safety, and this book is no exception. That is no excuse for skipping it, however. Making bamboo rods is far less hazardous than, say, hang gliding, but you will be working with things that can cut, burn, and poison you. A few basic precautions are warranted.

There are four basic safety items you should own and use. First, for those whose vision is not already optically enhanced, is a good pair of safety glasses. It's amazing how hard a lathe can throw things, and how much damage an itty bitty chip or spark can do once it gets into one of those windows to your soul. Wear shatterproof safety glasses when you chip out diaphragms, straighten nodes, or turn on a power tool.

Second, a good heavy pair of leather work gloves is mandatory because split bamboo is scary-sharp, and because few people have tough enough skin to handle bamboo when it gets hot enough to straighten nodes. Third, a professional quality respirator like those worn by auto-body repairmen is worth considering. This item is somewhat expensive and possibly optional, but I try to make myself wear mine when straightening nodes and varnishing. Bamboo smoke probably isn't any worse for you than any other wood smoke, but when you spend a few hours breathing it and suddenly realize that your throat is raw and your sinuses are full of soot, you may well ask yourself, as I did, "Is this smart?" Same deal with varnishing, only we *know* that solvents aren't good for us, and now we're talking possible carcinogens. This kind of danger is less apparent than smoke inhalation but more imminent. You might want to think about it. If you start turning your own reel seats on the lathe, watch out for wood dust. Most woods will make you miserable when ingested nasally, but some hardwood dust is definitely toxic and can really hurt you.

Speaking of solvents, most glues and finishes are highly flammable as well as toxic. Pay attention to warning labels and store dangerous stuff in an appropriate place.

The fourth item you must have is a fire extinguisher *in your shop*. Having one in the kitchen is not enough. The ten seconds it could take to fetch it might make all the difference.

Tools: What You Need to Build a Bamboo Rod

The items listed here are things you eventually will need to build a rod. You don't have to buy or make them all at once, and some of them you may be able to borrow from a fellow builder just to get started—an oven or binder, for instance. It isn't something you can expect, of course, but I know builders who have helped others get started by heat-treating or gluing a rod for them now and then. Some areas of the country are fairly densely populated with rod makers—if you live in the Northwest or Northeast you're in luck; out West we're a little more spread out. Although there are some tools that warrant getting the best you can afford, almost all of these items can be bought or built even if you can't afford much. Take your time and have fun.

Dial Calipers or Micrometer

Where an economy set of dial calipers or a micrometer costs about thirty dollars, a good set of calipers by a reputable manufacturer like Mitutoyo or Brown & Sharpe will easily run double that. Inexpensive micrometers are, all things being equal, likely to be more accurate than inexpensive calipers. Good micrometers are expensive because of features like ground threads and perfect flatness of arrival—things that don't make much difference to the rod maker. With good dial calipers you're paying for the quality of the gear, dial, and machining—things that could have a direct impact on accuracy to .001-inch, which you really should have. Even so, I prefer calipers because they are easier and faster to use than a micrometer, and good ones are, for my purposes, just as accurate. The smallest calipers generally available are 4 inches, which is fine, though 6-inch calipers are usually only a little more expensive and are pretty useful to have around for other things. If you can afford to

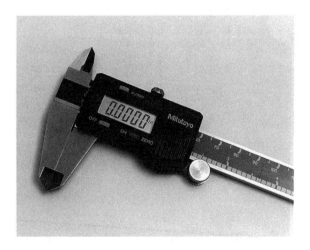

Figure 2.1. Digital calipers.

spend a hundred dollars or more, the new digital calipers are amazing (see Fig. 2.1). As I understand it, the digital unit reads a sort of microfine magnetic cloth in place of the rack. No gears to wear out, no moving parts other than the slide, and readings to .0005-inch. In a fit of self-indulgence I bought a set recently, and they're great. If you can't swallow the price tag, there are similar sets made in China that are rougher but apparently use the same technology and can be bought for much less. I'm not sure to what extent you get what you pay for in digital measuring equipment, but I'm more comfortable paying a little more to deal with a company I can gripe at if the product doesn't work well.

Dial Indicator Depth Gauge with 60-degree Conical Tip

This device allows you to read directly the depth of the groove in your forms to a thousandth of an inch, meaning that you can set them easily and with great accuracy. There are other ways to measure your form settings, but they all seem like a giant pain compared to the dial depth gauge. Again, you can spend whatever you want, starting at about fifty dollars for an economy model and going up to about three times that for a top brand. What you need is the kind that consists of a reverse-reading dial indicator mounted in a steel base with a precision ground and lapped bottom (see Fig. 2.2). You can also purchase the reverse-reading indicator alone and make your own base. You'll need to purchase the conical tip separately and either make sure that it measures exactly 60 degrees or take any error produced by its deviance into account.

Large Knife, Hammer, Screwdrivers, or Mallet (for Splitting)

Any large, cheap hunting knife will do. If you don't have one lying around, pick something up at the flea market for five dol-

Figure 2.2. *Left to right,* dial calipers, dial depth gauge with 60-degree point, and micrometer. You'll need the depth gauge, but you can get by just fine with either the calipers or the micrometer. Calipers are more convenient, but if money is tight, you'll get a more accurate instrument for the same money with a micrometer.

lars. There is a splitting tool called a *froe* that you could get, but I've never had one and never missed it. A couple of screwdrivers with sharp edges rounded are useful for making or extending check splits. A woodworker's mallet or a mechanic's hammer with a plastic face will avoid bunging up your knife and gouge.

Wood Gouge or Chisel

This tool is used to chip out the diaphragms at the nodes. The curved blade of a reasonably large (3/4-inch) gouge is perfect, but a regular old chisel will work if the former is unavailable.

Bench Vise

You need a vise, but you don't need much of one. If you use the same vise for just generally holding things and for flattening nodes, you need one with smooth jaws. Pony makes a little 4-inch clamp-on vise that is perfect for flattening nodes and adequate for any other rod-making job (see Fig. 2.3).

Heat Gun with Flat Diffuser

This tool is used for straightening nodes and rod sections. There are several different brands available. I have used a Milwaukee

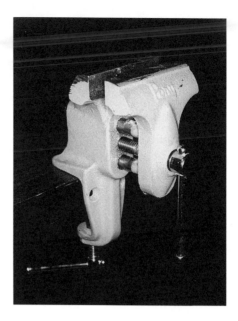

Figure 2.3. Small clamp-on vise by Pony. This model is widely available, usually for under twenty dollars as of this writing.

professional-model heat gun, a Wagner Powerstripper Plus, and a Black & Decker Heat 'n' Strip (I think they dropped the Heat 'n' Strip name, but the tool is the same). They all worked, but of the three, the Black & Decker was the least expensive, has worked the best, and has held up the longest (see Fig. 2.4).

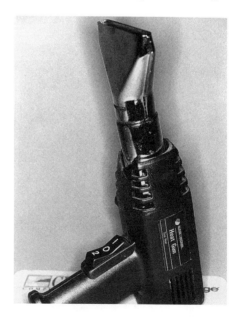

Figure 2.4. The Black & Decker electric heat gun with diffuser. Other heat sources will work fine for straightening nodes and rod sections, but the heat gun really does work beautifully, providing constant even heat. The only drawback is that it is noisy.

The flat diffuser comes as part of an accessory kit and is highly recommended, even though you may never use the rest of the stuff in the kit. You can skip the heat gun and use an alcohol lamp if you prefer. Some fine rod makers still do, and before the invention of heat guns most of them did. A kerosene lamp or small backpacking stove would work also, and I straightened the nodes for my first rod over an electric-stove burner.

Plane

The need for a plane should be self-evident. The best currently available plane for the job is the Record model 9 1/2, a nearly exact copy of the old Stanley no. 9 1/2 block plane. It normally costs about fifty dollars, but I've seen it on sale for forty dollars. An old Stanley 9 1/2 might turn up at a flea market for considerably less if it's a little rough. The modern Stanley, now called a G12-020, is not as well made as the Record but will work fine and is a little cheaper. Whichever plane you get, plan to spend some time flattening the plane's sole. Invest another twenty or twenty-five dollars and fit it with a Hock custom blade (see Appendix B, Resources). These blades cut better and stay

Figure 2.5. A few planing and scraping tools, *clockwise from left:* the Record 9 1/2, which I feel is the best modern plane available for rod building; an old Stanley 9 1/4; an even older Stanley knuckle model; a Lie-Nielsen bodied scraper; and—for those who really don't want to spend much money—a pocketknife for scraping enamel. The little bodied scraper from Conover Woodcraft in the center is my favorite.

sharp longer than the one that comes with either plane (see Fig. 2.5).

Sharpening Stones and Jig

A full discussion of stones is provided in Chapter 9, on sharpening. I've tried everything, and Japanese water stones work best. Combination 1000–6000-grit stones are relatively inexpensive, though a multiple stone setup with, say, 800-, 1200-, and 8000-grit stones will give a better edge quicker, albeit at a higher price. Combination stones can be found for twenty dollars or less, and individual stones will cost that much or more apiece. Finer stones are more expensive, and an ultrafine finishing or "gold" stone can cost sixty dollars or more. The importance of a razor-sharp plane blade to the final product can hardly be overemphasized, however, and you should avoid handicapping yourself with poor stones.

I used to think sharpening jigs were for wimps. I now use a Veritas jig and couldn't live without it. The jig made by General Tool works well also.

Rough Planing Forms (Wood)

Now we're getting into the stuff that you can't just walk into a hardware store and buy. I mention the wooden rough planing forms first because they are dead easy and cheap to make and will allow you to go a long way toward learning the rod-building craft while you're working on the other stuff. If you have a table saw or router table you can make a set in an hour. See Chapter 8 for instructions.

Final Planing Forms

These are the heart of your rod-making enterprise. The critical dimension is the 60-degree groove running down the center of the forms. Anything other than 60 degrees won't do (at least for making six-sided rods). You can make final planing forms or buy them, as mentioned earlier. They are relatively easy to make once you get past the idea that working with steel is inherently difficult. Workable forms can be made of steel, brass, aluminum, even wood. See Chapter 8 for a complete discussion. Several individuals and companies are offering forms for sale, with prices starting at about three hundred dollars. If you are interested, try to inspect a set before you buy. I've seen several sets in the three hundred dollar–range, and about half of them have been so poorly made as to be unusable.

Heat-Treating Apparatus or Propane Torch

Some bamboo is dense and tough enough in its naturally cured state to make a satisfactory rod. Although maybe one in one hundred culms is tough enough to make a good rod without heat-treating, no builder, even one willing to throw away lots of cane, can depend on that rare culm as a supply. Heat-treating cane, which increases its strength and elasticity by driving out moisture and toughening the fibers, is imperative. (Heat treating, as will be discussed in Chapter 5, does not eliminate the necessity of careful testing and selection. It will make bamboo of any quality better than it was, but much bamboo, even if heat-treated, is of insufficient quality to make a rod from.) Some makers heat treat their cane exclusively by flaming it with a large propane torch while it is still in the culm. This is perfectly acceptable, though I believe that the versatility and control afforded by a good oven is worth the expense and effort. Chapter 11 discusses several options for heat-treating rigs. If another rod maker lives nearby, there's always a chance that you can use his setup for a few rods until you can construct your own. If you build your own electric oven, plan on spending about one hundred fifty dollars for parts. Then again, Claude Kreider, in *The Bamboo Rod,* describes a method of heat treating using a steel pipe and a torch, so you can get by about as inexpensively as you need to. Just be careful.

Binder

Two words: build one. There are two main families of binding machines: the single-string type that winds one cord at a time, and the counter-rotating type that winds two or four cords simultaneously. I've had good luck with the former design (see Fig. 2.6). It's easy to make and, properly adjusted, works well and turns out straight blanks. Improperly adjusted—well, that's another story. Some makers swear by the four-string binder, though, and it does have some points to recommend it. If it is properly adjusted it should avoid the torque problems that can plague the single-string type, and it is much faster. And of course many rods have been glued without any sort of binder at all—just by the maker winding the string on by hand. Though this may have been tricky with relatively fast setting urea formaldehyde glues, modern epoxies make this method more practicable for those who don't want to commit to a binder.

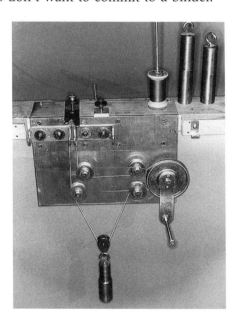

Figure 2.6. A single-string binder. All the wheels and pulleys were from a hardware or surplus store, but if you have a lathe it would be fairly simple to make them yourself.

Lathe with Three-Jaw Chuck

As mentioned earlier, a lathe is really useful (see Fig. 2.7). I've seen people rig turning outfits with electric drills, but those setups are quite limited. A lathe is the best tool for turning ferrule stations and cork grips, and having a good one enables you to make your own reel seats and ferrules if you wish. A small metal lathe is ideal, though a wood lathe will work as long as there is a hole completely through the headstock and it can be fitted with a three-jaw chuck. For the lathe to be as useful to you as it should be, get a dial indicator with an adjustable magnetic base that will allow you to check lathe setup and accuracy.

Figure 2.7. A small Craftsman lathe. A larger lathe may be better for metalworking, but any lathe with a hole through the headstock large enough to accommodate the butt section of a rod will work, including some of the larger "hobby" lathes.

Rod-Wrapping Device (Optional)

A variety of jigs and devices exist that make it easier to wrap the guides and trim onto a rod, usually by maintaining a constant tension on the thread. The time-honored method of running the thread through a closed book works, but bear in mind that silk (the preferred thread material for bamboo rods) frays rather easily. It is better to have a device that either applies resistance to the spool itself or uses a smooth-metal friction device like a sewing machine thread tensioner. These tensioners are available at any sewing machine repair shop, or you can buy commercial wrapping jigs from several companies listed in Appendix B. I use a wooden

wrapping stand from Cabela's, and other similar units are available (see Fig. 2.8). Thompson used to make a small wrapping vise that works well (see Fig. 2.9). It's been discontinued, but you may find one if you keep your eyes open.

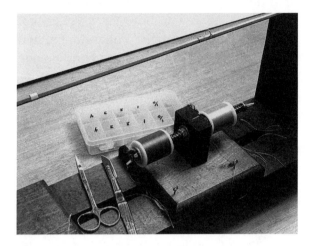

Figure 2.8. Cabela's wrapping jig. You can't really see it from this angle, but I added a sewing machine thread tensioner behind the spool on the right to smooth it out.

Figure 2.9. The Thompson wrapping vise, unfortunately discontinued.

Cork-Gluing Clamp

A special clamp for gluing cork rings onto the rod blank is necessary and is easily made or cheaply bought. The clamp consists

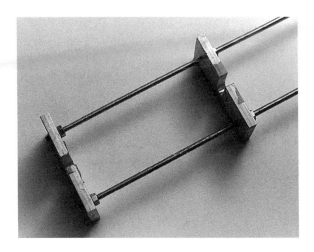

Figure 2.10. A cork-gluing clamp.

of two pieces of wood or metal with paired slots that center the blank and squeeze the cork rings together. Two threaded rods screw into the bottom and top pieces allowing for adjustment (see Fig. 2.10).

Dip-Varnishing Apparatus (Optional)

There are several ways to finish a rod if all you want to do is fish it, and some, such as a rubbed tung-oil finish, take no more than a bottle and a rag; an acceptable varnish coat can be applied with a brush. The best finish, however, is dipped varnish. If you've got the vertical space, perhaps in a stairwell, you're set. If your house is like mine, though, you'll wind up drilling a hole in your garage floor. The setup itself need not be expensive. The dip tank can be made from PVC piping, and a small geared rod-turning motor works fine to pull the sections. The main considerations for a dipping rig are that it has enough length to dip sections as long as you wish, that it be in a warm, dry location, and that you be able to shield it from airborne dust.

Drying Cabinet

Just how necessary this item is depends on how many rods you are likely to have going at one time and how humid your climate is. If you have a closet or alcove that is always warm, such as a closet housing a water

heater, you may not need a drying cabinet. If you do need one, a simple narrow wooden cabinet 5 or 6 feet long with a door, some small hooks in the top, and a light bulb in the bottom will provide a low-humidity environment for your rods while you aren't actually working on them. Some makers use a long cardboard tube. I found a bank of three old high school lockers at a junkyard for five dollars. I added hooks, insulation, light fixtures, and, *voila,* a drying cabinet. Improvise.

Miscellaneous

You'll need other stuff, especially if you start building equipment. You'll need a couple of files, a magic marker, an alcohol lamp (see Fig. 2.11), and so forth. I've tried to cover most of the outstanding items that might not be lying around your workshop, but don't get too mad at me if you have to make a couple of extra trips to the hardware store.

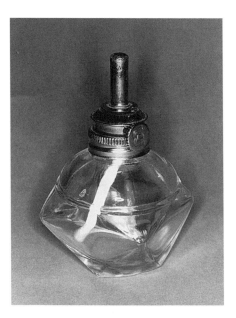

Figure 2.11. A standard alcohol lamp, used for gluing on tip-tops with thermal cement. Trim the wick down just flush with the tube for the smallest blue flame possible when working with the cement.

Materials: The Basic Ingredients of a Bamboo Rod

Although there seems to be some benefit to providing a checklist of materials needed to build a rod, an item-by-item discussion seems unnecessary. Sources for materials are listed in Appendix B. Buying in quantity almost always results in a lower overall price, but you'll have to decide for yourself how much money you can afford to save.

Bamboo
Cork rings
Epoxy for ferrules (Brownell's Acraglas Gel—the green box, not the red one)
Ferrules
Glue (Epoxy, URAC 185 or similar)
Reel seat
Sandpaper (wet or dry in grits from 240 through 600, plus 1,000 and 1,500 for finishing)
Silk thread
16/4 glace finish cotton thread
Snake guides
Stripping guides
Tape (Masking and Scotch "Magic")
Tip-tops
Varnish

3. PREPARING THE BAMBOO

The way this book is set up says more about how I do things than about how you will or should. This chapter discusses the manual skills—splitting, straightening, planing—that go into making a blank, but it does so without referring specifically to the blank. If you wish to get right to work on a rod, you can skim this chapter, go to the next one, start building a rod, then refer to this section when you have questions. However, I feel constrained to point out that the better your skills are, the better that rod will be, and it is an excellent idea to practice the basics on scrap bamboo.

As a professional orchestral musician, I feel reasonably qualified to hold forth on the virtues of practice. Every week I get a folder full of music to learn for the next concert. If I neglected to take the music out and play through it, or at least to look at it to identify the hard parts, I would show up at rehearsal unprepared. I might be able to sight-read the music and nobody would know I hadn't done my job, but if I were unlucky, if the music happened to be very difficult or I didn't already know it and therefore couldn't play it, no one would be the least bit sympathetic. My reputation would suffer at the very least, and I could lose my job if I made such behavior a habit.

Building a bamboo rod is different. Because you're doing it for yourself, it's going to be as good as you want it to be, and that's exclusively your business. Nobody is going to fire you. However, most people want their first rod to be as good as possible, and that's where practice comes in. Intelligent practice consists of breaking a task into its component parts, isolating the difficulties and solving them in isolation, then putting everything together again. Practicing straightening nodes before attempting an entire rod makes as much sense as hitting range balls before playing a round of golf. You don't have to do it, of course, but things have a way of turning out better when you feel prepared and confident. This chapter will help you master the basics. Given a little extra work, there's no reason your first rod can't be outstanding.

Splitting the Bamboo

Splitting is the first step in making a rod, and the success of subsequent operations depends on it being done well. It's not hard once you learn how, but you do need to learn. Pick out your worst culm for your first attempt, or, better yet, scrounge some scrap bamboo from another rod maker. We'll talk

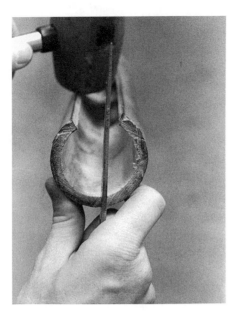

Figure 3.1. Starting the split that will divide the culm. Camera parallax got me; the knife should be tilted back toward the left just a little.

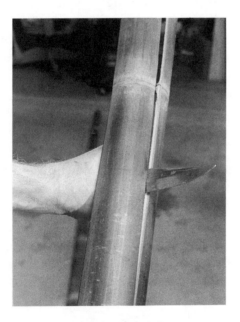

Figure 3.2. Continuing the split with the knife.

more about this in Chapter 5, but if you are starting with a whole 12-foot culm, you have a choice between splitting the whole 12-foot length and cutting it into 6-foot lengths first. When building a rod I normally choose the former because it affords me greater latitude in avoiding flaws and controlling cane thickness. For your first splitting job, though, I'd

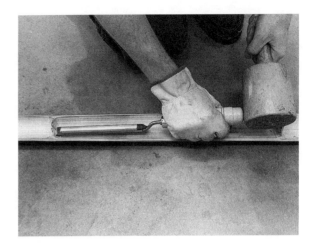

Figure 3.3. Knocking out diaphragms with mallet and gouge.

recommend cutting the tube in half, just to make the strips more manageable and to yield extra practice.

The first split divides the culm in half lengthwise. A check split probably extends most (if not all) of the way down the tube, so, using the center of that gap as a reference point, position your splitting tool (froe, big cheap knife) so that it bisects the culm at the butt end (see Fig. 3.1). After positioning your knife, tap it sharply with the mallet to start the split. Work the knife down the length of the culm, helping it along with the mallet when necessary (see Fig. 3.2). Once you achieve the two halves, use a gouge and mallet to knock out the diaphragms (see Fig. 3.3).

Because the halves with their diaphragms are very stiff, there is little danger of the split "walking," or wandering to one side or another. However, as the strips become smaller and more flexible, walking will become a problem. The central principle in splitting is that the split will walk in the direction of greater bend. If you start to split a 1-inch-wide strip exactly down the middle, without exerting any side pressure, the split should tend to continue straight down the middle because the two halves, being of equal width, will bend equally. It won't, though. Let the split wander just a tiny bit as it passes through a node or a sweep, and the situation changes. If the amount of cane on one side of the split narrows, it will bend more, causing the split to walk in its direction, making it more narrow so that it will bend still more. If a corrective bend to the thicker side is not applied, you'll wind up with one strip that tapers into nothing. This "steering" of the split soon becomes second nature, but I'm going into detail here because I initially had a tough time with it.

You now have two halves with the diaphragms cleaned out. The next step is to split the halves into six approximately inch-wide strips that will, in turn, be reduced to approximately quarter-inch-wide strips for straightening and planing. I say "approximately" because quarter-inch-wide strips, allowing some extra cane for good measure, will suffice for butt sections with a maximum diameter up to .340-inch, perhaps larger if your strips are even and you are careful. Larger butt sections will require wider strips. It would seem to follow that you could use smaller strips for smaller rods, and to some degree this is true, but 1/4- to 5/16-inch (even better if your culm will allow it) makes a convenient all-around size. Strips intended for tip sections could theoretically be much smaller than 1/4-inch, but such strips would be difficult to handle and easy to damage in splitting or node-straightening. I've worked with 3/16-inch-wide strips, but that's a bit too thin for comfort.

The best way to split cane, I have found, once you get the tube into sixths (and sometimes before), is to clamp a knife in your bench vise and don gloves. This leaves both hands free to control the split and gives very precise control. Start the split with a smaller knife, then transfer the operation to the knife in the vise (see Figs. 3.4 and 3.5). There are a lot of ways to get cut making bamboo rods, but letting your mind wander at a time like this is better than most. I repeat, wear gloves, and be careful.

Back to splitting into sixths. Take one

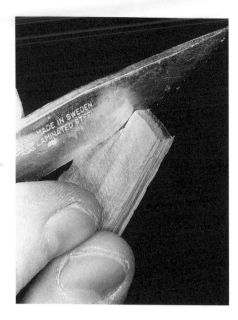

Figure 3.4. Starting a split in a large strip. If you start the split from the pith side, as shown, it's easier to make it perpendicular to the enamel. Keep the hand holding the bamboo well below the blade so you won't cut yourself if the cane splits suddenly.

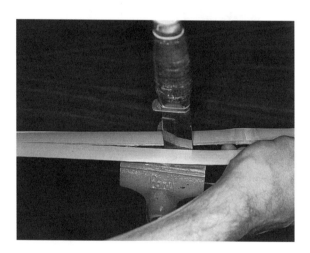

Figure 3.5. Splitting with a knife clamped in a vise. The advantage here is that you can use both hands and as much manual persuasion as is necessary to guide the split.

half of your culm and mark two points on the butt-end grain that divide the circumference into thirds. Position your knife on one mark so that it is perpendicular to the outer surface of the tube. Starting the split with this right angle is important, because you want your strips to have as sharp a square or rectangular cross section as possible (see Fig. 3.6). Start the split with hand pressure (don't

Preparing the Bamboo

cut yourself) or a tap with the mallet, and work the split down the culm as before. If the split starts to wander, clamp your knife in the vise and use as much body English as necessary to control the split. Repeat the process with the second mark, and with the other half of the culm. Mark the strips 1 through 6, maintaining their relative positions in the culm, and using magic marker slash marks across the entire width of the butt end (see Fig. 3.7). This is still practice, but you might get enough good strips for a couple of sections, so you should take the proper precautions.

To clarify what you're working toward, a two-piece rod with butt and two tips requires eighteen strips. A culm large enough to give you six inch-wide strips allows you to

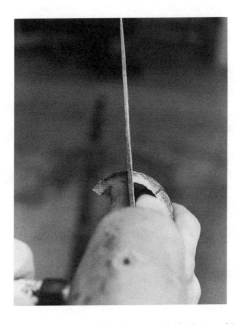

Figure 3.6. Starting the split that divides the half-culm into thirds.

split each strip in half twice (four strips), giving you six spares in addition to the requisite eighteen, assuming that you do not need strips wider than 1/4-inch. A smaller culm may not give you that luxury and may require you to split at least some of the six initial strips into thirds in order to achieve eighteen strips of sufficient width, never mind spares. Don't worry if you can't get

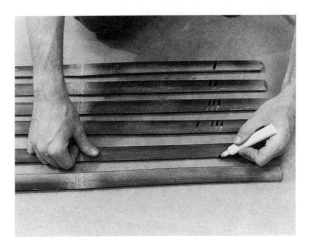

Figure 3.7. Marking the six strips with slash marks.

eighteen strips out of your first culm. This is practice, remember. If you get twelve good strips you can still build a rod, and you can use the defective strips to practice straightening nodes and planing with.

At any rate, you now have six strips that, depending on how large the culm was and how well the splitting went, measure somewhere around an inch in width. If you have a strip that measures an inch or more in width, use it now. All splitting, other than starting the split, will be done from now on with a knife clamped in the vise. Split the large strip exactly in the middle with a jack-knife or small sheath knife, again starting at the butt end, and use the knife clamped in the vise to continue the split, steering the split with your hands when it starts to wander. Split each resulting half in half again. The goal is to achieve four strips of a uniform quarter-inch width along the entire length. Repeat this process with all strips measuring an inch or more wide. If a strip measures just shy of 1 inch, go ahead and try to get four strips out of it, but try to make sure that at least one strip measures a full quarter-inch wide. The strips among the original six that measure much less than an inch wide will be split into thirds. Splitting a strip or two into quarters should have given you some feel for the sort of correction you need to make to keep the split running true.

To split a strip into thirds, you are beginning with unequal widths, so your correction will need to be constant and more forceful. Mark the strip, start the split, and go for it. Keep a steady compensating bend in the wider strip, relaxing your pressure when the split walks toward the wider strip. Once the first split is done, the wider strip is simply split in half.

This splitting into unequal strips is often necessary. Even when splitting into halves, it is common to want one strip to be slightly thicker than the other. Perhaps your initial strip is just a shade less than 3/4-inch wide. You'd like to have three strips 1/4-inch wide because they're easier to work with, but you know that you can get by with strips a little narrower for the tip as long as you have a solid 1/4-inch-wide strip for the butt. Your first split off the strip was supposed to give you a 1/4-inch strip, but things didn't work out the way you planned and it's too narrow. No big deal. You have a second chance, so you split the remaining strip slightly off center and you're back in business.

Although it's nice if you get enough decent strips to build at least a one-tip rod out of this process, the primary value of this exercise is to give you a feel for splitting. If a strip winds up varying so wildly in width along its length that it is unusable, split it again, even if the strips are only 1/8-inch wide. Controlling the split in such thin flexible strips is even harder, so it's great practice. Whether you have six, eight, twelve, or eighteen good strips is less important than the fact that you now know how to split accurately, and you also have the raw material to practice the next important skill: straightening nodes.

Straightening Nodes: Addressing Nature's Imperfections

Nodes appear innocent in the culm, but once the tube is split into narrow strips it becomes obvious that they are a problem. The ideal culm, in addition to having deep power fibers, great resilience, and no flaws, would have nodes that are straight and protrude very little to begin with. Unless you are prepared to throw away 99 percent of your cane, you need to learn to deal with culms that are less than ideal. Looking down at the surface of the cane, nodes often cause a bend in the cane, and viewed from the side they often create a troublesome hump (see Fig. 3.8). Controlling these nodes is the next fundamental skill in rod building, and perhaps the most difficult.

Nodes are straightened with heat and pressure in just the right amounts. The knowledge of what constitutes the right amount is contained mostly in your hands and can only be acquired through experience. While acquiring this experience you

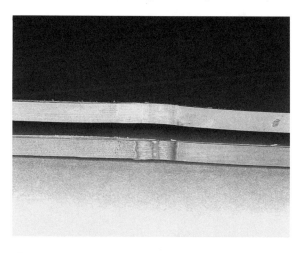

Figure 3.8. Two nodes: The one on top is fairly typical and needs straightening. The one on the bottom is the kind you pray for; any dip is so slight that no straightening is necessary, just pressing to flatten.

will probably bust a few nodes, so start with scrap. What you need to straighten are not the gentle sweeps between nodes but the sharp curves and kinks at the node itself. The sweeps will relax somewhat during heat treating when the rough-beveled strips are bound tightly together. If one sweep moves smoothly into another, the node may require very little or no work except for flattening.

Full treatment of the nodes involves both straightening and flattening. The tools needed consist of a file, a heat gun or other equivalent heat source, and a small smooth-jawed vise. As mentioned earlier, the Pony 4-inch clamp-on bench vise is ideal, though many similar hobby-type vises have been made throughout the years, and an amble through your local flea market will probably provide you with something usable. Whatever you get, be sure the vise jaws are parallel by working a file between them. Close the jaws until they barely touch the file. Work the file back and forth until it moves freely, then tighten the jaws a fraction and repeat the process until both jaws show smooth, bright metal across their entire surfaces.

How much the surface of the node needs to be filed depends on the node. Because we will flatten the node with heat and pressure, the surface needs to be filed so that the ridge is removed and the center depression just disappears, not so that the node is perfectly flush with the rest of the tube (see Figs. 3.9 and 3.10). The bit of enamel down in the very bottom of the depression or valley doesn't need to be completely removed, because the node will rise back slightly from flattening as a result of heat treating, and this protrusion will be removed with sandpaper along with the enamel before final planing.

Figure 3.10. The same node after filing.

(Filing the nodes may be done while the culm is intact. This may be desirable if the culm is flamed and the lightness of the nodes that results when the nodes are filed *after* flaming seems unappealing.) You also must file off any remaining protrusion from the diaphragm on the inside or pith side of the strip before you straighten the nodes (see Figs. 3.11 and 3.12). Some people use a disc sander or a plane to knock the diaphragm stubs off, and some use a disc sander to level the enamel side of the nodes as well.

Once the node is filed, the straightening-flattening sequence goes as follows: Heat and straighten the node; then, while it is still very hot from the straightening and still pli-

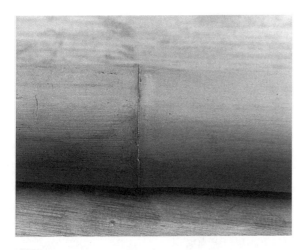

Figure 3.9. The enamel side of a node before filing. This can be done before splitting, as shown, or after. If you do it after, clamp the strip gently in a vise. It's a little faster to file before splitting, just because you don't have to do all the clamping and unclamping.

Figure 3.11. The stub from the diaphragm must be filed flush.

Figure 3.12. The strip after filing.

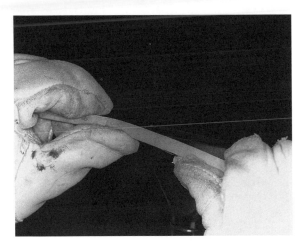

Figure 3.14. Some makers simply heat the node and clamp it in the vise from the sides, but I've found that a curve needs to be flexed beyond straight in order to stay straight. I also worry about cracking a node with pressure from the sides and prefer being able to feel what's going on.

able, clamp it gently but firmly in the vise to compress the "hump." Taking as an example a fairly typical bent node, you would heat and straighten the curve on one side (see Figs. 3.13 and 3.14), heat and straighten the curve on the other side, heat and straighten the now fairly severe bend in the center of the node (see Figs. 3.15 and 3.16), then quickly clamp the node in the vise while it is still hot (see Figs. 3.17 and 3.18). This may seem like a lot of manipulation, but it isn't and shouldn't take much time. The longer the node stays hot, the more likely you are to break it. With a heat gun, you need to find just the right distance from the nozzle to hold the strip so that it heats up fairly

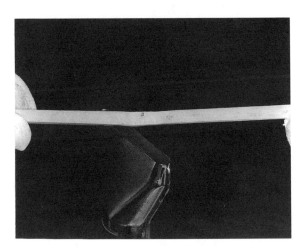

Figure 3.15. Heat the node itself and straighten the kink in the middle. Here's where you have to be most careful and where the node will fracture if you overheat or overstress it. The key is to get the node hot enough the first time around and go ahead and bend it with constant heat and gentle pressure, because the next time it'll be harder.

quickly but doesn't immediately char and burst into flame. Heat the node almost exclusively from the pith side so that the charring that inevitably occurs will not be visible on the surface of the finished rod. Unless you have very, very tough hands, wear gloves. You will need to touch the hot part of the node frequently to provide bending pressure or to put out fires. I use heavy leather gloves with cut-off fingers from worn-out

Figure 3.13. Heat the bend on one side of the node to straighten it.

Preparing the Bamboo

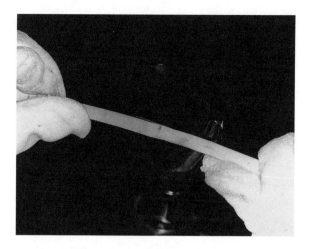

Figure 3.16. If you have to take back a little of the bend on each side of the kink to get it straight, that's okay.

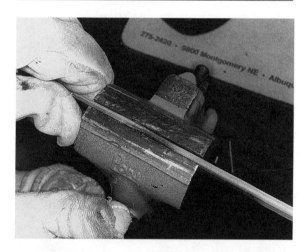

Figure 3.17. While the node is still hot from straightening, give it another shot with the heat gun to heat the whole node and clamp it in the vise to flatten it. Let the strip cool a minute or so before you remove it.

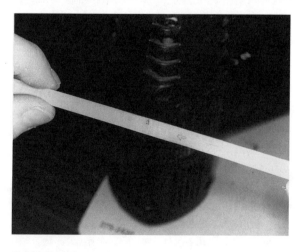

Figure 3.18. The straightened node.

gloves stuffed inside the thumbs for an extra layer of insulation.

There's a fine line between getting a node straight and harming it with too much heat. The more I build rods, the more I try to get away with straightening nodes as little as possible. Some nodes require almost no work at all. As long as the node winds up reasonably flat and provides a smooth transition from one bamboo segment to another, I find that a sharp plane blade can deal with the occasional dip.

Some rod makers do all of this differently, of course. I know some who do all their node straightening by squeezing the hot bamboo in a vise, and others who squeeze the bamboo in a heated vise. Then there are some who don't straighten nodes at all, but these folks usually use machines and don't have to worry about the plane blade getting under some angled grain and ripping out a chunk. However you wind up doing nodes is fine, though if you're just beginning let's assume you'll try my way first.

Ready? Put your flat diffuser on the heat gun, fire it up (I use the 2 or higher setting on the Black & Decker heat gun), put your gloves on (and your respirator), and give it a shot. With real ugly scrap pieces you might break a few nodes on purpose, just to get a feel for how much pressure and how much heat is too much. Too much and too little heat are equally destructive. The bamboo should give fairly easily when it is hot enough and will suddenly stiffen up and begin to crack when it gets too hot. Trying to bend the bamboo over too small an area can result in breakage as well. Be prepared to let some small bends escape for the larger good of a smooth transition and a sound node. When you have a good feel for the process, practice a little longer and then start on your good strips. Every node is different, so you need to cooperate with the cane, exerting some power, but not trying to take more than the material will give. It's a fascinating dance—try to remember that when it seems like unbearable drudgery.

Planing: Achieving Smooth, Accurate Cuts

Planing, as Yogi Berra might have said if he were a rod maker, is 90 percent equipment and the other half skill. An insufficiency of either will mess up the strip. The job of cutting smoothly is done by the plane but depends on your skill in sharpening the blade and in setting it up. The job of maintaining proper alignment of the plane with the forms is yours, but a poor plane or a poor set of forms can make it an impossible job. The idea behind planing the splines is simple. You put the strip in a planing form and plane away at the pith sides of the triangular strip in alternation until the plane blade touches steel (or wood or whatever). When the blade touches steel, you're done. There is, of course, more to it than that. Though an accomplished rod maker may claim that's all he does, he simply has forgotten all the things he had to learn and now does without thinking. I'll start off here with a discussion of planing that may seem excessively theoretical at first, but I think if you read the whole section before you pick up a plane, things will seem a little easier than they might otherwise.

There are three main requirements for accurate planing:

1. The plane must leave, particularly during final planing, a smooth surface without lifts or chips.
2. The final passes must take a fine enough shaving that overlapping cuts blend without visible gradations.
3. The sole of the plane, the edge of the blade, and the surface of the forms must be parallel, and the forms must provide a 60-degree triangular groove with one side of that triangle congruent with the surface of the forms.

Let's talk about how to satisfy each requirement. The smoothness of the cut, for example, is affected by 1. the sharpness of the tool, 2. the fragility of the grain of the material being cut, and 3. the blade's angle of attack. Without a razor sharp blade you are dependent upon the stability of the wood grain for a smooth cut without splits, and bamboo is notoriously easy to split. Because the fibers are very tough and long, and because the cut you are making lies in very nearly the same plane as the fibers themselves, the plane's cutting action will tend to get under them and lift them up rather than cut them cleanly. A sufficiently high angle of attack lessens this tendency.

The most commonly used plane in rod building is the Stanley or Record No. 9 1/2. This plane is popular not because its angle of attack (50 degrees, with its blade sharpened at the commonly recommended 30-degree bevel) is appropriate, but because it is easily managed with one hand, the other hand commonly being used to hold and flip the bamboo strip. A jack or smooth plane has a better angle of attack but is too large to use with one hand (at least for me—some makers do use them). A block plane carries a fairly low angle of attack because it is intended for planing across end grain. Considering how much its rod-building use differs from its intended use, it's a testament to the stubborness of rod makers that it works at all. The no. 60 1/2 low-angle block plane is even worse. Some rod builders use it, but they're making things much harder than necessary. (All other things being equal, of course. No matter what model plane you use, some just cut better than others, and it doesn't seem to have anything to do with the sole being flat or the blade or anything else I can identify. I have several 9 1/2-type planes, and one is discernibly the best. Geometry has no opinion, and a 9 1/2 is by design a better plane for this job than a 60 1/2, but a maker who has a bad 9 1/2 and a good 60 1/2 might come to the opposite conclusion.)

Still, the no. 9 1/2 fits nicely in the hand, and it can work well because sharpening the blade at a higher angle than the commonly recommended 30 degrees will give a higher angle of attack and a correspondingly better cut. If you have problems with lifting grain and chipped nodes, try sharpening the blade at 40 degrees, giving a 60-degree angle of attack. Much better. Try 45 degrees—better still. Some makers sharpen their no. 9 1/2 blades at 55 to 60 degrees. I've tried it, and even though I keep one blade sharpened that way for particularly troublesome nodes, I feel that my best balance between keeness and smoothness of cut occurs around 45 degrees. Experiment.

Of course, the angle of attack is not particularly relevant unless the blade is absolutely razor sharp, and it is virtually impossible to place too much emphasis on this. How to sharpen a blade is a matter of some debate. Well, an edge that is sharp to pine or oak is not necessarily sharp to bamboo (Chapter 9 discusses sharpening at some length). Also, the sole of your plane must be flat, which they rarely are out of the box. Check and roughly correct the sole with a file, then use sandpaper affixed to 3/8-inch plate glass with spray adhesive as a final flattening surface. Do your flattening with a blade tightened in the plane, because that extra tension makes a difference.

If you have a no. 9 1/2, you've noticed that there is an adjustment for throat opening. I just keep the opening set as close as possible for a given cut. A narrow throat opening seems to help reduce chips and lifts.

The second requirement, that the final passes be fine enough that overlapping cuts blend, depends (surprise!) on sharpness as well. The sharper the blade, the less material it requires to take a bite and form a shaving. Your final passes should take a shaving of .001-inch or less. With a sharp, high angle blade and a fine cut on the final passes, I have found no need for sanding or scraping to smooth out nodes or blend planing cuts. Let me restate that for emphasis. If your plane is correctly sharpened and truly sharp, you won't need to touch the pith sides of your strip with any tool other than your no. 9 1/2 plane.

Once your plane will take a smooth, fine cut, the next imperative is to maintain perfect alignment of your plane with the forms throughout the stroke (see Figs. 3.19 and 3.20). A brief consideration of the geometry involved should render this necessity obvious. The objective in hand-planing strips for a six-sided rod is to maintain a perfect (or nearly so) equilateral triangular cross section for the entire length of the strips. The planing forms, if properly made, supply two sides of this equilateral triangle in the form of the groove, the third side being the plane created by the face of the forms. In planing, your task is to keep the plane (the one with the blade in it) aligned parallel to the face of the forms, even when the blade is still some fraction of an inch above it. This is harder than it sounds, and it's amazing how quickly an error of a couple of degrees in holding the

Figure 3.19. Starting the planing stroke. Hold the strip down just ahead of the plane.

Figure 3.20. Finishing the planing stroke. Hold the strip down behind the plane, shifting your grip as necessary.

Figure 3.21. Using a mirror to check plane alignment. It's a perfectly obvious thing to do, but if you hadn't thought of it yourself, the trick alone is worth the price of the book.

plane can add up to a strip that is completely out of whack. An invaluable aid for me has been the trick of mounting a mirror at the end of my workbench at such an angle that I can see the gap between the plane and forms as I go (see Fig. 3.21). Immediate visual feedback is the best kind.

Another possible source of planing errors is misalignment of the blade within the plane. It is not impossible (it happened to me) for the surface that the blade rests on inside the body of the plane to be higher on one side than the other. This condition, once detected, is easily remedied by disassembling the plane and having at it with a file. A small unevenness can be compensated for by skewing the blade, but anything larger should be fixed. Even if all is well here, attention must be paid to the lateral position of the blade. The blade pivots on its adjusting notch, and a misalignment will result in one side of the blade sitting lower than the other. Again, it takes only a small misalignment to, over the course of twenty or thirty strokes, result in a skewed strip. Check blade alignment by sighting down the plane sole, from the front, against a strong light. The blade should show as an even thin line. An even more sensitive test is to check the blade exposure from edge to edge by running your thumb over it as though you were testing its sharpness, but this is obviously another fine way to cut yourself if you aren't careful.

To review briefly, there are two alignment issues: how you hold the plane through the stroke and how the blade is aligned in the plane. If you hold the plane straight (look in the mirror) and your strips consistently measure one way or the other, the blade is probably misaligned. If your strips measure one way at the butt and the other way at the tip, you're rolling your wrist during the stroke and you've just got to stop it. Of course, you can shift the blade alignment to compensate for a consistent error in the way you hold the plane. I like the idea of eliminating variables, of keeping everything square to the world, but do what works for you.

Even if everything is perfect, you won't know it unless you check the strips regularly with your dial calipers for equilateral cross section. Select a point on the strip, and take all three measurements from that point. Be

Preparing the Bamboo

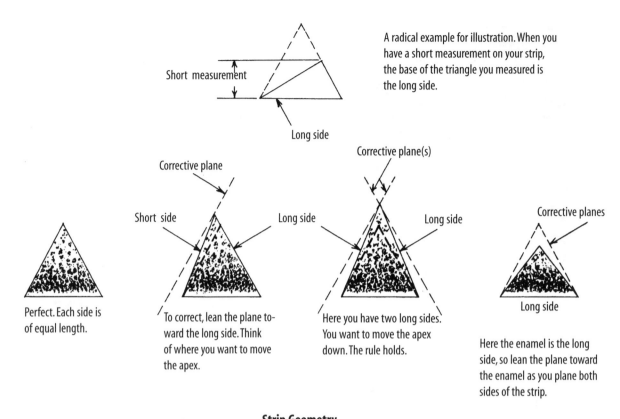

A radical example for illustration. When you have a short measurement on your strip, the base of the triangle you measured is the long side.

Short measurement

Long side

Corrective plane

Short side

Long side

Corrective plane(s)

Long side

Corrective planes

Perfect. Each side is of equal length.

To correct, lean the plane toward the long side. Think of where you want to move the apex.

Here you have two long sides. You want to move the apex down. The rule holds.

Long side

Here the enamel is the long side, so lean the plane toward the enamel as you plane both sides of the strip.

Strip Geometry

careful not to squeeze too hard and crush the delicate pith apex. Since we're dealing with an equilateral triangle, meaning that all three sides are of equal length, a line running from the center of any side to the apex should equal the same measurement from any other side. So, if all three measurements from your strip are the same, or within a couple of thousandths of each other, you are in good shape. Deviations will illustrate, by their placement and magnitude, just how your strip is out, by how much, and what you should do to correct it. The accompanying drawing shows the geometry. The general idea is that when a greater measurement occurs with one of the two pith sides as the base of the triangle, that side is too short, the other pith side is too long, and to correct it you need to put the strip in the forms with the short side up and angle the plane toward the pith apex. My simple rule: Lean (the plane) toward the long side. And which is the long side? The long side is the base of the

lesser measurement. Confused? Don't worry. When you practice planing, try angling the plane to one side or the other, and note the errors produced. Reversing the angle corrects the errors.

After each correction you need to resume planing normally (or accurately, with the plane held level) for a few strokes so that you don't wind up with a triangle in which the enamel side is drastically longer than the other two. What if this happens? Lean toward the long side, which in this case means leaning the plane toward the enamel when planing both pith sides. (All of this discussion is conducted as though the three sides of the triangle were perfectly flat, which, of course, they are not. The enamel side is slightly curved, at least until the enamel is removed, assuming that you remove the enamel in such a way as to flatten it. This is not something I worry greatly about, because by the time I get really serious about equilateral triangles [during final planing] the enamel has been removed and the enamel side of the strip thus flattened to a large degree. Even then, my primary concern is that the two measurements taken with the pith sides as the base of the triangle are as nearly equal as possible. If they are the same and within a couple of thousandths of the third measurement, there will be no glue gaps. If, however, they are more than a few thousandths smaller than the measurement taken with the enamel side as the base of the triangle, this means that the enamel side is too narrow. This error will give you glue gaps fairly quickly. If you decide to glue before you remove the enamel, keep this little bit of geometry in mind.)

It would be hard to overemphasize the importance of being able to detect, diagnose, and correct planing errors. If you can hold a

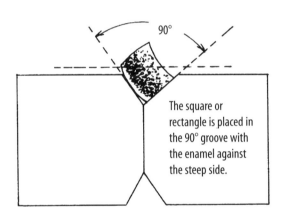

The square or rectangle is placed in the 90° groove with the enamel against the steep side.

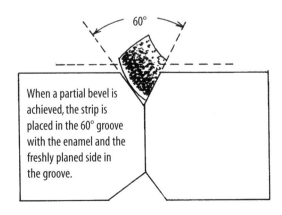

When a partial bevel is achieved, the strip is placed in the 60° groove with the enamel and the freshly planed side in the groove.

Rough Planing End View

reasonably equilateral cross section, your rod sections will turn out great. If you can't, they won't. Fortunately, holding a good cross section is a skill that is attainable by anyone with the patience to measure strips and apply a few simple principles.

Practice Planing

To start planing, you need at least the rough planing forms described in Chapter 8. These forms have one side with a tilted 90-degree groove to get the bevel started on one side of the strip, and a 60-degree groove on the other side to make the 60-degree equilateral triangular strip we all know and love. To begin, take a strip you have prepared by straightening and flattening the nodes, and take a few passes with your plane over the pith side to remove whatever irregularities remain. The length of the strip isn't critical, but you might as well make it at least 3 feet long so that you will get accustomed to making complete strokes. Take a few passes on each side of the strip (if it isn't too narrow already) for the same reason. Now, place the strip in the 90-degree groove of your rough planing forms with the enamel side pressed against the steeper side of the groove (see illustration). Holding the strip in place with your nondominant hand (as a left-hander, I'm going to get back at a right-handed world by talking this way), take a few strokes with your plane the whole length of the strip. For planing in general, I like to take long smooth strokes, making one long shaving from butt to tip, shifting the hand pressing the strip into the groove and taking a step or so along the forms as necessary (this is not as necessary for me as it might be for others, since I'm 6 foot 4 and have correspondingly long arms). When first establishing the bevel, however, short overlapping strokes often are more efficient, helping you locate and eliminate high spots. Planing the sides of the rectangular strip as discussed earlier minimizes such high spots to start with, but you'll see what I mean.

Until you get used to this work you may find it advisable to wear a glove on the hand holding the cane, and perhaps on both hands. The blade should be set for a fairly hefty cut, since the first few strokes only take off the high spots. Stop as soon as you have a fairly even bevel along the edge of the strip. You don't want to go too far, because it is nearly impossible to establish an exact bevel at this stage, and you want to transfer the operation to the 60-degree groove, where formation of an accurate triangle begins, as soon as possible.

Once you switch to the 60-degree side, place your strip in the groove with the bevel side down, and plane the as yet untouched pith side until the bevel more or less matches the first side. Then alternate sides, flipping the strip over every few strokes, enamel side always down. (Never plane the enamel side. That's where the power fibers live, and any scraping or sanding of the enamel side of the strip will be done with the utmost caution to avoid removing or damaging them.) Or alternate sides at every stroke. If you're having trouble maintaining a correct cross section, switching sides every stroke seems to help. As the triangular strip emerges (it's a lot more exciting than it sounds), back the blade in for a finer cut. Since you're still practicing, try to see just how fine a shaving you can produce, or see how heavy a cut you can take without chipping the nodes. Once you get three sharp corners, start measuring for equilateralness at several points on each strip. Correct and measure, correct and measure. Try to identify tendencies or consistently appearing errors and figure out whether they are the result of your equipment or your technique.

If your equipment is fine, information from regular measurement will help you even out your planing stroke to counter the natural tendency to roll your hand to one side or the other. Remember the mirror trick. Using a finger or thumb as a dragging brace on the forms will help, but if your plane digs in and raises a shaving from the steel forms, and you run your thumb over it on the next pass, it will open you up. Knock those shavings off with a file immediately. Eventually you will maintain the plane in the proper relationship with the forms for the whole stroke more or less automatically. Even then, however, you should check the strips with the dial calipers periodically. It's a good cautious habit, like feeling for your wallet or keeping an eye peeled for the State Patrol.

The end result of this stage, using your wooden forms, is an untapered triangular strip. For practice purposes, it really doesn't matter what your measurements are, just as long as they indicate an equilateral triangle. If you start working on strips that may eventually be part of a rod (you'll need to read ahead and check out node staggering), however, you want to stop at a dimension about .050-inch larger than the largest dimension of the finished strip. This will allow some room for shrinkage during heat treating, enamel removal, and further correction during final planing. At some point you will want to transfer your practice to adjustable forms and practice final planing. I normally remove the enamel before final planing, but so long as you're just practicing, it doesn't make much difference whether you remove the enamel or not. (If you start working on a rod section you'll want to read Chapter 5 first anyway, which includes a section on enamel removal.) Anyway, back to final planing practice. Plane until you are taking tiny shavings of steel, then compare your strip measurements with the form setting according to your dial depth gauge. If a consistent difference between the two emerges, you will need to account for it in your form settings. Because the point on my depth gauge is slightly off, for instance, I include a correction of minus .003-inch to .005-inch, depending on the measurement, when I set my forms.

Just so you know, your steel forms will get scratched and scarred by the plane on the final passes, but (except for the chips that can slice your thumb open) it's not anything to worry about. If you're careless and really hack away it's possible that you may make some pretty impressive gouges, and you should try to avoid that. If you think they need it, you can touch up your forms between rods with a file or a hard sanding block and 400 or 320 grit paper. Eventually, though, your stroke will be level enough and your final passes fine enough that the plane won't dig into the steel and you will smooth the forms only very occasionally.

Planing Accuracy

It is often stated that all the strips for a rod should be perfectly equilateral for their entire length. This is true; they should be, and in a perfect world they would be. All the rods out there with glue gaps and egg-shaped cross sections bear witness to reality. You should, of course, strive to keep your strips equilateral because you don't *want* glue gaps or egg-shaped cross sections. You're supposed to do your best; that's what all this practice is about. It is possible, however, to beat yourself up trying to achieve strips that are perfectly equilateral, or at least within .001-inch of it, when such an achievement is not only practically impossible on an ongoing basis, but superfluous.

We're working with wood—well, a grass, actually, but wood is close enough for this discussion. Wood expands and shrinks, it flexes and compresses. If your strips are within .004-inch of equilateral at their worst, you won't have glue gaps. If they are within .002-inch of equilateral, the rod will be unimpeachable. And you know that perfect construction isn't everything. I've examined beautiful rods that felt like CB whips (I really shouldn't malign CB whips), and great-casting rods that looked as though they were made with stone tools. I wouldn't want to put my name on either kind of rod, but I know which one I'd rather fish with.

Your rod is an expression of your best effort. You should do your best to maintain consistent dimensions because doing so is a mark of good craftsmanship, because the better your dimensions are the better you can evaluate and predictably modify your rod designs, because it's a kick to make a rod that turns out just the way you intended, and because, all other things being equal, good construction means a good rod. Do your best, but don't get hung up over a thousandth of an inch when you could be varnishing your rod or fishing with it.

Practice planing until you feel confident. Then, let's build a fly rod.

4. Rod Design

One of the most captivating things about building bamboo fly rods is that you are virtually unlimited in your choice of designs. You can build any bamboo rod that your heart desires, and if that thought doesn't bump your pulse up a little, maybe you should take a minute and let it sink in. If you have always wanted a rod with the action of a classic Payne or Dickerson or Garrison or Leonard, all you have to do is determine the taper (or locate the rod itself and measure it) and build it. Once you get to know a few rod makers, it will be a rare taper indeed that you can't obtain. If your interests run more to experimentation, you can go wild—that's why the forms are adjustable.

What Makes a Good Bamboo Rod?

Rod building is a lot like homebrewing: Maybe nobody has made a raspberry-honey-spruce-espresso porter before (someone probably has), but that's not to say it wouldn't be good. The endless possibilities are intoxicating, and whether you get the urge to build a 4-foot 1-weight or a 10-foot, one-piece, hollow-built nodeless salmon rod, there's nothing stopping you. A little madness is probably

therapeutic, and some rod builders seem to be engaged in an unspoken competition to see who can build the weirdest rod.

As any angler knows, there are many different kinds of rods, because different kinds of fishing require rods with specific qualities and dimensions, and because people like different things. Not only is a good rod for 10-inch high-country brookies different from a good rod for Umpqua steelhead, but one steelhead fisherman's ideal rod may be quite different from his partner's. An important part of a rod maker's education is his development of a keen sense of rod action and utility, his ability to judge rods and to translate that judgment into rod design.

This means, among other things, learning to cast well if you do not already do so. I approach this subject with some caution, because I have plenty of work to do myself in this regard. Still, the better caster you are, the better you will be at determining the limits, capabilities, and shortcomings of a particular rod, and the better your rods will be. It's certainly not necessary to be a champion caster to build great rods, but then again, it doesn't hurt, and what I'm talking about is a continuum—every little bit helps. Having great casters (or *other* great casters, if you are one) try your rods and offer opinions is one measure that you should probably consider no matter how good you are, but it's not a very satisfying substitute in the end for using your own muscles and trusting your own senses. The pure sensation of throwing a beautiful line with a bamboo rod is something that you deserve to experience, especially if you made the rod. I don't consider myself to be a particularly good caster, but one of my ambitions is to become as good as my late start and limited aptitude will allow, so I try to spend at least a little time practicing every day. There are lots of books and videos available on casting, as well as some fine instructors but, once your mechanics are decent, it all boils down to the same thing: Practice.

Just as there are various qualities, often expressed in terms of absolutes, that one might hope to find in a friend, there are absolute qualities that any good rod is said to possess, though the mixture of qualities that any one person finds satisfying may seem inexplicable. It is well that this is so. Otherwise, there would be only one good rod design in the world and the overwhelming majority of us would be friendless. If you ask any angler whether his favorite rod has enough power for the fishing he does, he will say yes. If not, the rod would not be his favorite. Does the rod have a pleasant action? Does it throw a smooth line? Can he achieve adequate accuracy with it, and mend line effectively? Does it roll cast well?

Absolutes, though, are useful only to a point. Affirmative answers to the above questions tell you little about the rod, other than that the angler likes it, no matter what you think. Here's my own ideal: a rod that is powerful and crisp without sacrificing delicacy, accuracy, smoothness, or the ability to make short, soft presentations. Who could argue with that? The problem is that those are just words. My ideal fly rod, should I ever achieve it, might be too slow for one judge, or too fast for another. This is why an appreciation for and the ability to cast a variety of rod actions is valuable if you really want to

learn, or if you wish to build custom rods for others.

There have been a few attempts here and there to quantify rod action, to assign a numerical rating of fast or slow based upon stress curves, rate-of-change graphs, static deflection tests, oscillation frequencies, and so forth. I certainly would not discourage anyone from pursuing such standards. Anyone who improves them significantly or who discovers new and useful ones, will do the rod-building world a service.

What a fly rod should be seems to be an even more inexhaustible subject than how to make it, which is a large part of why this stuff is so much fun. Although this section includes quite a few tapers, it seems in order to discuss rod design in general, because sooner or later you'll want to try your hand at it. There aren't any charts and graphs in this section because I'm not an engineer. If you're really interested in numbers I'll try to point you in the right direction, but my approach has always been to try to build great rods by hook or by crook, and if my limited work with numbers has taught me anything about rod design it's that numbers don't tell the whole story.

Creating a Design: Preferences and Functionality

There are two readily identifiable approaches to rod design. (This doesn't mean there aren't more than two, just that most others fall in between and are a blend.) One approach is empirical, meaning "relying on experience or observation alone, often without due regard for system and theory." The empiricist builds a rod by copying one he likes, then changes subsequent rods until he comes up with one he likes better. This approach has resulted in a lot of fantastic rods.

The other school is championed by the engineering types. This builder is excited by the mathematical challenge of employing or, better yet, devising an elegant numerical formula for determining the measurements of a rod possessing certain qualities. Where the empiricist will say, "I made the butt section a little stiffer, and that rod seemed to handle wind better than the previous one," the engineer will say, "to compensate for certain deficiencies in the previous rod, I decreased the stress values in the butt from a minimum of 15,000 oz./in. to a minimum of 13,000 oz./in., and increased the maximum for the tip from 20,000 to 22,000 oz./in. Assuming that the tip impact factor remains the same, this rod will handle wind better than the previous one." Some makers say things like that, and some of them make mighty nice rods. You need to build a rod that makes *you* happy, which is what this is all about.

You will notice that, except for some salmon and steelhead rods, the rods presented at the end of the chapter are mostly of moderate length, ranging from 6 1/2 feet to 8 1/2 feet, and of moderate weight, mostly 4- and 5-weights. There's a reason for that, and this seems as good a place as any to discuss the general parameters of bamboo fly rod design. To a great extent, length and line weight in a rod are dictated by personal preference. Lee Wulff caught more salmon than most of us will ever dream about on 6-foot cane rods, but that was a matter of his preference and ability. You may want a short light rod for tiny streams, or a longer, heavier rod for all-around use, or a long light rod just because you like the feel of it. There's another side to the coin, though, which is that bamboo is a natural material with a fairly consistent range of strength and elasticity, and it is possible to build rods that are outside of its usual design envelope.

Bamboo in rod construction needs a certain thickness to assure integrity and longevity. A 2-weight bamboo rod with a doting owner and small fish might survive a long time. Used by an angler who treated it like a graphite 2-weight, odds would be against it. This is all my opinion, of course,

and I'd invite anyone who disagrees with me to build the rods to prove me wrong, but I think that a 3-weight is about the lower practical limit for a light rod, and then only in shorter lengths. A good rod must have enough strength and elasticity to control a line, not just flop it out there in the general direction of forward, and something like an 8 1/2-foot 3-weight uses up too much of its material strength simply controlling itself. I'm not saying you can't do it, just that it will be a noodle.

The upper limits of bamboo rod length and line weight are governed by the same physics. To control x weight at the tip of the rod, you need y stiffness at the butt, and the longer the rod, the more leverage it must have and the stiffer the butt must be. However, since bamboo's strength is more or less constant, a rod's diameter reaches a point of diminishing returns where the increased strength of the larger diameter no longer justifies its increased weight. The result is a slower rod—not necessarily bad, but perhaps not exactly what you want. A generation or two ago, builders tried to get around this point of diminishing returns by double- and triple-building butt (and sometimes mid) sections. They would laminate strips containing only power fibers to other strips in order to obtain the effect of a double-thick layer of power fibers. The problem is that power fibers are heavy, and the fibers that really do the work are those that are farthest from the neutral axis (center) of the rod. Putting more power fibers at the center of the rod increases the solidity of the section but doesn't make that outer skin of fibers any stronger. The opposite approach, removing weight from the center of the rod by hollow-building, was more successful, but the advent of graphite pretty much made it a moot point for all but the most serious bamboo nuts. Since graphite has become part of our lives, it seems to me that there is an upper limit to how long and heavy a rod that is viable by modern standards can be built.

Let me clarify what I mean by modern standards. These days, 4 ounces, corresponding to about a 10-foot 8-weight graphite rod, is considered fairly heavy. An 8- or 8 1/2-foot 6-weight bamboo rod of plain construction may weigh 5 or 6 ounces, which seems to be about the upper limit of what most anglers today are willing to handle. I've just been reading a book by George Dawson (circa 1860), in which he talks about the fairy-wand lightness of his *8-ounce* solid wood trout rod, as compared to his *heavy* salmon rod. If you are willing to fish an 8-ounce rod, you may never lay hand on a graphite rod again. However, there are few anglers these days who will fish a 7- or 8-ounce bamboo rod when the same or longer casts can be accomplished with a graphite rod weighing half as much. In smaller rods, weight is not really a concern, because a 7-foot 3- or 4-weight will probably weigh 3 ounces or less, and the slight extra weight (as compared to graphite) will actually feel good, lending timing to the cast and making a light line more controllable.

I think bamboo starts to diminish in terms of fishing pleasure and performance at around an 8 1/2- or 9-foot 7-weight rod. A heavier rod than that feels ponderous to me and I wouldn't relish the thought of fishing all day with it, but I know makers who are busy at work on 13- or 14-foot 9- or 10-weight bamboo spey rods. You can draw the line wherever you like—it's your rod.

Those are the extremes. Between them, bamboo seems to have a definite sweet spot when it comes to rod length and line weight: 3-weights from 6 to 7 feet; 4-weights from 6 1/2 to 7 1/2 (okay, 8) feet; 5-weights from 7 to 8 feet; and 6-weights from 7 1/2 to 8 1/2 feet. Nine-foot rods in 5- to 7-weight can be nice, but for some reason I've never really gotten too excited about them. Frankly, you could happily build 6- to 8-foot 3- to 5-weight rods for the rest of your life, and you may never even have a request for a long, heavy bamboo rod. But if you're like me

you'll build a few, because you just might have a chance to fish for summer steelhead in British Columbia or monster brook trout in Labrador, and it would be nice to do it on a bamboo rod.

The Empirical (Seat of the Pants) Design

To design rods empirically, the instructions are simple. Find a rod you like and measure it. Or, since it probably belongs to someone else, obtain permission from the owner to measure it. In either case, cover the jaws of your micrometer or dial calipers with clear plastic "magic" tape to protect the varnish. This tape usually measures .0025-inch, but all you have to do is put the tape on the jaws, close them, and reset the caliper dial (or micrometer spindle) back to zero. Remember to reset the device after you take the tape off.

Once you have the taper for a rod you like, there are a number of things you can do with it. Within limits, you can beef it up, lighten it, lengthen it, shorten it, increase or decrease the drop over the ferrule, make a two-piece into a three-piece or vice versa. Whatever you do, keep careful notes, so that if the rod turns out well (or not so well), you'll know what you did.

If you are a truly dedicated empiricist, you can measure the rod any old way you want, but if there's a chance you might want to make some comparison with or investigation of the taper, it's best to put the rod together and measure in one continuous string of 5-inch increments. Start with measuring the overall length of the rod. Then, starting at the tip, measure across each set of opposing flats at each 5-inch interval. Where a guide, tip-top, ferrule, or decorative wrap prevents taking a measurement directly from the varnish, simply measure at the closest available point and make a note. If, for instance, you are measuring a 7-foot 6-inch rod, the ferrule will be in the way of the 45-inch tip measurement. Consequently, you will make a measurement at the top of the ferrule wrap, noting that the measurements at, say, 44.25 inches were .184-inch, .186-inch, and .183-inch. Later, when you build the rod, you can make an educated guess as to the dimension at 45 inches, as well as making the appropriate measurement at 44.25 inches on your forms.

On our hypothetical 7-foot 6-inch rod, the last two or three measurements will be obstructed by the grip and reel seat. This is not a problem, because the action on most rods ends ahead of the grip, and the dimension of the wood under the grip is not critical. Lyle Dickerson, for instance, made most of his rods an even 3/8-inch under the grip so that he only had to deal with one size of hole in his reel seat spacers. Measure right at the end of the grip, and unless you're dealing with a pronounced swell, continue the slope of the rod to the reel seat. Measure carefully at the ferrule(s), because many rods incorporate a certain amount of "drop" over the ferrule, and this is an important aspect of the rod's design. Many of the old-style ferrules dictated a drop of 1/64-inch over the ferrule, which tended to speed up the action of the rod, making it feel livelier and more powerful. (The drop over the ferrule is an aspect of rod design that can be varied intentionally. A drop of .010-inch over the ferrule will make the rod feel like it is bending through the ferrule more, and will give the rod a faster feel. Too much drop, or extra drop in a rod that is already fairly fast, can give the casting impulse too much acceleration and overpower the tip or create an unwanted "hinge" effect. This overpowering is manifested by extra or objectionable waves in the line but also can be caused by a tip that is simply too light. Some Dickersons had a drop over the ferrule of .020-inch or more, but a drop of this magnitude makes fitting Super Z ferrules a problem. I've mostly confined my experiments with this

variable to drops of .012-inch or less.) Note the dimensions and type of ferrule. While you're at it, measure the exact placement of the guides. You may want to use your own guide spacing, but then again, maybe the original builder got it just right. Best to have the information just in case. Other notes to make include dimensions and a description of the reel seat and grip.

If you have the great good fortune to measure a rod with the varnish stripped off, congratulate yourself. Measurements taken directly from the wood are the most accurate. Otherwise, you will need to make an informed guess about the thickness of the varnish. Over time, you will learn to guess fairly accurately. Thick varnish adds a total of .008- to 010-inch to a blank. Thin varnish adds .003- to .005-inch. If you're unsure, taking a figure of .006-inch (.003-inch per side) and subtracting it from the measurement over varnish will put you within a couple of thousandths either way.

When you measure across each of the three opposing sets of flats on a six-sided rod, you will probably get at least two different numbers. You shouldn't get too excited if there's a variation of .004-inch or even .006-inch. Such variation is especially common in machine-built factory rods, and the thing to do is to make the best average you can of the three numbers and go on from there. If your numbers are, say .184-, .186-, and .183-inch, I would be happy with a value of either .184 or .185. If the values are really whacked out, say, .184, .186, .192, I would tend to treat the most aberrant number as an outright goof—maybe a node sticking out or a run in the varnish—and ignore it, writing down .186-inch. Assuming, of course, that there are only a couple of measurements like that. If more than a few are significantly out, you're most likely dealing with an egg-shaped cross section, and you have to recognize that if you want to make a rod with similar action.

When you find a discrepancy, check several other points on the rod close to the designated point. If a significant part of a section is egg-shaped, take note of which flat the guides are on. This is the casting plane, and if the measurements from the casting plane are consistently higher, you may want to bump the average up a couple of thousandths. If they are consistently lower, bump them down a bit.

All of this talk about variations leads to the question of how important those couple of thousandths actually are. Inevitably, there is a certain amount of disagreement. Some feel that every thousandth of an inch at any given point on a rod is critical and that the slightest deviation will change the end result. Others argue that the inherent variation of bamboo stiffness and elasticity is great enough to render dimensional variations of .001-inch (up to .004-inch, some say) meaningless. I'd have to observe that people tend to make rods in their own images, and that I've cast great (and not-so-great) rods made by meticulous, obsessive people and by laid-back, general-idea people. I feel that measurements at a few points—namely where the action ends ahead of the grip, at the ferrule, and at the tip—*are* critical, and controlling your dimensions as closely as possible at all points in between reduces variables and is a mark of good craftsmanship. However, bamboo does vary quite a bit, and the Law of Parsimony stipulates that, given two different explanations for a single phenomenon, the simpler one must be true. I suspect that a bamboo rod is a kind of averaging mechanism for all these measurements, meaning that a slight change in dimension at a given point will make a difference mostly because of the change over a greater area that it represents. That may sound complex, but it's simpler than believing that every thousandth of an inch at every point on a rod can be felt. Also, I've measured quite a few rods, and anybody who holds tolerances of plus or minus .002-inch is doing fine work, anybody who holds plus or minus .001-inch is doing fantastically precise work, and any-

body who claims to hold tolerances closer than that perhaps has an exaggerated sense of his own competence.

Rod Action for Empiricists

Rod action can be as simple or as complex as you want it to be. An engineer rodbuilder friend of mine once said that he simply couldn't figure out a way to model the construction and behavior of a bamboo rod accurately, what with the varying densities of cane, the varying thicknesses of power fibers as the thickness of the rod changed and as you went from point to point on the culm, et cetera. I could see his point, in a way, but at the time it seemed like a classic case of someone being too smart for his own good. What a fly rod does, in layman's terms, is pretty obvious. It's been said often enough that a fly rod is both a lever and a spring. As a lever, it amplifies the relatively small movement of your arm into the large movement of the rod tip. As a spring, it stores the inertial energy of the fly line. Good rod design is a balancing act between these two functions. A good lever is stiff, but a fly rod that is too stiff won't bend enough to store the line's energy as tension and compression of the bamboo. A good spring is compliant enough to store a lot of energy, but a fly rod that is too compliant can't effectively transmit the arm's motion to the tip. This covers only the gross behavior of a fly rod, of course.

How a rod bends is generally referred to as its action. A tip-action rod is just that—most of the bend is in the tip, or roughly the last one-third of the rod's length, whereas the remainder of the rod is relatively stiff. A tip-action rod manages the trick of being both a stiff lever and a compliant spring, so it lends itself to a quick casting stroke. It produces tight loops with somewhat greater ease than slower, more full-flexing actions, making it good in wind and normally very accurate. In bamboo rods, though, this action is hard on tips, and it took the advent of graphite to really make the tip-action rod a going concern. At the other end of the scale is the full-flexing parabolic action. "Parabolic" is what Charles Ritz dubbed rods of his own design that flexed very deeply and easily into the butt; some of his rod designs had butt sections that were radically shorter than the tips in order to place the ferrules lower and encourage this full flex. These rods are typically very powerful but require exquisite timing to cast well—the sort of timing that, in my case, is the first thing to go when the wind kicks up, I have a high brushy bank behind me, and I need to make a really good cast in order to have the slightest chance of catching a particular fish. I don't mean to be dismissive, because some fine anglers (beginning with Ritz) have loved this sort of action. I like casting them on a lawn very well, I just can't fish with them.

In between the tip-action and the parabolic rods lies a large middle ground of medium to medium-fast, where most of the popular and enduring bamboo rod actions fall. Generally speaking, such rods are more full-flexing than tip-action rods, carrying a decent flex at least into the lower third of the rod on a reasonably long cast. Garrison, for instance, called his designs "semiparabolic" or "progressive." They were designed to flex into the butt, and did so more under progressively increasing casting loads, giving them a reserve of power without sacrificing crispness and castability within a wide range of conditions and casting strokes. This is a simplification, of course, and if you're interested in rod design the best thing to do is to read Garrison's own ideas on the subject. Since the publication of *A Master's Guide,* more of these progressive tapers have probably been built by hobbyists than any other type, and it's hard to go wrong with one of them. A medium to medium-fast bamboo rod action is, in my opinion, the best use of the material. A very fast bamboo rod can be made, but durability and longevity suffer. A very slow full-flexing rod that distributes stress over its whole length may be very strong and durable, but it seems to me to be needlessly demanding for fishing.

So how do you judge what kind of rod action you have in a particular rod? Well, you can tell a little by waggling it, but the best way is to cast it. If you want pictures but don't want to mess with a lot of icky math or computers, just graphing the dimensions of various rods will provide a fairly illuminating means of comparing different rod actions. After a short while you will begin to correlate various graph shapes with corresponding actions and to modify your designs by adjusting the graphs. That's beginning with an existing rod, of course. If you want to design rods from scratch, you need to make a slightly greater investment in time.

The Theoretical (I Want to Know Why) Design

There's a certain satisfaction in designing your own rod taper. Hoagy Carmichael wrote that Everett Garrison considered himself a rod designer first, that he built the rods because people wanted them. Considering that Garrison is our most storied craftsman, whose rods are most often held up as paragons of meticulous and uncompromising perfectionism, that's a pretty powerful statement.

We might as well get the argument over using computers to design fly rods out of the way right now. A number of people I have spoken to have all but condemned the idea of using something as newfangled as a computer to design something as traditional and romantic as a fly rod. Look, folks, computers are not taking over the world—they just do math, and do a whole lot of it almost unimaginably fast. Did Everett Garrison compromise the aesthetic purity of the bamboo fly rod by introducing logical and clear engineering principles and by using math? Try talking the price down on one of his rods with that argument. If a personal computer had been around when Garrison was designing fly rods you can bet he would have been all over it.

If you're interested in understanding the engineering approach to rod design, you should obtain or at least borrow a copy of the Garrison and Carmichael *A Master's Guide to Building a Bamboo Fly Rod.* Everett Garrison was the first to set forth a logical, comprehensive guide to calculating rod tapers, and virtually all the methods I have encountered use his math in one form or another. The pertinent chapter in *A Master's Guide* is pretty heavy sledding for those of us without technical backgrounds. I had to go through it a number of times before I felt I knew what was going on, and I still don't trust myself to explain it in anything more than general terms. Read the chapter, and don't give up or be intimidated by the math.

One reason not to be intimidated by the math is that although you really should understand it, you don't actually have to do it. If you want to get into rod design and you have a computer, buy Wayne Cattanach's book, *Handcrafting Bamboo Fly Rods.* It's a good book with good information, and it contains MS/DOS software that runs Garrison's math, allowing you to specify tip impact factors and stress-curve values and design a rod from scratch or enter the measurements of an existing rod in order to investigate the stress curve. Wayne's program is plain but effective. From this point on, I will discuss the process under the assumption that you either have or will get a copy of this book and program.

Earlier, fly rod design was discussed in terms of wood. Here, we're discussing it in terms of physical forces. In these terms, a fly rod works by storing energy supplied when your arm accelerates it against the weight and inertia of the moving fly line. The load of the line is dynamic; its movement (inertia) in the direction opposite the direction the rod tip is traveling increases its effective weight.

The tension between the fly line traveling one way (because of inertia) and the rod grip traveling the other (because of your arm) is what bends the fly rod, storing the energy that shoots the line forward when the caster stops his stroke and the energy in the rod is released. How much a rod bends at any given point under a given load is described by a "stress curve," a numerical representation in ounce-inches (a measure of force like foot-pounds, only smaller) of the rod's action. You know how a fly rod is thin and limber at the tip? It bends a lot there, so it is under a lot of stress. This translates into a high number, like 22,000 inch-ounces. The rod gets progressively thicker toward the butt because if it didn't, it would be unable to resist the stress of casting and would collapse, not responding to the energy and timing provided by your arm. So, at the butt, where the rod bends relatively little, the bamboo is under less stress, say, 14,000 ounce-inches. The trick in designing a rod is to put enough bamboo at every point in the rod so that the energy provided by your body can be transmitted to the tip, but not so much that it cannot bend enough to store the energy provided by the fly line. Remember that a fly rod is both a lever and a spring? If it's too weak, it can't act as a lever. If it's too stiff, it can't act as a spring. The stress curve tells you how strong it is and where.

If you don't know what sort of stress curve to use, I would recommend starting with Garrison's or Cattanach's and making modifications as you gain experience. A stress curve applies to a rod of specific length, but you can lengthen or shorten the stress curve to apply to different length rods as well. There are discussions of how to do this in the Garrison and Carmichael book and in Wayne Cattanach's. The idea is to keep the tip and butt values the same but to stretch or compress the spacing of the values in between, as though you were looking at them through a convex or concave lens.

If you are an engineer, as a fair number

of rod makers seem to be, you probably have your own ideas for generating a really sexy stress curve, though you have to start somewhere and actually build a rod to see if your stress curve works. At any rate, once you have chosen a rod length and stress curve, the next step is to decide what weight line you want to cast, and how much of it. Let's say you want to design a rod that will perform best when casting a DT4 line 30 feet. To do this, you figure out what 30 feet of DT4 weighs, then you multiply that figure by four to account for the increased weight the line will present to the rod due to inertia. This figure is resolved into what Garrison called the "tip impact factor," a number that represents the dynamic weight presented to the rod tip. (I'm glossing over how this is actually done because the Garrison book explains it well and Wayne's program does it for you.) Now comes the math. You work down the rod, calculating how much bamboo you need in order to move that line, including the things that add weight and also need to be moved, such as the tip-top and guides, varnish and wraps, ferrules, and the weight of the bamboo itself. You know, thanks to Garrison, what bamboo weighs and how strong it is for a given diameter in six-sided construction. You know, or soon will, what all the rest of the stuff weighs.

Once you figure in the stress curve that describes how your desired rod will store its casting energy over its length, it's the math that tells you what diameter your rod needs to be at 5 inches to cast the line, the tip-top, the first snake guide, wraps and varnish, plus the bamboo weight of the first 5 inches of the rod. Then you do the math for the 10-inch station, which has to move all of the above plus the stuff between 5 and 10 inches, and so on, for each 5-inch segment of rod. Actually, it's not as though you start at 5 inches and do the math and keep going down the rod and then you're done. You start by assuming the rod has a straight taper and

then run the calculations a couple more times to arrive at the final taper. That's a lot of math, and the advantages of a computer program should be obvious. Wayne's program asks you all the right questions, so it's possible to design a rod by putting in numbers without having a clear idea of how it works. Of course, if you truly have no idea how it works, you probably won't wind up with much of a rod, but you never know. Actually, I think this is what gets anticomputer folks upset. For a computer to save you time is one thing. For it to substitute for understanding seems degenerate. I don't feel bad using a computer, but I would recommend reading Garrison if at all possible, and maybe doing the math with a calculator once to get a feel for the problem.

If you are comfortable with computers, stay tuned. Some bright people are working on this, and mathematical tools that weren't around forty years ago will soon be applied to rod design. One of these days, someone is going to put together a computer program that uses finite difference equations (or another of the half-dozen new and perfectly unfamiliar mathematical tools that engineers have told me would be perfect for figuring tapers), that runs under Windows, that saves all of the taper and stress-curve information to file, and that either has graphing capability or links to a spreadsheet program like Excel.

Empirical or theoretical? It's up to you. Personally, I need both, the first because numbers aren't always the whole story; the second because math is such a valuable predictive tool. It's true that a whole lot of rods, including many great ones, were built before rod builders had heard of a stress curve. Great rods are still being built, as a matter of fact, by people who have no use for stress curves. (What's more, the stress curves for many great rods absolutely look like hell.) However, though a lot of wonderful things have been accomplished by trial and error, it seems sensible to do whatever you can to minimize the number of errors.

Designing the Rod Tip

The tip of the rod seems to be a particularly critical area, and I'm discussing it last because it is a specific topic that is pertinent regardless of how you design a rod.

Making the tip an appropriate size for the rod, the line, and the user can be a little tricky. Theoretically, the rod diameter at the tip-top can be very small, smaller even than the .040-inch that is about the smallest I have seen. The very light Leonards were known for exquisitely thin tips, and such tips, properly integrated into a rod's design, can be wonderful indeed. Such a rod often excels at very soft accurate presentations at close range, what some instructors refer to as "casting off the tip." A light tip, properly done, often is associated with delicacy and a rod's light, crisp feel, but that delicacy can sometimes also mean fragility. Further, the very tip of the rod is the last thing the casting wave or impulse "sees" as it travels into the line. It is possible to make a tip so thin that it fails to control that impulse and cannot dampen its own vibration after the stroke, or that it cannot transmit the quick, sharp impulse necessary for a cast into a strong wind. If you make a rod that casts well except that it has a tendency to throw humps in the line, try beefing up the last 5 or 10 inches of tip by .002- to 004-inch on the next similar rod. If you make a rod that casts well except that it has difficulty forming nice tight loops, particularly at short range, try thinning the last 10 inches of the tip by a couple of thousandths on the next one.

A tip that is too heavy can be a problem as well. A heavier tip will shift the casting stress for short casts lower on the rod, which can be good or bad, depending of course on what the rest of the rod is like. A heavier tip usually dampens quickly and helps throw a smooth line but can give the rod a clubby feel if overdone and also can produce extra oscillations if the middle of the rod is too weak. The trick is to find the happy medium for the desired rod and purpose. The figure of .070-inch is often used as a good generic tip measurement, and, all other things being equal, I'd tend to agree with it. It's maybe a bit heavy for a 3- or 4-weight and maybe a bit light for a 6 and certainly too light for a 7, but I rarely make a 5-weight tip smaller than .070-inch anymore. I've made 5-weights with tips as thin as .062-inch, but felt they did not dampen well enough for everyday use. I might make a 3-weight with a tip smaller than .060-inch, but probably wouldn't make a 4-weight smaller than .065-inch.

Remember, though, that these "standards" are just mine. Most of my rods are for myself or for other western anglers, and even a light rod for the West normally is made with the idea that it may have to punch a cast into a stiff wind or throw a weighted Woolly Bugger in an emergency. If you are building a midge rod for sheltered eastern streams and feel that a .042-inch tip will be just the thing for delicate presentation of tiny flies, by all means try it. My intent here is not to dictate but to establish the tip of the rod as a critical area, and to alert you to the fact that changing the tip dimension a relatively small amount can make a noticeable difference in the rod's behavior.

Determining Taper

The tapers here, all taken from fine rods, are the result of one builder's collecting mania as well as his generosity. My first customer had something very specific in mind. He wanted a rod that cast like a Dickerson 7012. He had cast a 7012 at one point and loved it, but couldn't afford an original, assuming that one could be found for sale. "Can you build that rod?" he asked. "Sure," I replied. I didn't have the taper, of course, but my first call was to Daryll Whitehead, and a week later I had the taper in my mailbox, and a couple of months later I had a satisfied customer. Quite a few makers have discovered Daryll and his hoard of tapers, which includes Dickersons, Paynes, Gillums, Leonards, F. E. Thomases, Grangers, Heddons, you name it. Daryll has handled and cast many more rods than he's measured; he has only measured the best ones.

And the best of those are here. Partly as a tremendous act of generosity—to me and to all of us—and partly in an attempt to get out from under all the requests for tapers, Daryll offered to let me include his catalogue in this book—at least the good ones. Talk about an easy decision. This array is likely to be of interest to any maker but will be particularly valuable to someone just starting out. Once a maker is established and knows a few other makers, there is literally no taper (assuming the rod was offered commercially) he can't obtain. And the more rods he builds, the more likely he is to leave these tapers behind and strike out on his own. Of course, there are lots of other good tapers out there. There are Garrison's and Cattanach's, and a few in Kreider's book, though they are mostly large rods and you will have to convert them from 6-inch to 5-inch centers. If you subscribe to *The Planing Form,* a rod maker's newsletter, you will find tapers in nearly every issue.

One caveat. These tapers are just numbers, sets of values taken from existing rods. The measurements from a particular rod of a given model by a given maker may not be the same as any other rod of the same model by the same maker. They are just the measurement for that one rod. What's more, it is craftsmanship and materials that make a rod good, not the taper. The fact that you build a rod using a set of numbers taken from a Payne doesn't make a Payne. Yours may not be as good, or it may be better.

A note about how rods are measured. When you look at Garrison's tapers, they all start with the tip of the rod as zero and march down the rod in one continuous string of 5-inch intervals. That's because of the way Garrison derived his tapers: a series of calculations based on a stress curve and starting at the tip. If Garrison ever made rods with a

drop over the ferrule, he didn't note it in the tapers that made it into his book. Even when you're measuring a finished rod, it makes a certain amount sense to take your measurements that way in case you want to play around with computer programs or graphs. Lots of people measure each section starting from the butt, including Daryll. Because most of these tapers came from him, they're done that way. A few are measured from the tip, but that's not really confusing because it's readily apparent from the numbers how you need to set the forms.

All of the ferrule recommendations are made with the assumption that you'll use a Super Z–style ferrule, but we should explore that just a bit. A lot of these rods were made before Super Z ferrules were available, or before the maker made his own ferrules. Most non–Super Z ferrules were made with a difference of 1/64-inch internal diameter between the male and female, which is expressed in rod tapers that show a large drop over the ferrule. Dickerson, for instance, made his own ferrules, and the ferrule size is part of the rod model number: a 7613 rod is 7 feet 6 inches long with a 13/64-inch ferrule, but that's a ferrule made by Dickerson himself, not a Super Z. I've simply translated the model number into the ferrule recommendation, but you may want to make adjustments—for rods where the model number translated into Super Z ferrule size may make a weak ferrule joint because you'd have to remove a lot of wood to get the Super Z to fit, I've included the next size up in parentheses. In many instances a large drop over the ferrule is attractive; it can make a rod feel faster and more lively, as if it bends through the ferrule more. It can also be tough to fit with a Super Z, though, and if you wind up looking at a situation where using a Super Z will mean either cutting into the power fibers of the butt or not cutting enough off the corners of the tip, you have a couple of options.

First, you can tinker with the taper just a little. This is a bit of a gamble: If you want to build a given rod and want to duplicate it exactly, you'll have enough variables to deal with without departing from the taper. Still, I've taken that risk and had it work out pretty well. It just depends on how great the departure is. A second option is to use a Super Z that fits the butt dimension and build up the tip ferrule station with slivers of bamboo power fiber before turning. To do this, take a strip of clear cane a shade narrower than the flats and heat-treat it. Remove the enamel, then plane away the pith side until you have a bamboo shim .040-inch or .030-inch thick. Cut this strip into lengths that match the ferrule length, and glue them (epoxy is recommended) to the ferrule end of the tip, binding them tightly with cord until the glue cures. Then, turn the ferrule station as you normally would, blending the shims into the blank with a file so the ferrule serrations taper down to meet the blank. This works very well, though it's kind of a pain. Some makers use this method exclusively, even when there's no drop over the ferrule, believing that it's best to remove no power fibers at all, ever, in order to install ferrules.

A third option is to make or obtain ferrules that fit the taper. Classic Sporting Enterprises makes Super-SD ferrules of the old step-down style and for a price will make you anything you need. I suppose if you really want to duplicate a given rod faithfully this would be the way to go, even though step-down ferrules mean a weaker joint. I'd rather give up a little authenticity and use a Super Z.

A word about varnish thickness: Most of the rods were measured over varnish and are so indicated, along with a guess at how thick that varnish might be. Varnish figures are total thickness, meaning you subtract that number from the diameter, then divide by two to get the form setting. You'll find as you mess around with rods that you can fine-tune the varnish numbers a bit. Varnish seems to be thicker on the butt than on the tips—the butt usually needs an extra coat of

varnish to look good, and it also seems that the smaller diameter of the tip holds less varnish and winds up with thinner coats than the larger diameter sections anyway. So I might subtract an extra thousandth or so from the lower part of the butt and subtract a thousandth or so less from the very tip. Building rods from tapers taken from existing rods is far from an exact science; you've got averages instead of actual diameters, you've got different cane, glues, heat treating, building environments—in short, a taper is a starting point, not etched in stone.

Despite the fact that a taper is just a set of numbers (and a patent has never been granted for a rod taper), there are no tapers here from rods by living makers. Have fun!

Fred Devine
7-foot 6-inch 3-piece, 3/4-weight
15/64-inch and 10/64-inch ferrules

Measured over varnish: Deduct .004-inch. A rod from the 1920s, so it's what would be called medium to slow today, but a beautiful old rod, a delight to cast.

	Butt	Mid	Tip
0	.295	.230	.152
5	.290	.215	.140
10	.288	.203	.128
15	.280	.188	.116
20	.265	.182	.100
25	.244	.168	.084
30	.230	.162	.064

Dickerson 6611 (1948)
6-foot 6-inch 2-piece, 4-weight
11/64-inch ferrule

Measured over original varnish: Deduct .004-inch from butt and tips. This is one of the nicest, most useful short rods I've cast. Six and a half feet may seem too short to some, but the 4-weight line is enough for lots of different situations, and the rod is both delicate enough to cast short and powerful enough to punch out 50 feet with relative ease. A delightful rod.

	Butt	Tip
0	.285	.170
5	.285	.162
10	.285	.147
15	.230	.137
20	.220	.120
25	.206	.105
30	.196	.090
35	.188	.075
40	.180	.064

Dickerson 7012 (1954)

7-foot 2-piece, 4-weight
12/64-inch ferrule

Measured over original varnish: Deduct .006-inch from butt, .004-inch from tips. Another fine rod. Actually a little more delicate than the 6611; this rod might not be my choice for a windy western river, but I've built several and Daryll's built many more, and they've all been hits.

	Butt	Tip
0	.326	.180
5	.326	.168
10	.310	.159
15	.258	.144
20	.245	.130
25	.232	.115
30	.216	.099
35	.207	.086
40	.200	.070
42	.194	.066

Dickerson 7612 (1946)

7-foot 6-inch 2-piece, 4-weight
12/64-inch ferrule (13/64-inch)

Measured over original varnish: Deduct .006-inch (.003-inch per side) from butt and tips.

	Butt	Tip
0	.375	.198
5	.375	.182
10	.360	.167
15	.285	.154
20	.276	.140
25	.268	.130
30	.255	.114
35	.248	.100
40	.224	.086
45	.216	.070

Dickerson 7613 (1952 and 1970)

7-foot 6-inch 2-piece, 5-weight
13/64-inch ferrule

Two fine examples of a very nice Dickerson rod, and an illustration of how two rods of the same model can be quite different. The first, built in 1952, is a very powerful rod that could easily take a 6-weight and might be thought of as a 7613 "Special." I've built this rod and it's been a big hit. The second, as is obvious from the measurements, is a lighter, slightly slower, deeper-flexing 5-weight.

	1952			1970	
	Butt	Tip		Butt	Tip
0	.360	.208	0	.360	.198
5	.360	.198	5	.360	.185
10	.344	.180	10	.355	.175
15	.298	.170	15	.288	.158
20	.288	.155	20	.278	.142
25	.274	.140	25	.272	.128
30	.256	.122	30	.252	.115
35	.238	.104	35	.238	.098
40	.220	.090	40	.222	.082
45	.213	.068	45	.213	.068

Dickerson 7614

7-foot 6-inch 2-piece, 6-weight
14/64-inch ferrule

An even heavier, faster version of the 1952 7613. Measured with no varnish. There was only one 7614—built by Dickerson and left without finish, then given by the Dickerson family to Jim Schaaf.

	Butt	Tip
0	.375	.210
5	.375	.199
10	.340	.182
15	.313	.163
20	.300	.149
25	.293	.143
30	.272	.123
35	.252	.107
40	.222	.093
45	.218	.080

Dickerson 8013 (1949, 1951)

8-foot 2-piece, 5-weight
13/64-inch ferrule

Measured over original varnish: Deduct .006-inch from butt, .004-inch from tips. The 8013 was one of Dickerson's most popular rods, and as readers of *Dickerson, The Man and His Rods,* by Jerry Stein and Jim Schaaf, will know, there were quite a few different versions. The 1949 rod below obviously is heavier, but they're both good rods, just different.

	1949			1951	
	Butt	Tip		Butt	Tip
0	.375	.202	0	.375	.202
5	.375	.198	5	.375	.190
10	.370	.183	10	.360	.178
15	.322	.172	15	.312	.161
20	.310	.160	20	.297	.148
25	.296	.145	25	.283	.135
30	.280	.128	30	.266	.120
35	.260	.112	35	.252	.106
40	.238	.092	40	.232	.090
45	.217	.074	45	.215	.077
48	.212	.066	48	.212	.070

Dickerson 8014 (1949 and 1952)

8-foot 2-piece, 6-weight
14/64-inch ferrule (15/64-inch)

Measured over original varnish: Deduct .006-inch. A very nice 6-weight.

	1949			1952	
	Butt	Tip		Butt	Tip
0	.375	.222	0	.375	.222
5	.375	.212	5	.375	.208
10	.360	.200	10	.360	.196
15	.332	.187	15	.328	.182
20	.320	.174	20	.316	.170
25	.303	.160	25	.298	.156
30	.287	.145	30	.282	.141
35	.276	.125	35	.272	.121
40	.260	.106	40	.256	.102
45	.242	.090	45	.238	.086
48	.236	.081	48	.232	.077

Dickerson 8014 Guide (1951)

8-foot 2-piece, 7-weight
14/64-inch ferrule (15/64-inch)

Very powerful, very nice rod. Could take a 6, but really blasts it out there with a 7. A good streamer rod or a light steelhead rod—very stiff. Measured over varnish: Deduct .006-inch.

	Butt	Tip
0	.375	.224
5	.375	.216
10	.375	.202
15	.332	.188
20	.322	.174
25	.308	.160
30	.292	.143
35	.274	.128
40	.254	.110
45	.242	.092
48	.238	.084

Dickerson 8015 "Guide" and "Guide Special" (1950 and 1955)
8-foot 2-piece, 7-weight
15/64-inch ferrule (16/64-inch)

These are probably the most famous Dickersons; they are very stiff and very, very powerful. Made for shooting long casts behind sweepers from a canoe, they can pick up a long line and a heavy fly from the water and pop it back out there with ease. Everybody talks about the 8015 Guide Special's power, and it would make a fine steelhead rod.

	Guide (1950)			Guide Special (1955)	
	Butt	Tip		Butt	Tip
0	.375	.232	0	.375	.236
5	.375	.222	5	.375	.225
10	.375	.208	10	.375	.208
15	.350	.194	15	.353	.197
20	.338	.180	20	.342	.181
25	.328	.165	25	.325	.168
30	.308	.150	30	.309	.154
35	.292	.135	35	.294	.137
40	.272	.120	40	.274	.122
45	.255	.102	45	.257	.104
48	.250	.095	48	.250	.096

Dickerson 8615
8-foot 6-inch 2-piece, 6-weight
15/64-inch ferrule

Measured over original varnish: Deduct .006-inch from butt and tips. A nice trout rod. A little less stout than the 8-foot rods and not something you'd use for steelhead, but a very nice 8-1/2-foot 6-weight.

	Tip	Butt
0	.375	.228
5	.375	.212
10	.264	.197
15	.320	.186
20	.306	.170
25	.295	.156
30	.287	.138
35	.276	.117
40	.266	.101
45	.254	.088
50	.240	.074
51	.238	.073

Dickerson 9016
9-foot 2-piece, 8-weight
16/64-inch ferrule (17/64-inch)

Measured over original varnish: Deduct .006-inch from butt and tips. Good steelhead or light salmon rod. Medium-fast action.

	Butt	Tip
0	.375	.256
5	.375	.246
10	.375	.230
15	.360	.215
20	.346	.198
25	.336	.182
30	.326	.165
35	.315	.150
40	.300	.134
45	.290	.118
50	.274	.110
54	.268	.100

Gillum

7-foot 3-piece, 4/5-weight
15/64-inch and 11/64-inch ferrule

Measured over varnish: Deduct .004-inch from each section. Deep flexing, fairly powerful rod.

	Butt	Mid	Tip
0	.320	.228	.160
5	.316	.217	.146
10	.310	.208	.132
15	.290	.196	.112
20	.268	.190	.096
25	.242	.175	.082
28	.233	.170	.070

Gillum 1–983

7-foot 6-inch 2-piece, 5/6-weight
14/64-inch ferrule

Measured over original varnish: Deduct .006-inch from each section. Rather heavy and powerful for its size. This is a tough one to fit with a Super Z; if I were building it I'd probably scale it down a bit so the ferrule would be a better fit. Cutting the butt ferrule station .004-inch into the power fibers might not hurt anything, but making the whole rod .004-inch smaller probably wouldn't hurt anything either and seems to me the better choice.

	Butt	Tip
0	.350	.214
5	.350	.210
10	.328	.202
15	.318	.186
20	.297	.176
25	.267	.158
30	.250	.142
35	.240	.122
40	.228	.100
45	.223	.082

Gillum 1–974

7-foot 8-inch 3-piece, 5/6-weight
16–17/64-inch and 11/64-inch ferrule

Measured over original varnish: Deduct .006-inch from each section. Another fairly representative Gillum rod. Rather heavy, very powerful. Slightly tip-heavy, but that means a full flex and a smooth line. This is another one where you probably should build the butt ferrule station up with bamboo or scale the rod down.

	Butt	Mid	Tip
0	.360	.254	.168
5	.360	.252	.158
10	.348	.244	.146
15	.306	.232	.132
20	.290	.224	.116
25	.270	.206	.088
30	.260	.184	.071
31	.258	.172	.070

Gillum 1–685

8-foot 2-piece, 6-weight
15–16/64-inch ferrule

Measured over heavy varnish: Deduct .008-inch from butt section, .006-inch from tips. A very nice 6-weight. A drop of .028-inch over the ferrule is huge. Probably a good idea to build the tip ferrule station up with bamboo slivers, or consider making or ordering a custom ferrule.

	Butt	Tip
0	.375	.220
5	.375	.210
10	.370	.192
15	.335	.187
20	.306	.170
25	.295	.152
30	.287	.136
35	.276	.116
40	.270	.096
45	.255	.078
48	.248	.073

Gillum 506

8-foot 6-inch 3-piece, 6-weight
17/64-inch and 11/64-inch ferrules

Measured over varnish: Deduct .006-inch from each section. Medium action, what today might be considered a slower rod. Very nice, though.

	Butt	Mid	Tip
0	.385	.264	.170
5	.385	.250	.158
10	.375	.236	.150
15	.312	.230	.129
20	.300	.212	.112
25	.286	.196	.100
30	.272	.180	.086
35	.266	.178	.074

Gillum 584

8-foot 6-inch 3-piece, 6/7-weight
19/64-inch and 12/64-inch ferrules

Measured over original varnish: Deduct .006-inch from each section. Sections measured 34 3/4 inches.

	Butt	Mid	Tip
0	.390	.282	.180
5	.390	.276	.170
10	.388	.260	.148
15	.346	.248	.136
20	.330	.232	.118
25	.315	.214	.104
30	.303	.202	.088
35	.294	.194	.074

Gillum 1–730

8-foot 6-inch 2-piece, 7-weight
15/64-inch ferrule

Measured over original varnish: Deduct .006-inch from each section.

	Butt	Tip
0	.370	.220
5	.370	.218
10	.370	.208
15	.362	.196
20	.340	.178
25	.314	.156
30	.302	.140
35	.288	.124
40	.266	.108
45	.250	.094
50	.226	.082
51	.225	.076

Gillum Salmon Rod

8-foot 6-inch 2-piece, 7-weight
17/64-inch ferrule

Measured over original varnish: Deduct .006-inch from each section. Salmon rod with fighting butt.

	Butt	Tip
0	.385	.258
5	.385	.242
10	.380	.223
15	.375	.212
20	.358	.193
25	.354	.174
30	.322	.160
35	.310	.136
40	.288	.127
45	.277	.104
50	.264	.093
51	.262	.086

Gillum

8-foot 10-inch 2-piece, 8-weight
16/64-inch ferrule

Measured without varnish.

	Butt	Tip
0	.392	.235
5	.392	.230
10	.386	.218
15	.378	.204
20	.358	.186
25	.332	.166
30	.316	.146
35	.294	.130
40	.282	.114
45	.272	.100
50	.256	.090
53	.242	.082

Granger (Wright McGill) Victory

7-foot 2-piece, 4-weight
13/64-inch ferrule

Measured over varnish, apparently original but quite thin: Deduct .004-inch.

	Butt	Tip
0	.335	.180
5	.335	.168
10	.335	.156
15	.270	.144
20	.260	.130
25	.245	.120
30	.239	.105
35	.225	.090
40	.203	.072
42	.200	.070

Granger (Wright McGill) Special and Aristocrat

7-foot 6-inch 3-piece, 4-weight
15/64-inch and 10/64-inch ferrules

Measured over original varnish but quite thin: Deduct .004-inch.

	Special				Aristocrat		
	Butt	Mid	Tip		Butt	Mid	Tip
0	.325	.228	.146	0	.325	.228	.153
5	.325	.215	.140	5	.325	.224	.148
10	.320	.210	.126	10	.325	.215	.124
15	.276	.202	.112	15	.274	.211	.111
20	.264	.190	.096	20	.262	.197	.094
25	.254	.176	.080	25	.253	.185	.084
30	.248	.162	.064	30	.246	.166	.067

Granger (Wright McGill) Victory

8-foot 3-piece, 5-weight
16/64-inch and 10–11/64-inch ferrules

Measured over varnish: Deduct .004-inch. Very nice rod, this particular one seemed more comfortable with a 6-weight, so if you want a 5-weight you should make sure not to overcut it.

	Butt	Mid	Tip
0	.360	.240	.156
5	.355	.232	.152
10	.350	.222	.142
15	.295	.212	.128
20	.280	.200	.114
25	.262	.190	.094
30	.250	.172	.078
32	.246	.168	.076

Halstead

8-foot 2-piece, 6-weight
15/64-inch ferrule

Measured over varnish: Deduct .006-inch.

Measured from tip

0	.080
5	.092
10	.111
15	.130
20	.150
25	.156
30	.185
35	.195
40	.199
45	.218
48	.225

Butt

48	.235
50	.240
55	.258
60	.272
65	.287
70	.298
75	.305
80	.323
85	.370
90	.370

Heddon Bill Stanley Favorite (Model 20 Featherweight)

7-foot 2-piece, 3/4-weight
12–13/64-inch ferrule

Measured over varnish: Deduct .006-inch. A beautiful 3-weight dry-fly rod.

	Butt	Tip
0	.365	.182
5	.365	.170
10	.344	.158
15	.272	.144
20	.254	.128
25	.243	.112
30	.230	.098
35	.215	.079
40	.203	.068
42	.200	.066

Heddon Deluxe Model 50

7-foot 6-inch 2-piece, 4/5-weight
14/64-inch ferrule

Measured over varnish: Deduct .006-inch.

	Butt	Tip
0	.380	.200
5	.380	.185
10	.380	.170
15	.291	.154
20	.272	.142
25	.265	.124
30	.254	.116
35	.238	.100
40	.228	.086
45	.210	.080

Heddon Black Beauty (Model 17)

7-foot 6-inch 2-piece, 5-weight
13/64-inch ferrule

Measured over varnish: Deduct .006-inch.

	Butt	Tip
0	.390	.198
5	.390	.188
10	.386	.172
15	.284	.160
20	.272	.145
25	.250	.127
30	.232	.116
35	.226	.103
40	.214	.090
45	.208	.082

Heddon Deluxe Model 50
8-foot 3-piece, 5/6-weight
16/64-inch and 11/64-inch ferrules

Measured with no varnish on butt, varnish on midsection and tip. Deduct .004-inch from midsection and tip.

	Butt	Mid	Tip
0	.375	.250	.160
5	.375	.244	.146
10	.375	.230	.134
15	.294	.220	.122
20	.286	.206	.106
25	.272	.188	.092
30	.260	.174	.078
32	.252	.170	.070

Leonard
6-foot 6-inch 2-piece, 3 weight
10/64-inch ferrule

Measured over varnish, but quite thin: Deduct .004-inch. A very delicate rod, miniature reel seat and grip. Very typical of the tiny midge rods that were all the rage in the 1960s, and a rod that would be a hell of a lot of fun on small streams.

	Butt	Tip
0	.250	.145
5	.250	.137
7.5	.245 (front of grip)	
10	.238	.130
15	.238	.122
20	.212	.109
25	.200	.096
30	.180	.084
35	.163	.068
39	.154	.060

Leonard 39L
7-foot 6-inch 2-piece, 4-weight
13/64-inch ferrule

Measured over original varnish: Deduct .004-inch.

	Butt	Tip
0	.380	.190
5	.380	.182
10	.362	.164
15	.280	.146
20	.268	.136
25	.258	.128
30	.246	.108
35	.230	.096
40	.210	.082
45	.200	.062

Leonard 39DH
7-foot 6-inch 2-piece, 4-weight
13/64-inch ferrule

Measured over varnish: Deduct .004-inch. A very smooth rod, one of the nicest Leonards I've ever cast.

	Tip	Butt
0	.066	.202
5	.078	.213
10	.097	.228
15	.110	.238
20	.124	.250
25	.135	.256
30	.143	.264
35	.162	.350
40	.178	.350
45	.192	.350

Payne

7-foot 2-piece, 3/4-weight
10/64-inch ferrule

Measured over varnish: Deduct .006-inch from each section.

	Butt	Tip
0	.310	.162
5	.310	.159
10	.302	.144
15	.237	.138
20	.226	.122
25	.209	.107
30	.194	.092
35	.180	.079
40	.168	.067
42	.166	.061

Payne

7-foot 9-inch 2-piece, 4/5-weight
13/64-inch ferrule

Measured over varnish: Deduct .006-inch from each section.

	Butt	Tip
0	.350	.196
5	.350	.192
10	.330	.179
15	.292	.178
20	.276	.172
25	.258	.160
30	.246	.148
35	.235	.132
40	.222	.114
45	.205	.083
47	.204	.073

Payne

8-foot 3-piece, 6-weight
16/64-inch and 11/64-inch ferrules

Measured over varnish: Deduct .006-inch from each section.

	Butt	Mid	Tip
0	.350	.246	.164
5	.350	.236	.156
10	.350	.230	.144
15	.305	.218	.132
20	.292	.205	.114
25	.275	.192	.096
30	.265	.180	.080
32	.260	.174	.070

Payne

8-foot 3-piece, 5-weight
16/64-inch and 11/64-inch ferrules

Measured over varnish: Deduct .006-inch from each section.

	Butt	Mid	Tip
0	.360	.246	.160
5	.360	.240	.148
10	.360	.230	.137
15	.310	.219	.125
20	.288	.206	.113
25	.274	.194	.094
30	.262	.180	.073
32	.258	.174	.068

Payne

8-foot 2-piece, 7-weight
15/64-inch ferrule

Measured over varnish: Deduct .006-inch from each section.

	Butt	Tip
0	.375	.226
5	.375	.216
10	.365	.206
15	.324	.196
20	.308	.180
25	.294	.169
30	.282	.150
35	.269	.137
40	.260	.114
45	.243	.095
48	.238	.085

Payne Canadian Canoe

8-foot 6-inch 3-piece, 7-weight
17/64-inch and 12/64-inch ferrules

Measured over varnish: Deduct .006-inch. This is a really fine rod. Not particularly fast, but smooth and powerful. The ones I have made from this taper have cast a weight-forward 7 with authority. This is one case where deducting .006-inch from the tip dimension would make it too light. I've made the ones on my rods .072-inch, and that seems to work well.

	Butt	Mid	Tip
0	.385	.264	.170
5	.385	.260	.164
10	.385	.253	.153
15	.333	.237	.139
20	.311	.228	.125
25	.300	.215	.108
30	.289	.195	.085
34	.275	.186	.071

Payne Two-Handed Salmon Rod

13-foot 3-piece, 10-weight
Custom ferrules

Daryll and I thought we'd throw this one in for general interest. If you want to build it you'll need to make your own ferrules. Measured over varnish: Deduct .006-inch. Detachable 7-inch fighting butt; butt, grip, and reel seat 22 inches total.

	Butt	Mid	Tip
0	.575	.415	.270
5	.575	.406	.264
10	.575	.396	.258
15	.575	.388	.238
20	.570	.376	.220
25	.515	.364	.200
30	.500	.356	.190
35	.480	.343	.170
40	.466	.325	.152
45	.434	.306	.132
50	.425	.292	.110
52	.420	.290	.108

Paul Young Midge

6-foot 3-inch 2-piece, 4-weight
12/64-inch ferrule

Measured with no varnish. Really a lovely little rod, very positive and crisp.

	Butt	Tip
0	.248	.172
5	.248	.160
10	.240	.146
15	.234	.130
20	.218	.110
25	.206	.100
30	.196	.082
35	.190	.066
38	.188	.065

Paul Young Perfectionist

7-foot 6-inch 2-piece, 4/5-weight
14/64-inch ferrule

Measured without varnish. There's not much need to dwell upon the positive virtues of this rod—its praises have been sung by many others.

	Butt	Tip
0	.288	.218
5	.284	.202
10	.278	.184
15	.274	.158
20	.264	.142
25	.250	.132
30	.244	.116
35	.230	.106
40	.224	.090
45	.218	.066

Paul Young Martha Marie

7-foot 6-inch 2-piece, 5-weight
15/64-inch ferrule

Measured over varnish: Deduct .006-inch from each section.

	Butt	Tip
0	.325	.220
5	.325	.212
10	.305	.197
15	.300	.182
20	.290	.166
25	.274	.150
30	.258	.139
35	.247	.120
40	.239	.102
45	.234	.072

Paul Young Para 17

8-foot 6-inch 2-piece, 8-weight
17/64-inch ferrule

Measured over varnish: Deduct .006-inch from each section.

	Butt	Tip
0	.330	.258
5	.330	.248
10	.330	.225
15	.320	.210
20	.314	.202
25	.296	.182
30	.288	.176
35	.284	.144
40	.270	.122
45	.266	.102
50	.264	.086
52	.262	.084

Paul Young (Unmarked)

8-foot 6-inch 2-piece, 7/8-weight
15/64-inch ferrule

Measured over original varnish: Deduct .006-inch from each section. This was evidently a prototype of some kind, with no model designation. Would make a good steelhead or light salmon rod.

	Butt	Tip (wet)	Tip (dry)
0	.375	.234	.228
5	.375	.228	.228
10	.360	.222	.212
15	.346	.216	.208
20	.317	.200	.194
25	.302	.178	.168
30	.284	.158	.148
35	.276	.145	.135
40	.276	.135	.125
45	.256	.110	.100
50	.236	.084	.078
52	.234	.082	.077

Phillipson Premier

7-foot 6-inch 2-piece, 4-weight
13/64-inch ferrule

Measured over varnish: Deduct .006-inch.

	Butt	Tip
0	.350	.202
5	.350	.186
10	.350	.176
15	.304	.162
20	.294	.152
25	.280	.142
30	.264	.126
35	.242	.112
40	.216	.098
45	.206	.078

F. E. Thomas

6-foot 8-inch 2-piece, 3-weight
11/64-inch ferrule

Measured with no varnish. According to Daryll, the best 3-weight he's ever cast.

	Butt	Tip
0	.325	.158
5	.310	.153
8	.305 (beginning of swell)	
10	.244	.140
15	.226	.128
20	.214	.118
25	.202	.109
30	.188	.088
35	.178	.074
40	.170	.050

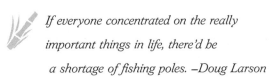
5. Making the Blank: The Rod from Start to Finish

Now it's time to get down to business. You know what rod you want to build, and you have either practiced the basic skills and are ready to go or you just read Chapter 3 and figured you'd take your chances and tackle a rod. Either way, your first job is to select a culm for the rod you have in mind.

Selecting, Flaming, and Splitting the Culm

Bamboo for a rod is not like 2 X 4 lumber for a house. Bamboo varies in a number of respects, the most important of which is the quality and depth of power fibers in the culm. In observing the end grain of a culm, it will be seen that the dense, compact nature of power fibers immediately under the enamel gives way to somewhat dispersed fibers and finally to white pith (see Fig. 5.1). It is difficult to describe how large and deep power fibers should be for a given rod, but in general, culms displaying deeper, larger power fibers are better suited for longer, heavier rods. A fairly useful rule of thumb is that solid power fibers should make up at least two-thirds of a strip's thickness at the rod's greatest diameter (see Fig. 5.2). The reason for this is that the pith is soft, and if

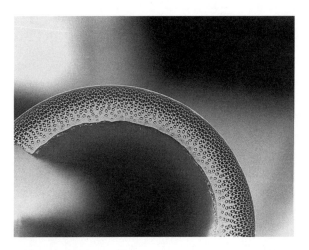

Figure 5.1. A close-up of the end grain of a decent culm. Culms with very thin layers of power fibers should be avoided or, at the least, not used for large rods.

there is too much of it, it can become crushed and break down quickly. In a graphite rod, the fibers push against the scrim, the material (graphite or fiberglass) wound at right angles to the long fibers. In a bamboo rod, the power fibers are held together by lignin and push against the center of the rod. If the pith becomes crushed because it is overabundant, there is nothing solid for the outer fibers to push against as they oppose one another in tension and compression, and they lose power.

No rule is absolute, of course. A smaller rod with a dramatic swell at the butt would

Figure 5.2. An end view of butt section cutoffs from two different rods built on the same taper but from different culms. Notice the subtle differences: The section on the left has dense power fibers that suddenly break off into pith, whereas the section on the right has slightly larger fibers and a more gradual transition into pith. I don't know that I'd care to postulate a rule, but I would prefer the rod represented by the section on the left.

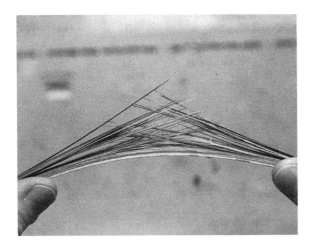

Figure 5.3. Breaking a piece of cane helps test its quality. It should break into long spikes, but most decent cane will do this. Pay attention to how the piece resists bending, whether it feels weak and spongy or stiff and resilient, and to how it springs back from a bend before you actually break it.

break this one, as would a culm with a layer of power fibers of moderate thickness but exceptional strength and density. The more you work with the material, the more astute you will become at choosing culms appropriate to the intended rod. I've had a couple of makers tell me that they judge cane by its

weight: A relatively heavy culm means more and denser power fibers, whereas a light culm means more pith. You can't argue with success, but the size, wall thickness, and curing state of bamboo varies enough that "weight" has to be shorthand for a fairly complex and intuitive evaluation. I'd guess that there aren't too many builders out there who handle enough culms day in and day out to be able to make that judgment accurately and consistently.

My suggestion is to look at the power fibers at the butt first to make sure they are deep enough for the intended rod; then, when you're splitting the cane and cutting the strips to length, take a cut-off piece and torture it. Note how springy and resistant it is to bending, how much of a bend it will sustain and still spring back, how much it resists bending when already in a deep bend, and how it breaks when it finally does break. Good bamboo breaks gradually, with individual fibers popping out into long spikes (see Fig. 5.3). These are the sorts of cues you can remember, even if you only handle bamboo enough to select a culm a few times a year.

Part of the selection process is deciding how you're going to use the culm. The power fibers in the culm are at their thickest at the butt of the culm and at their thinnest at the tip. Keeping that fact in mind, let's say you want to build an 8-foot 6-weight, which will put you at either a 14/64-inch or 15/64-inch ferrule. That's a fairly heavy rod these days, and you'll want dense, deep power fibers. The best way to get them will be to use a fairly large culm—one with deep fibers and with a diameter that will allow you to get at least eighteen strips of adequate width—and just use the lower part of the culm for the rod. My friend Daryll Whitehead builds all his rods like that. He plans on only one rod per culm, uses fairly large culms, and simply cuts his 6- or 7-foot piece out of the culm as low as possible. If it turns out to be the bottom half, fine. If he has to take 6 feet out of the middle to avoid grower marks or other flaws, that's fine too. Of course, that means that half the culm is thrown away no matter what, but that doesn't bother him. "I've never thought of bamboo as a scarce commodity," he told me. For my part, I've made some very nice light rods out of the top parts of culms, so I don't like to throw that much cane away, and I approach this task with the goal of preserving as much undamaged cane with sufficient power-fiber depth as possible.

To get back on track, you're building a heavy rod, so you make it a point to use the lower part of the 12-foot culm for all the strips in the rod, and you've picked a culm that will allow you to do that. For a particularly heavy rod, you can beef it up just a shade more by reversing ends for your butt-section strips before you stagger the nodes. The very densest cane is already at the ferrule for the tips, and reversing the butt strips puts the same most dense cane at the ferrule in the butt. There is comparatively little stress on the butt down by the grip anyway, so it does you little good to have your best cane under the cork. Of course, you don't have to do this just for heavy rods. I know some builders who do it as standard operating procedure.

Bamboo runs quite a bit smaller today than it did fifty years ago, I hear, perhaps mostly because it's impossible to go to a warehouse and high-grade the big pieces. Even if you order a bale of "large" cane that supposedly measures 2 to 2 1/2 inches in diameter, you will get very few pieces that actually approach the upper figure. Most of them will be barely over 2 inches, and a couple may be smaller. If you get the small size, well, you get the idea. There's nothing wrong with small diameter cane—some makers prefer it. However, a culm reaches a minimum size below which it is impossible to get eighteen adjacent strips of adequate width, even if there are absolutely no flaws and your splitting is perfect. Or, if you are

building a three-piece rod, flaws may make it impossible to get twenty-four adjacent strips out of even a very large culm.

Let's say you're building a light rod, a 7-foot 4-weight, for instance. If the top half of the large-diameter culm you used for the heavy rod has power fibers deep enough to meet the two-thirds rule of thumb expressed earlier, I'd use it. However, let's say you have a different culm that seems nice and dense but is too small in diameter to yield eighteen strips. Or maybe it will give you eighteen strips, but just barely, and you're nervous without a few spares. You can lay out the rod using the top part of the culm for tips and spares, and the bottom part for the butt and spares.

This business of matching the culm to the rod, or vice versa, is really little more than common sense, but it helps to take a "big picture" approach to the process, and to be flexible.

Flaming

Flaming, if you wish to do it, should be done with the entire culm, or with half-culms at most. When you flame, the cane will char at any edges that exist. Flaming a whole culm means two charred edges (assuming that there is only the check split), flaming half-culms means four charred edges, and so on. Also, it seems to me that flaming the whole culm results in a more even color overall. If you wanted to flame your rod but have already split the culm into strips, I don't feel obligated to apologize, because flaming is something else that takes practice and perhaps shouldn't be tackled on your first rod—unless you were going to use it as your sole means of heat treating. In that case, I'm sorry. Flaming can make a gorgeous rod and can, I believe, improve its casting qualities, but it also can wreck it. Too much heat applied too quickly makes cane brittle.

The proper tool for flaming is a propane torch or some other source of a big, soft flame. I use a big industrial torch, but there are smaller ones available that would work. What you want to avoid are torches that throw a little blue flame. You want a big yellow flame (see Fig. 5.4).

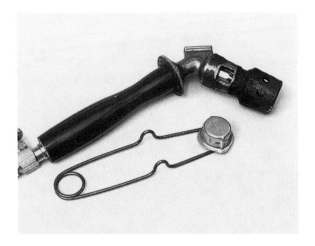

Figure 5.4. An industrial propane torch. I got this one by mail from McMaster-Carr after a long search through local welding and industrial supply houses.

Flaming is best done outside for obvious reasons, and you need some sort of stand to support the culm at about chest height. You must wear heavy gloves, again for obvious reasons. Start with small discarded pieces of bamboo, and experiment with the amount of flame directed against the culm and with the rate at which you move the flame. I try to keep the culm in the edge of the yellow part of the flame, and I move the flame back and forth fairly slowly. Experiment. Start with flaming a piece to a light caramel and test it. Flame another to a dark caramel and test, then another to a light mahogany and test, and so on. Your tests should include both breaking strips and straightening nodes. The first culm I flamed (be aware that I didn't start with scrap) was a gorgeous uniform reddish walnut color, but every single node I tried to straighten snapped in my hands. Learn ye from my experience.

You should start flaming at the middle of the culm and gradually work toward the ends to force the moisture out. On culms that haven't seasoned a long time—or that *have* seasoned a long time, though not in a particularly dry place—you may actually have water fizzing and popping out of the ends (which is fine, don't worry). The color and pattern that results from flaming is largely a matter of taste. Some people like cinder black rods, others don't. I think cinder black rods may be taking things too far, but that's just me. Some people like even-toned rods, others like mottled or tiger-striped flaming. If you like the nodes to stand out as light spots, flame before you file the nodes. If you want the rod to be an even tone overall, file the nodes on the whole culm, then flame.

It's a little tempting to try to give some concrete advice on flaming—move the torch so many inches per second, something like that. The fact is, though, that it's something you have to learn yourself, and even seeing it done only helps so much. I've already given you the best possible advice: Practice on scrap.

Splitting

The process of splitting the culm into halves and then into sixths was discussed at some length in Chapter 4. In the section on cane selection I mentioned that there are different ways to lay out a rod, and that a lot depends on the culm. If you've read everything up to this point, you know that you can cut a section of the culm out—or cut the culm in half—and use a single section for all the strips in the rod, or you can use the upper part of the culm for tips and the lower part for the butt. If you wanted to make two rods whose action matched perfectly, you could select a large culm and make four tips from the top and two butts from the bottom.

Your splitting will be governed by how you want to lay out your rod and stagger nodes. This section is about splitting, but we've already covered the mechanics. This is more about strategy, because you can start splitting with the 12-foot culm, or you can cut it into shorter lengths first. My favorite way to lay out a rod is to split the entire 12-foot culm into six large strips (assuming that some severe flaw or damage doesn't give me a 6- or 7-foot culm to begin with), mark them 1 through 6, lay them on the floor, and stagger the nodes, by which I mean slipping the strips one way or another so that no two nodes are adjacent in the finished rod. We'll get to exact methods of staggering nodes in a minute, but right now we need to talk about when, not how. So, back to 12-foot-long inch-wide strips. Staggering nodes at this point allows maximum flexibility in utilizing the culm, in placing the ferrules and tips well clear of nodes, and in dodging problems in the cane. The long strips are more awkward than 6-foot ones, but, well, a lot of things in life are awkward.

With long strips, the best way to handle them is to stagger the nodes and lay out the rod(s) with the six strips, mark the sections, cut them to length, and then split them into smaller denominations.

If you choose to work with shorter sections of the culm for splitting and staggering, you can stagger nodes with either six large strips or eighteen small ones. If you have good, clear cane and confidence in your splitting ability, it is quicker to stagger the nodes using the large strips. This is actually the same procedure that you would follow with 12-foot strips, but let's go over it again just for insurance. After staggering the nodes and marking the layout, cut the large strips to length, then split them into strips for the butt and tip sections. You only need to make twelve cuts, and the short sections are easier to split than long ones. The drawback to this is that if your number 3 large strip has a leaf node in it, or if you make a splitting mistake and get only two usable strips, or if somewhere down the line you ruin a strip, you may be caught with no backup.

The other method is to use 6-foot lengths

and to split all of the large strips into small strips to begin with, then to pick one strip from each large strip (1, 2, 3, 4, 5, and 6) for each rod section, then stagger the nodes for each section individually. This method involves more splitting, sorting, and cutting (and, it hardly needs to be said, doesn't work well with 12-foot lengths), but if you wind up with some spares, you can use them in a pinch to replace any spline by matching up the node locations and cutting the new piece to length.

There is another possibility, if you have a large enough culm. If your culm will give you seven or even eight 3/4-inch or wider strips, you can stagger nodes and cut sections from six large strips and still have one or two large strips in reserve to split and cut as necessary in an emergency. This *does* work with 12-foot culms.

This replacement strategy will seem obvious to some and heretical to others. Though I try to arrange the rod splines in the same relationship as they grew in the culm, I simply won't throw out an entire culm because a spare from the number 4 large strip must be pressed into duty as a number 2 spline. I'm not absolutely sure it makes a noticeable difference. I've seen plenty of old rods—some even by famous makers—where strips from totally different

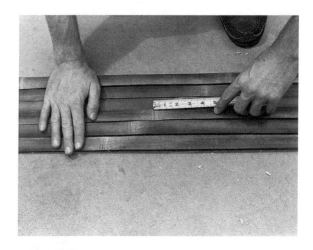

Figure 5.5. After marking the split strips to keep them in order, stagger the nodes.

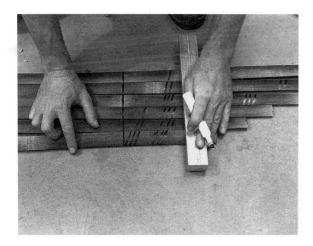

Figure 5.6. Mark section lengths and cutoff points, then remark the strips.

Figure 5.7. Large strips ready to cut to length.

Figure 5.8. The strips cut to length.

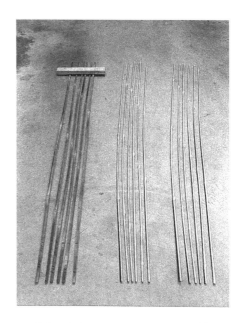

Figure 5.9. Strips split into narrower strips and sorted for sections, ready for node straightening.

culms were apparently grabbed more or less at random and glued together, and some of them cast great and stayed straight. You probably won't see stuff like that today, because good, even node spacing is one of the first things bamboo rod people look for, but it's a fact that if all of the strips in your rod come from the same culm, you are paying more attention than a lot of the old companies did. Maintaining the "culm relationship" in each rod section may or may not make a difference; it's one of those things that you do because it's the most intellectually satisfying and precise way, and it just might make a difference. (See the accompanying photo sequence, Figs. 5.5 through 5.9.)

Staggering and Straightening Nodes

The nodes, meaning the areas of interlaced fibers that, along with the diaphragms, divide the stalk into segments, are the most vulnerable part of a bamboo strip. In the growing cane the nodes ring the tube, are buttressed by the diaphragm, and are very strong. In fact, these periodic reinforcements are a primary reason for the whole cane's tremendous resilience. As part of a narrow strip and thus deprived of its natural environment, the node is relatively brittle. For the sake of distributing whatever vulnerability or effect the nodes may produce throughout the rod, as well as for the sake of appearance, the nodes must be staggered. The accompanying photos show the more popular node-staggering arrangements (Figs. 5.10 through 5.13). Obviously, the usable length of your strips is decreased by node staggering. This should be taken into account in reckoning the length of rod sections obtainable from a given culm using the desired pattern, or, alternatively, in selecting a pattern to yield sections of a desired length from a given culm.

Figure 5.10. Nodes staggered for a straight spiral. This spacing and the Garrison variation use the most cane but have a nice look and leave only one node at a given point in the rod. It's the method I normally use.

Figure 5.11. Nodes staggered in what is commonly called a "3/3" arrangement, meaning that there are three nodes aligned at a given point in the rod. If you're worried about the nodes being weak, this would be the least desirable staggering method. However, some of the most prominent rod makers (whose rods now command the highest prices), including Lyle Dickerson, have used it.

Figure 5.12. Nodes staggered in what is commonly called a "2/2/2" arrangement. It's sort of halfway between the straight spiral and the 3/3.

If, for instance, you have a 6-foot culm and wish to make an 8-foot two-piece rod, you will need 48-inch strips after staggering. Even with a spiral pattern, this should pose no problem: An offset of, say, 2 inches per strip for six strips still leaves a foot for end allowances and waste. (The distance that you displace the strips should probably be greater than 1 3/4 inches, but beyond that the distance is not critical. Just be sure you

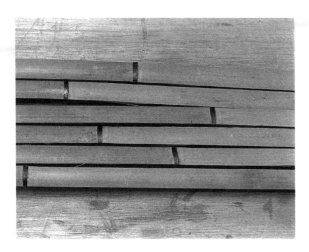

Figure 5.13. Nodes staggered according to Garrison's spiral variation. Using this method, the strips are placed in the order 1, 5, 3, 6, 2, 4—the firing order of many six-cylinder engines—and staggered as though a straight spiral were intended. When the strips are placed in their normal 1–6 orientation, they will look as shown. I guess the thought is that if the nodes are spiraled their resistance may produce some torsion.

don't ignore the offset between strips 1 and 6.) However, perhaps the lower foot of the culm is scarred by a grower's mark, or the top foot and a half was crushed during shipping. Perhaps the distribution of the nodes in the culm is awkward; you should try to have clear, node-free cane under the ferrules and within at least 3 inches of the tip-top. Accommodation of any of the above conditions may require a shift in the staggering or the use of the culm for a different rod. Of course, all of this depends on how strongly you feel about using a particular pattern or a particular culm.

As I mentioned above, the freedom of node spacing is one reason I prefer to work with 12-foot culms. I almost always use some form of spiral stagger (Payne or Garrison), and it is not until I have six 12-foot-long inch-wide strips lying side by side on the shop floor that I decide exactly how the nodes will be staggered and where the rod sections will fall. This gives me the most latitude in avoiding scars or flaws, situating clear cane at the section ends, and maintaining adequate fiber depth for the intended rod

while leaving open the possibility of getting more than one rod out of the culm.

When you lay out the node spacing and mark the strips for cutting, allow at least an inch and preferably a couple of inches excess at each end beyond the nominal length of the rod section so that eventually you'll wind up trimming off a few inches on each end of the glued-up section. You'll need the space when gluing, if not before; you may want to locate your ferrule a bit to either side of the originally designated point if your final dimensions are a little over or under spec, and it's neat to have pieces of glued-up cane on hand. You can make ferrule plugs out of them, or give them to friends or acquaintances who just don't understand what you mean about gluing together six triangular strips. For a while I considered writing my name and phone number on them, varnishing them, and using them as business cards, but in a rare moment of sober reflection I decided that the last thing I needed was a twenty-five-dollar business card. If you build rods and *still* have a lot of time on your hands, the idea is yours, no charge.

Straightening Nodes

Once your three rod sections consist of six strips each with nodes staggered and ends trimmed, it's time to straighten the nodes. This will go pretty fast, both here in this book and in real life, because we've discussed it before and because you've practiced. If it's been a while since you heated a node, start with one of the butt-section nodes that will be under the reel seat or grip or, better yet, give yourself a quick refresher course with a piece of scrap. Remember, you don't need to worry too much about the sweeps between nodes. This isn't a specific injunction against straightening strips between the nodes, because I've straightened such places when they were especially bad, and because the straighter your strips are the straighter the section will be. It is, however, a warning not to damage the strip by heating and reheating it trying to get it perfect.

Rough-Beveling and Heat-Treating Bamboo Strips

Using your wooden forms, plane the rectangular strips into untapered triangular ones. As was discussed earlier, use the 90-degree side of the forms to put a slight bevel on one side (enamel against the steep side of the groove), then switch to the 60-degree side and begin alternating strokes from one side to the other as soon as the new bevel more or less matches the first one. At this stage, accuracy and avoiding chipped nodes are considerations, but not major ones. The only thing you really need to worry about is making the strips for your butt section too small. Add at least .040-inch to the butt section's largest dimension and use that as your minimum. If all of your square strips start out more or less the same width, there's nothing wrong with making butt and tip sections the same diameter before heat treating. That way you can heat-treat the sections equally without having to worry about taking the tips out too soon or too late. If your rough-beveled tips are a little smaller, that will save you some effort in final planing because heat-treated cane is a little harder to cut, but you will have to pay extra attention during heat treating because thinner sections heat up faster than thicker ones, just like a roast.

When you do your rough beveling with nonadjustable wooden forms, the basic idea is to plane down just to the wood or just shy of it. Of course, this raises the question of how you change the thickness of the rough-beveled strips for different rods. Well, for the most part, you don't. You make your rough forms large enough to yield strips of adequate size for the average rod you intend to make. For smaller rods you will do a little more planing after heat treating, and for larger rods you will leave the strips raised from the rough-beveling forms. Or you can make a smaller or larger set of rough forms. Garrison had a set of adjustable straight steel forms, and certainly that is an option if you wish to make them. Just follow the instructions in Chapter 8 for making adjustable forms, only make them a little shorter, put adjustments every 10 inches instead of every 5, and make the groove straight instead of tapered.

Heat Treating

Once your strips are beveled, you will use your binder to secure them together for heat treating, assuming that you are using an oven. Remember, some makers flame their cane and perform no other heat treating. I prefer to heat-treat cane in the oven after rough beveling even when I've flamed it. The strips turn out straighter, because the sweeps between nodes relax to some extent when all six strips are held tightly together and heated. This makes final planing easier and makes the blank straighter. Flaming seems to add stiffness to a rod and gives a wide range of possible colors, but even a rod that has been flamed will discharge quite a bit of moisture when subsequently oven-treated.

When binding for heat treating, use plenty of pressure and tension on the thread. While I use a fairly light weight on my single-thread binder for gluing, for this first binding job I use a weight of about 4 pounds and crank the tensioners down just short of the thread's breaking point. I usually add a couple of extra wraps of thread, too. Part of the benefit of heat treating is to straighten the splines, and the more tightly they are held, the straighter they will turn out. Another thing that will make the rod section straighter (or more easily made straight) is to bundle the strips together for heat treating in a different order than they will be when assembled in the finished rod. If you've read the Garrison and Carmichael book, you may remember that Garrison staggered nodes by placing the strips in the order 1, 5, 3, 6, 2, 4 (the firing order of many six-cylinder engines, which evens out vibration), then staggering the nodes in a regular Payne-style spiral. That way, when the rod was assembled with the strips in the usual 1, 2, 3, 4, 5, 6 order, the nodes would be apparently even more widely dispersed. You may also remember reading that Garrison would gather the strips in the old 1, 5, 3, 6, 2, 4 order when binding the strips together for heat treating, though he didn't convey a clear reason for it other than that the finished section came out straighter than it would otherwise.

There *is* a clear reason for it, though I can't say for sure that it's the one Garrison had in mind. If, when you put the bound-together sections into the oven for heat treating, there happens to be a bend in a section, that bend will be there when the strips cool down. And after you plane the strips and apply glue, guess what? That bend will still be there, each bent strip nestled in with its mates. If you displace the strips before binding and heat treating, however, and replace them for gluing, the bends in the strips will cancel one another out to some degree. This is not to say that the section will be straight, or even easy to straighten. A lot of other factors have some effect on that, but they will be straighter or easier to straighten than if you were fighting bends that were put there during heat treating.

Now, the $64,000 question. How much heat, and for how long? Let's tackle this in general terms first. A lot of it has to do with the cane's inherent quality and strength, because considerable variation exists. Some makers have maintained that the best cane doesn't need to be heat-treated at all. This may be true to some extent. I have run across culms of extraordinary resilience (at wide intervals), but I would hate to base my operation on such a small percentage of available cane. Even the biggest fans of light-colored cane concede that heat treating in-

creases the strength and elasticity of cane and reduces its weight. This makes a better rod, in my opinion, no matter how good the cane was to begin with. So, enough heat has to be applied and for sufficient time that most of the cane's natural moisture is driven out and the fibers toughened. Application of heat shrinks the cane, partly because most of the moisture in the cane seems to be in the pith between fibers, and when the water leaves, the pith shrinks. The resulting cane is denser and tougher in fiber and lighter for the absence of water.

Again, how much heat and for how long? With my oven, I heat-treat most rod sections at 375 degrees for a minimum of about twenty minutes. Once a minimum amount of time has elapsed, I'm more concerned about the color of the cane and how much steam it is pushing through the oven vent holes than how much time has elapsed to the dot. Some rods come out after twenty minutes, some stay in up to thirty. You will need to experiment.

Although just setting your oven at 375 and your timer at twenty minutes and sticking the sections in might work, it might also provide a painfully clear illustration of the "look before you leap" principle so central to rod making. The universal stove thermostats that most of us use are not unimpeachably accurate, and getting an accurate temperature reading may be difficult. I have a small dial-face thermometer that reads up to 500 degrees, but don't trust my readings. Your setup and conditions will be different. Again, experiment with some scrap pieces of cane.

Take a half-inch-wide strip a foot or so long with at least one complete section between nodes. Split it in half and put one half in the oven for, say, ten minutes at 375 degrees. After this baking, note its color, then compare it with the untreated half for strength and resilience by flexing and even breaking both of them. If you really want to be scientific, weigh the treated piece before and after baking and note the percentage of weight loss. Repeat this process, increasing (or decreasing) time and temperature, until you are satisfied that you have achieved the best results in both lightness and strength, keeping in mind that it is possible to heat cane too much and damage it, making it brittle. If you're going to discover the point where that occurs, you want to do it on scrap.

Remember that when you put rod sections in the oven, there may be a greater initial temperature drop, again depending on your oven, than there was with small test pieces, so don't be too disturbed if your first rod sections seem underdone after your test time has passed. You'll probably find, eventually, that your time and temperature figures will serve as a minimum, and that you will pay closer attention to the color of the cane and the way the end grain looks than anything else when determining when to take the sections out of the oven.

I have found that, for cane that is not flamed, the end grain will look darker and denser and the enamel will darken a shade, perhaps from pale straw to medium or dark straw, when the heat treatment is sufficient. For cane that *is* flamed, oven treating is an extra process that removes most of any moisture that lingers after flaming or that has crept back in since. Consequently, for flamed sections I rely more on time and temperature standards and less on a definite color change.

Speaking of color, most cane-rod users and makers have a preference, and heat treating is the time when the color of the rod is primarily determined. Heat treating in an oven can produce rods in a fairly narrow spectrum, from light straw to light brown or caramel. Within limits, you can get the moisture out of a rod and keep it light colored by decreasing the temperature and increasing the time, though the rod will be softer than a darker one, and I am told that it is possible to ruin cane by cooking it for too long at lower temperatures. Increasing the tempera-

ture will give you a progessively darker (and stiffer) rod, up to a point. However, if you want a rod that is darker than a light brown, you should flame it with a torch.

The process of experimenting on scrap is the only substitute I know of for experimenting on the rods themselves. You want to get as much moisture out of the cane as possible without damaging it, *and* you want to subject it to a high enough temperature to toughen it, but there are no absolutes, because the climate where you live and how your cane is stored (and for how long) will have an effect on how much moisture there is in the cane already. Further, your conditions will be different from anyone else's. Garrison's tables indicate that he treated cane at 350 degrees Fahrenheit for a maximum of eight minutes and thirty seconds. With my oven, eight minutes and thirty seconds at 350 does next to nothing. With Garrison's setup, twenty minutes at 375 would probably have made charcoal. Just guessing, I would say that Garrison's oven, a propane-fired hunk of steel furnace pipe, probably carried a great deal more thermal inertia than my electric oven, which is not powerful enough to prevent a noticeable drop in temperature when sections are added. You may have better insulation, a more powerful heater, or a different mechanism altogether.

Although I would recommend an electric oven as compact, effective, and safe, it is far from your only option. Garrison, as I mentioned earlier, used a length of pipe heated by a row of propane jets underneath. Claude Kreider used a section of heavy steel pipe suspended from the ceiling by wires and heated by passing the flame from a torch along its length. Mike Clark uses a vertical oven fashioned from a length of stove pipe fastened like a chimney on a kerosene heater. Whichever method you use (except for Kreider's), it is a good idea to rotate the sections and swap them end for end at intervals to assure even heating.

One last thing about heat treating. Once

your strips are heat-treated, it is helpful to think of them as long skinny sponges waiting for any opportunity to soak up moisture. Keeping them in a dry place until they are glued, and keeping the sections in a dry place until they are varnished, will reduce the bamboo's opportunities for reabsorbing the moisture you have driven out, and strengthen its opportunity for stabilizing at its optimum level of lightness and strength.

Setting Forms

Before final planing, you need to set your forms (see Fig. 5.14). If you have a single set of forms, you probably will set them for the butt section, plane out the butt section and then reset the forms for the tips, though there's no law that says you can't do the tips first. The tips are actually easier to plane accurately than the butt but seem scarier because they are so thin. It's up to you. If you use a dial indicator depth gauge, the process of setting forms is pretty obvious. Mark the measurements on a strip of masking tape alongside the forms or with a felt tip pen on the forms themselves (the final passes will scrape the ink off). Go through the stations, measuring and adjusting, at least twice, because each station's ad-

justment will affect the stations to either side. I usually set the forms once, go through again and fine tune the settings, and let the forms sit on my workbench overnight. The next day (or whenever), I will check the settings one more time before I start final planing. Each time you use the depth gauge, check it for proper zero by setting it lengthways on the forms or a piece of plate glass. Make sure that the tip is screwed on tightly and that there is no dust or crud on the base. Clean the forms, too. If the indicator tip stays securely fastened, the zero should not drift, and most changes in zero are the result of dirt. If the zero drifts consistently, something is wrong with the instrument or it is receiving excessively rough handling.

If you have made enough test strips and test sections to understand any consistent discrepancies between what your indicator reads, what the strips measure, and what the glued-up section measures, set the forms as your experience informs you. If you haven't, set the forms .003-inch over, then adjust them during final planing based on the measurements you get from the strips.

Removing Enamel from the Bamboo

Let's start with the rough-beveled strips for the butt section. As mentioned earlier, they should be somewhat larger than the largest final dimension. Your next task is to remove the enamel, but it's a good idea to plane a few strokes on each pith side first to take out any roughness and to true up the strip. Then, placing a strip enamel side up in the forms (with the forms adjusted for the butt section, a rough-beveled strip should sit well raised of even the butt groove in the forms), remove the enamel first by scraping, then by sanding. You may choose to leave the enamel on and remove it after the rod is glued, in which case you will need to add an allowance of approximately .003-inch per

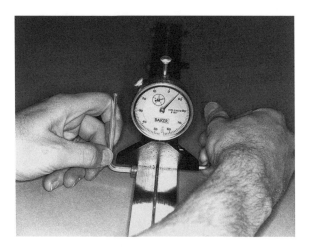

Figure 5.14. Setting forms. As with everything else, don't try to do too much at once. Steel bars will only bend so much, and you don't want to strip something.

side when setting the forms. I much prefer to take the enamel off prior to final planing for a couple of reasons. First, it is not uncommon for worm holes and other flaws to hide under the enamel. If you discover them before you glue up the sections you may be able to make a replacement strip and save the rod. Second, removing the enamel and sanding before final planing evens out numerous small irregularities, including protrusions from the nodes after heat treating, which otherwise would interfere with accurate planing and measurement. The net effect of all of this is a smoother, flatter, better-looking rod. The sacrifice in time is that you scrape and sand off the enamel, then sand off the glue, whereas if you left the enamel on, you would just have to scrape and sand once.

When scraping, your objective should be not to scrape down to the power fibers but merely to remove the hard glossy part of the enamel so that your sandpaper can bite. You want to leave the thin layer between the enamel and the power fibers intact as much as possible. Scraping all the way down to the power fibers puts you in a bind, because if you sand at all to remove the scraping marks you will be cutting into the power fibers. You should gauge your efforts so that your last pass with the sandpaper removes all but the very last trace of the cambium and just reveals the power fibers. Don't scrape the nodes; you will finish and level them with sandpaper. For scraping, I use a small-bodied thumb scraper made by Conover Woodcraft (see Fig. 5.15). It is very controllable and cuts smoothly. I own other scrapers, including a beautifully made and expensive one, but I always wind up reaching for the little thumb scraper.

As an aside, if you flame the culm dark enough, the enamel will become very fragile, almost chalky, and there may be no need to scrape at all. If the enamel looks almost black and sort of blistered, 240 or 320 grit sandpaper will probably bite just fine.

On to the sandpaper. You will need a

Figure 5.15. Breaking through the enamel with a little bodied scraper by Conover Woodcraft. Unless you don't mind chatter marks on the rod or taking the risk of breaking through the power fibers, take it easy with the scraper and do the real work with sandpaper.

sanding block of some kind. A rubber sanding block will flex and round the corners, so a piece of wood, plexiglass, or metal would be a better choice. The larger the sanding block, the harder it is to control, but the smaller the block, the harder it is on your fingers. I opt for maximum control and use a very small block, but I'll probably change my tune somewhere on down the road. I usually start with 240 grit wet or dry sandpaper (used dry, of course) to even out the scraping and use 400 grit to finish (see Fig. 5.16).

Figure 5.16. Sanding a node using a small glass plaque. I like to hit the nodes before moving on to the enamel, but I use the same rig for both.

I usually hit the nodes with sandpaper first. With short, light strokes, I knock them down to the level of the enamel, then sand the whole strip. Remember back when you filed, straightened, and flattened the nodes, you filed them until there was a narrow band of enamel in the middle of the node, not until the node was completely bare. The nodes were flattened, and now, after heat treating (assuming that you are heat-treating at this point—if you don't heat-treat after rough beveling, you naturally should file the nodes bare to start with), they will have pushed back out just a tiny fraction of an inch. This sanding step takes off that little bit of raised-up node and takes the tiny bit of remaining enamel with it. Leveling the nodes like this makes a hard sanding block especially important. It takes some time, but if you do it right the nodes will be invisible when you sight down the rod and undetectable when you run your fingers down it, and there will be no cut power fibers.

Final Planing of the Bamboo Strips

Place a mark on your forms with an ink marker where the butt end of the strips will be placed, and perhaps another at the tip. We discussed planing at some length earlier, so the main idea here is to remind you of a few of the more crucial points. Your blade must be very, very sharp, and you must be prepared to resharpen it or switch to a fresh blade frequently, perhaps on every strip. I prefer to sharpen several blades at a stretch, then, when planing, pop in a fresh blade as needed. I can usually get through a section on three blades. I use the first blade to take all six strips down to within .010-inch or so of the forms. Then I use a fresh blade to make the final passes on three strips, and another fresh blade for the other three. Sometimes I run into a very tough piece of cane and wind up using four or five blades per

section. You can work out your own system, but when you get down to the final passes, taking off transparent .001-inch shavings, your blade has to be sharp or you will chip nodes and tear off fibers. If you are chipping nodes on what should be your final passes, either your plane is set for too coarse a cut, your blade is dull, or it is sharpened with an insufficiently steep bevel.

During final planing, it is a good idea to pay especially close attention to plane alignment and to make frequent measurements to ensure that your strips are maintaining their equilateral cross section. When you start final planing you will be turning a straight strip into a tapered one. I think it makes some sense, after taking a few strokes over the whole length of the strip, to start at the tip and plane for a number of strokes on the first foot or two of the strip (alternating sides, of course), then move the starting point for your planing stroke 6 inches back, take a few strokes, move the starting point back, and so on. This builds some taper into the strip before you get down to the steel, and you wind up taking longer final strokes and digging into the forms with your plane less. I guess avoiding hacking your forms up is less of an issue than the desirability of long, smooth final cuts, but the proper method is the same in either case.

This is mostly important for butt sections, since for tips you can use the butt side of the forms as a preliminary step, planing down to steel (or almost) to establish the taper and triangle. When you flip the forms over to the tip groove, you should have little to do except make fine, even strokes from butt to tip until you reach the surface of the forms. Unless you build a separate set of forms for both butt and tip sections, the above solution doesn't help much for butt sections, but that's fine. I've used one set of forms for all my rods and never felt deprived. If you feel a serious need for a preliminary planing step for butt sections, you might set a .020-inch oversize taper into the forms initially, then reset the forms for the final passes. However, this step is really advisable only if you are very rough with the plane. If you take the butt strips down to final size with an ordinary degree of caution and finesse, such precautions should be unnecessary.

All right, you're planing along, planing along. When do you stop? The short version is that you plane until the plane blade just touches steel, but there's more to it that you will discover. When you start with the rough beveled strip, you want a cut from your plane that will remove material somewhat quickly but will not chew up the nodes. Actually, you can chew up the nodes a little bit when you're removing material quickly, so long as you go to a finer cut soon enough that any chipped areas will be removed before the final dimension is reached. It's a waste of time, effort and blades to start out with a .001-inch cut when you have .020- to .060-inch worth of cane to remove. Then again, haste has spoiled more rods than anything else. Just how coarse your initial cut can be depends on the bamboo, so you'll have to experiment. I'd say that .005- to .010-inch is an acceptable range, but if you get really nasty deep chips and lifts with .005-inch shavings, then that's obviously too coarse or your blade is dull, or both. Also, some bamboo is just tougher to cut cleanly than the rest. The closer you get to the steel, the finer you want the cut to be, partly to ensure that the start of a cut doesn't show up in the glue joint, and partly as insurance against chips and lifts that, if they occur this late in the game, cannot be remedied (see Figs. 5.17 and 5.18).

You should test your strips for hidden weaknesses by bending them, not enough to damage them, but enough that any deviations from a smooth normal curve become apparent. You should do this at least once during or after final planing for the butt strips, and before final planing for the tip strips. The tip strips after final planing are too small and fragile to offer much resistance on their own, so bending them then tells you

Figure 5.17. Final passes should take the finest possible shaving.

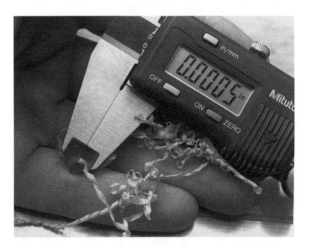

Figure 5.18. A properly sharpened blade in a properly set up plane should take a shaving as fine as .0005-inch. You may not absolutely need to take a shaving this fine, but it's good to be able to do so in case you run into a really troublesome node.

little. Come to think of it, I make it a habit to flex each strip before straightening nodes and before and after rough beveling as well. The idea is to catch bad strips as early as possible (see Fig. 5.19). Catching one during or after final planing is discouraging, but less so then than finding it later by breaking a rod.

When you have finished planing and the strips measure to your satisfaction, place each strip (one at a time) enamel side down on one of the bars of your planing forms and take a couple of passes with your plane (fine cut) on the pith apex (see Fig. 5.20). Taking

Figure 5.19. A worm hole in a strip. You really hate to see this during final planing. If you don't have a spare, sometimes you can save the strip by planing away just the side with the flaw, but you need enough cane to completely remove the flaw and you also need to have some confidence that the flaw is an isolated one.

Figure 5.20. Planing the pith apex.

the edge off this apex makes it easier for the strips to nestle together and gives a space for a tiny glue bead to run down the center of the rod. You're now ready to glue.

Gluing the Strips Together

Glues

It is tempting to say that your choice and use of an adhesive is the most important factor in your rod building. The characteris-tics of glues that are most important to a rod builder are film thickness, shear strength, and water resistance (complete). Obviously, if your glue fails, your rod comes apart—perhaps the most conclusive and complete failure that can occur. However, there are several different glues being used today, and all of them must work to some degree or no one would use them. The trick is to find the adhesive in which you have the most confidence, keeping in mind that any glue can fail if your strips are not well made and if the glue is not properly used.

Alphatic Resin Glues. My first reaction to what most people know as yellow carpenter's glue is not enthusiastic. Other glues are intrinsically stronger and have greater shear strength and water resistance, so I have more confidence in them. On the other hand, my predjudice may be based on a previous generation of adhesives and may not do justice to recent developments in this field. New alphatics like Titebond II are inexpensive, widely available, very low in toxicity, essentially waterproof, and although not as strong as URAC 185 or epoxy, they are certainly stronger than many glues that were used in the old days. One well-known rod maker has glued hundreds of rods with Titebond II and tells me that he has had no problems. He loves the stuff because of the previously mentioned attributes, plus the convenience of no mixing and the easy cleanup with wa-ter. For him and doubtless for others, Tite-bond II is perfect. Although stronger adhesives exist, Titebond II is strong, and if he is willing to trust his reputation to it, it must be strong enough.

Epoxies. Epoxies are almost my favorite chemicals. They can be created to cover a wide range of needs with formulations for extreme heat resistance, extreme flexibility, extreme hardness, extreme resistance to sol-vents, and on and on. They can contain toluene and other solvents, so if the label says "use only with adequate ventilation," do it.

As mentioned, there are many different brands and types of epoxy for different applications, which would indicate that it is important to choose the right one for bamboo fly rods. The one I use, Nyatex parts 10EH008 and 10E007, is in fairly widespread use among rod makers. This is a very strong long-curing epoxy. Because it takes about three hours to set initially, it affords the builder plenty of time for the gluing and straightening process. Frankly, I'm not sure I would trade this open time for anything. At normal room temperatures it takes five to seven days to fully cure. It can be force-cured at higher temperatures, and the common recipe among rod builders is three hours at 235 degrees. However, I've started simply hanging the sticks in my drying box for a week or two. It has been said that heat-curing the glue will increase its strength and heat-deflection temperature, and this may be, but the folks at Nyatex didn't seem to think so. "When the stuff is cured, it's cured," the tech fellow said. "It doesn't care how long it took to get there." The point is probably moot, because even without heat curing it's incredibly strong and quite heat resistant.

A side benefit to using the full curing time is that it makes getting the binding string off a snap. Wait a couple of days, until the epoxy is firmly set but not glass-hard, and the string comes off easily. Wait until the glue is completely cured and you're stuck sanding the string off. Or you can use poly kite string for binding: Glue doesn't stick to it and it is much stronger than cotton, so it will come off easier. On the other hand, it is more expensive and may not stand up to the temperatures of heat curing as well as cotton. Cleanup is easy with white vinegar or rubbing alcohol.

URAC 185. Since about 1940, more rods have been glued with URAC 185 than with any other adhesive, for reasons that are fully evident. It is very strong, quite heat resistant, completely water resistant, has outstanding shear strength, and is a nice tan color. This tan color certainly doesn't hide open seams in a rod, but it doesn't hurt, either.

A lot of great rod makers continue to use URAC, and I would encourage anyone who feels comfortable with it to do so. I've used it but have never been able to get completely at home with it. Part of the problem is that, in my experience and in my particular environment, when the glue is mixed for optimum strength it is too thick and sets too fast for it to be sufficiently squeezed out during binding, leaving small, uniform but visible glue lines. The rods with these glue lines have performed well, but I'd rather not have the lines at all. The time-honored rod-building recipe of four parts liquid to one part powder gives a thinner glue (thus thinner glue lines and a longer working time) and an extended set-up time but weakens the glue. Even in its weakened state URAC may be strong enough, and certainly there are plenty of rods out there to indicate that it is. The success or failure of URAC probably depends upon getting the perfect ratio of powder to liquid for your needs and your environment, and upon the speed with which you can get string on the blank. Fine, but I for one don't need that kind of pressure.

Resorcinol. You don't see many Resorcinol-glued rods these days, though a lot of rods were glued with it and you still see it in hardware stores and woodworking catalogs. Garrison used it, and the deep wine purple glue line it leaves is one of the evident characteristics of his rods. It has all of the positive attributes as well as drawbacks of URAC 185. It is a formaldehyde catalyzing glue as well, and is extremely strong, virtually waterproof, and insoluble. A few makers still use it, but most probably stay away from it as much because of the color as anything else. Some people may think the purple line left by the glue soaking into the bamboo is neat, but others may not. If you find some and don't mind the color, give it a shot. The Garrison and Carmichael book contains comprehensive instructions for its use.

The Moment of Truth

It takes a lot of rods until you feel comfortable with gluing, and even then there can be surprises. As Nolan Ryan said, "Some days are just better than others." As far as just getting the glue on and the thread wrapped, it's pretty easy. However, your best single shot at getting the rod straight comes when you glue it, and that's when things can get interesting. There are three major contributors to gluing a rod up straight. The first is relatively straight splines, particularly for large-diameter butt sections. The second is the alignment, tuning, and adjustment of your binder. The third is your skill and persistence at manipulating the rod section once it's glued and wrapped but before the glue sets. The matter of straight splines was discussed a little earlier under heat treating, and there's not a whole lot to add. Heat treating usually results in splines that are adequately straight, but if they seem less straight than you would like, it is better to accept the challenge of gluing them up straight than to try to fix them at this point. The only time this might not be true is when you are trying to build something truly enormous, like a 13-foot spey rod. The larger the strip, the less cooperative it becomes when gluing.

Perhaps the most important part in gluing sections up straight is the tuning of your binder. A properly set up single-string binder will help straighten the rod sections as you glue them. If the guides on your binder are aligned in a straight line, so that the rod section is not bent as it passes through, the twirling motion of the rod against the pressure of the belt, the thread, and the guides will perform much the same task as rolling on a flat surface. It follows, of course, that a binder whose guides do not provide such an alignment will produce a straight rod only accidentally. Another important consideration is the weight on the drive belt—it should be as light as possible, a half-pound or so, and certainly not more than a pound for normal trout rods. A heavy weight will distort the section even if the guides and the strips are perfect. I'm operating here on the assumption that you are using a single-string binder. Other kinds have much to recommend them, but I've built all my rods using the single-string, and it's a case where the devil you know is better than the devil you don't. Also, the single-string binder is very easy to build, and it's my strong suspicion that the vast majority of individual rod makers use some variation of it. (For those interested in alternatives, there is a brief discussion of two- or four-string binders in Chapter 10.)

The next gluing bogey is thread torque. When you wind the binding thread on under tension, it stretches. This is good, because it keeps the strips bound tightly together, but the effect of a stretched thread spiraled around the section and tied at both ends is twist. This is bad. The thread tension is opposed to some extent by the countering twist of the drive belt, and by the use of opposing thread wraps. It's a delicate balance. The first wrap of thread compresses the strips and forces the glue out. This takes up some of the stretch in the thread, so although there is some twist, the thread is not particularly tight. The second wrap, in the opposite direction, is made on a section that is made solid and unyielding by the first wrap, so the thread retains most of its tension and voila, twist in the opposite direction. There are three different ways to combat this. The first is to increase the driving-belt weight for the second pass, which increases the counter-twist of the belt. The second is to decrease the thread tension, which effectively does the same thing. The third is to make additional wraps to balance out the twist. Another thing you can do is use a heavier thread or string, which will stretch less. This would seem like the simplest solution, but I like the 16/4 cotton thread because its low bulk makes the rod easier to straighten (once I've dealt with the twist).

I have talked to a number of makers

about this subject, and it is telling that almost all of them have different solutions and some even see the problem differently. Some makers change tension, some change weights, some change both, and some just don't find it a problem (which makes me almost unbearably envious). Since almost all of the binders in the world are home-built, this variety should come as no surprise. If you understand the principles behind the undesirable phenomenon, you can diagnose your binding system and find the best solution.

For what it's worth, here's what works for me. With 16/4 cotton thread for binding and 80-pound Spectra kite line for a belt, I make the first two passes without changing anything in the setup. There is usually some twist after the second pass, so I make a third pass in the direction of the first pass. Depending on the severity of the twist, I may slightly decrease the thread tension. If the third pass has put its own twist in, I will decrease the thread tension slightly and run it through a fourth time, countering the third wrap. This may sound like a lot of extra work, but I actually like having four light wraps on the blank because that makes it less floppy and easier to straighten. Put another way, I plan on using four wraps but stop if the section is twist-free after three.

So, with that little bit of perspective, let's glue.

1. Make sure you have plenty of time. Gluing can't be hurried. Well, I suppose you *can* hurry it, but man, will you ever pay. It has taken me anywhere from one to four hours to glue a rod. Of course, the reason some rods have taken four hours is that with epoxy, one has that long. If you use glue that sets in an hour, you're done in an hour, for better or worse. If (using epoxy) you plan on four hours and everything just falls into place and it takes one and a half, consider it a gift and do something fun. If this is your first rod, consider gluing just one section at a time. This will allow you to concentrate better on each step and will give you two or three shots at the drill. Actually, it's a good idea to plane out and glue a couple of test sections before you try it on a rod. Do it. You can thank me later.

2. Lay out everything you'll need: newspaper, cheap toothbrush for spreading glue, glue, rod sections, binder. Set the thread tension by hanging the driving belt weight on a loop in the end of the thread and increasing the tension until the weight just pulls the thread through the tensioners.

3. Carefully clean all dust and debris from each strip. Don't use a rag. A rag will catch fibers on the edge of the strip and remove them. I use a small piece of soft leather from an old golf glove. While you're at it, thoroughly clean your workbench or wherever you're gluing. It doesn't take much of a chip to screw up a glue joint.

4. Bundle the strips together in order, and even the butts by pressing them against the edge of your workbench (see Fig. 5.21).

5. Wrap masking tape around the section at approximately 12-inch intervals, closer if

Figure 5.21. Evening bundled strips by pushing against the edge of a workbench.

Figure 5.22. Wrap the section at intervals with masking tape. Start each wrap on the same strip and end each wrap on the strip on the other side of the rod. For instance, begin on strip 4 and end on strip 1 so that there will be one joint with only one thickness of tape over it.

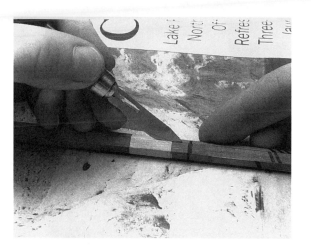

Figure 5.23. Slice carefully through the tape at the joint with only one tape thickness. A scalpel blade is ideal because of the curvature, but you can use a straight razor blade and stick toothpicks in the crack, if necessary.

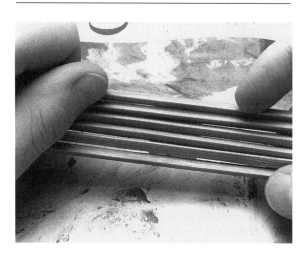

Figure 5.24. Spread the strips, flexing the tape so the section stays open.

needed (see Fig. 5.22). If you start each wrap on the same flat, say, number 6, and end it after one and a half turns, you will have a joint with only one thickness of masking tape to cut through. Garrison did that, and Carmichael included it in his book. Now that's the kind of thing you *might* figure out for yourself, but being told up front sure helps. It also helps to use narrower masking tape for the tips. If possible, buy a premium tape from an auto-body-supply store. The tape you get in most hardware stores is too thin and the adhesive is either so puny that the tape falls off or so gummy that it sticks to the blank. The best tape is Scotch Brand Masking Tape. It will cost about twice as much as hardware store tape, but it's at least twice as good.

6. Using a scalpel, run down the joint that has only one thickness of masking tape covering it. A scalpel works better than a razor blade because it is thinner and curved, so that the whole thickness of the blade need not penetrate the gap in order to cut the tape. With a thin, fresh scalpel blade you should have no trouble. If you seem to be having trouble, slow down, or use a bamboo splinter or toothpick to wedge the sections apart while you cut the tape (see Fig. 5.23).

7. You now have rod sections that are held together with tape but that will open up for gluing (see Fig. 5.24). Bend the tape segments until the strips stay open, then lay them on newspaper, enamel side down. Inspect the sections to make sure all the strips are oriented correctly and in the right order. Using a soft brush, go over them one more time to remove any lingering dust.

8. Mix the glue (see Fig. 5.25). If you're using Nyatex epoxy, you should mix it, wait fifteen minutes, then mix it again before using. Later on, you will mix it earlier and do

Figure 5.25. Mix the glue. This is sort of a hint from Heloise—I use an old ice cube tray for mixing epoxy. Once the tray is full, I pop out the old glue cubes and start over.

brush, but the local Osco store has these store-brand brushes that occasionally go on sale for nineteen cents, so I've been using them. Acid brushes work well too and are even cheaper. Don't skimp on the glue; it's better to have to clean up some drippings than not to use enough. If you're using Nyatex, wait a few minutes to let the adhesive sink into the bamboo. See Fig. 5.26.

10. Pick up the butt section from the newspaper and gently close the strips back into a hexagon (see Fig. 5.27). Place the section in the binder, ferrule end first. (The tips will go ferrule end first as well.) Loop the drive belt twice over the end of the rod sec-

Figure 5.26. Spreading the glue. It's probably best to stroke the brush from butt to tip to avoid catching fibers or, on the tips, catching the fragile ends.

some of the other preceding stuff during that fifteen minutes. If this is your first rod, though, the last thing you need to do is imitate a busy chef. If you must do something, double-check to make everything is working right on your binder. No knots in the thread? Good. If you're using a nonepoxy adhesive, forget about the waiting. You probably need to move at a pace that approximates purposeful relaxed urgency. With any two-part glue, measurement is important and often critical. I measure epoxy with plastic spoons most of the time. Two teaspoons of each part seems to make plenty for one rod. Be very, very careful not to stick the spoon you used for part A into part B. The slightest contamination will ruin the whole can. I mix the epoxy according to a strict ritual, using separate tools to pry the lid off each container, and discarding each spoon immediately after use.

If I'm gluing a lot, I'll put the epoxy in separate pump dispensers that measure out 1 ounce per pump, regardless of viscosity.

9. Using a toothbrush, spread glue on the splines. You could probably use any

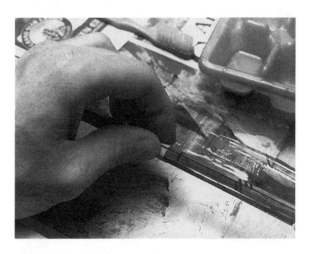

Figure 5.27. Carefully close the strips back.

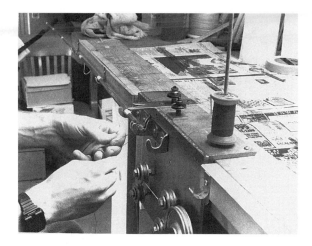

Figure 5.28. Bind the strips together in your binder, or whatever device you're using.

Figure 5.29. A single-string binder.

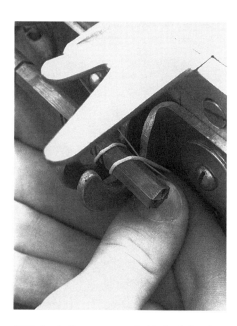

Figure 5.30. For the first wrap, wrap the binding belt twice around the blank in a clockwise direction when viewing from the end (wrap away from yourself), and pass the thread under the belt as shown.

tion clockwise. Pass the binding thread under the drive belt and make four or five half hitches over the end of the section (see Fig. 5.28). Turn the handle slowly, allowing time for the glue to squeeze out as you go, and pulling the pieces of tape off as they approach the drive belt. When you come to the end of the strip, disengage the strip from the belt, pull out an extra couple of feet of thread, and make another four or five half hitches to secure it. When you bind tip sections, the pressure of the driving belt may put a dangerous-looking bend in the section as the diameter diminishes. If, when this begins to happen, you put your finger between the strands of the belt directly under the rod section, the pressure will be transferred somewhat to the sides and the section won't be distorted as much. See the accompanying photo sequence, Figs. 5.29 through 5.34.

11. Reversing the direction of the drive belt and the binding thread, repeat the process. If there is no twist after this pass, you have been living right. It's time to wipe off the excess glue and straighten. If there is some twist, you need to employ some or all of the remedies discussed earlier.

12. The final hurdle in gluing is straightening. This doesn't have to take as much

time and trouble as what I'm about to describe, but it's a real pay-me-now-or-pay-me-later situation. Any crookedness you don't get out in gluing you'll have to take out with heat later, and that can be dangerous. I'd rather spend the time up front and save the rod from the heat, if possible. Of course,

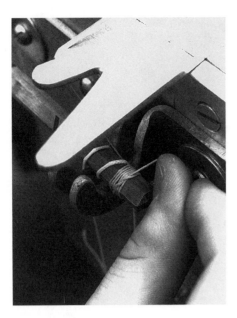

Figure 5.31. Wrap the thread around the blank clockwise once or twice and make several half hitches. When you turn the binder crank, the thread will be wound onto the blank between the turns of the belt. After the wrap is complete, tie off with half hitches.

Figure 5.32. For the second wrap, wrap the binding belt twice around the blank in a counterclockwise direction and pass the thread under the belt as shown.

that's not always possible. Some rods are just straight from the word go, and others fight you down to the wire—which doesn't mean that they will be bad rods. So do your best to get the sections straight. If you can't, the problem is not necessarily you.

Figure 5.33. Make a few counterclockwise half hitches to tie off.

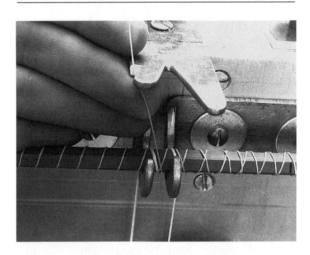

Figure 5.34. The wrap spacing is governed by the spacing of the rod-cradle guides. The thread guide must place the thread between the turns of the belt, which means you'll need at least two different guide notches to accommodate sections of large and small diameters.

When the section is bound, your best friend for straightening is a good flat surface. I'm lucky—I have a piece of glass that must have been an old bank door. It's a full inch thick, about 7 feet long, and 2 1/2 feet wide, and it makes a perfect straightening table. Your workbench or kitchen counter, protected by a sheet of glass, formica, or masonite, will work fine. Just remember that flatter is better. The first step is to roll the section on the table. This will show you what degree of crookedness you must deal with right off the bat. If it rolls smoothly, you're home free; if it flops and wobbles, you have work to do.

You can accomplish a lot simply by rolling the rod section on the flat surface with your hands (see Fig. 5.35). (When straightening the ends, hang the inch or so with the half hitches over the edge so they don't screw things up.) Still, it's a good idea to find a small piece of plywood or glass (I use glass—the dimensions are not critical but I would think a foot square would be about minimum) for rolling out bends that cover larger areas (see Fig. 5.36), and an artist's hard rubber or plastic roller (see Fig. 5.37). When I'm gluing a rod, I will carefully observe the way the rod passes through the binder. If the end flops

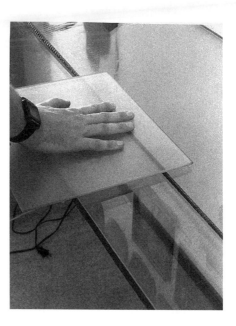

Figure 5.36. Using a square of glass for straightening.

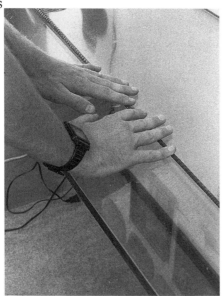

Figure 5.35. Straightening the section by rolling on a flat surface. A flat surface is your best friend for straightening.

Figure 5.37. Straightening with an artist's hard rubber roller.

around, that's a bad sign, and I will usually take it to the table to straighten it as much as I can by rolling and pressing between wraps. If the section runs true through the binder, I will usually go ahead and put all the wraps on, then straighten.

If there's one area of the rod section that you want to have straight right out of the string, it's the ferrule end. It doesn't mat-

ter how long you have to roll and press and tweak (this is why I like epoxy so much), having the last foot or so of the ferrule end of the section perfect is worth the effort. When the glue is freshly applied, the strips will slide against one another pretty easily, which is why the section may feel like a wet noodle and why trying to make adjustments with your hands alone at this point is normally pretty frustrating. Unless the section is braced against a flat surface, the bend you remove will simply reappear somewhere else with equal severity. When the glue starts to set a little, you can be more aggressive.

One of Wayne Cattanach's tricks that I use is to place the section on the table with the convex side of a bend facing up. Visualize the rod section as a pool cue. Place your fingers on the section just where the bend starts and press gently. With the other hand, lift the butt of the section slightly and draw it back, as if you were drawing back a pool cue. The degree to which you lift the butt of the section, the amount of pressure you apply with your fingers, and the length of the stroke will determine the amount of correction. Any correction you make will probably affect the area of the section directly ahead of it somewhat. Once you start manipulating the rod in this way you're pretty much committed to chasing the bend all the way to the tip, because the sections have to slide, and the motion has to be released somewhere. Resistance to sliding grows with section diameter, both because of the stiffness of the strips and their surface area. That's why you need to start at the butt and progress toward the tip when trying to stroke out problems.

You can see the larger problems just by rolling on the flat surface, but some bends are slight enough that the weight of the blank itself will press them down and render them invisible. Once the section rolls smoothly, carefully pick it up and suspend it by holding the tip of the section. Sighting down the section from this vantage point (above) will expose lingering bends. For a surefire test, spin the section slowly by twirling the tip gently between your fingers. If it wobbles noticeably, you need to find out why.

Once the rod sections are straight, or as straight as you can get them, hang them up in a warm, dry place. Congratulations! You've got the blank all but done.

That's a lot to swallow about straightening at one time if you're just beginning.

However, a lot of things that are difficult and maybe a little tedious to describe in words become fully evident when you actually do them. In a sense, it sounds harder than it is. In another sense, being able to produce straight sections out of the string is a matter of time and experience, and the most voluminous instructions can only point you in the right (one would hope) direction. Having a wet, sticky, freshly glued bamboo rod section in your hand is the best teacher.

Removing String and Glue

After the glue has cured you will need to remove the string and excess glue. Boy, if that's not self-evident, I don't know what is. With most glues, you can simply nick the half hitches loose and unwind the string. It will stick, of course, but it will come off nonetheless. If you use Nyatex and heat-cure it or wait a week until it is completely cured, you are stuck sanding the string off. As mentioned earlier, I usually peel the string off after a day or so, then put the section back in the drying cabinet for a week or two.

Either way, you are faced with some sanding. In order to preserve the flatness and sharp corners of the rod section, you need to use a sanding block of some kind, just as when you removed the enamel. You'll probably start sanding with 240 grit wet or dry paper. The glue bond on regular open coat garnet paper is not tough enough. You should wind up sanding off the very last skim of glue residue and only polishing the bamboo itself with 600 grit sandpaper, so take it easy with the 240. If you go all the way to the wood with the 240, you'll have to take off a couple of thousandths of your power fibers just to get the 240 grit scratches out. So, using the 240 grit and a sanding block, work over the section, one flat at a time, and remove most of the excess glue (see Fig. 5.38). Switch to 320 or 400 grit, and remove all but the last traces, then finish up with 600 grit. If your sandpaper shows white dust, you're removing glue. If it shows tan or

Figure 5.38. Sanding away glue residue with a small block.

brown, you're removing bamboo and should halt or proceed with utmost caution. The objective is to get the smoothest, flattest surface you can without sanding away the power fibers.

Straightening

Once you have removed the string and glue, you have an unobstructed view of the blank and can accomplish any necessary straightening that remains with heat. Actually, I check the blank after the string comes off but before the glue does. I correct any visible bends at this stage with the glue still on; the glue helps protect the blank against scorching. However, it doesn't take much junk on the rod to prevent you from seeing a slight bend.

If you see a bend, mark it in pencil with an X on the convex apex of the bend. That way you can tell exactly where the bend is, center it between your hands, and, with the X facing you, bend outward with both thumbs. That is, at least for me, the most natural and controllable way to apply a bend. Once the bend is marked, heat the section very carefully in the area of the bend and apply just enough pressure to correct the

problem. How much heat and pressure is enough is hard to describe. From your experience straightening nodes, you will have a pretty good idea of when the bamboo is ready to bend. You don't have to get the section quite as hot as you did the node because you're applying heat over a larger area and directly to the power fibers. That's good, because you don't have the pith to char, so too much heat means that you burn the power fibers. This can be tricky, but I'll bet you don't have a problem right away. On your first rod, you will be so cautious that you will barely get enough heat and apply enough pressure to do the job. Bit by bit, the rod will become perfectly straight. When you will get bitten is on your third, fourth, or seventh rod, when you start to feel comfortable and maybe allow yourself to hurry or to let your mind wander. You'll be working on a bend, rotating and sliding the section over the heat gun, when the phone will ring, and you'll stop to wonder whether you should answer it, or your spouse will ask you what you did with the checkbook, and the next thing you know, you will look at the section you were supposed to be moving and turning and there's a big black spot.

Or maybe not. You may heed my warning, or just be an extremely diligent, focused person, or just lucky. If it does happen, it likely will do so only once. Such a mistake is an extremely effective and pointed lesson in patience and concentration and will last a long, long time.

Assuming that everything has gone well, and no doubt it has, you now have a blank. With the addition of ferrules and a few other things, you will have a rod. Take a break, have a beer or something. Make it substantial, with enough gravity to celebrate the fact that you have accomplished a whale of a lot and are about to enter the home stretch.

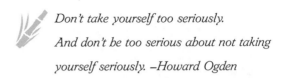

Don't take yourself too seriously.
And don't be too serious about not taking
yourself seriously. –Howard Ogden

6. Transforming the Blank to a Fly Rod

Other than the fine double shotgun, there is no tool of sport that is more highly refined, more subtly harmonized, or more cherished by its owner than the top-grade bamboo fly rod. When I read the following, from *Good Guns,* by Steve Bodio, I couldn't help mentally substituting "rod" for "gun."

> Good guns are fine things, so perfect in their fusion of form and function that non-, even anti-hunters can be moved by their shape and grace. To want to own and use a few is a natural outcome of good hunting, related neither to conspicuous consumption nor to the neurotic "completionism" of collectors. Such a desire implies an intelligent and almost sensuous delight in the tools and craft of the sporting life.

This is not to imply that making a bamboo fly rod is anywhere near as complex or demanding as building a handmade double. To speak of fly rods in terms of aesthetics at all is to plunge into murky waters, made so because tastes vary so wildly, and clouded still further by the often indistinct line between craft and art. It is argued not infrequently that for crafts like rod building or fly tying to lay any claim to artistry is pretentious. Flies, for example, to actually qualify as flies, must be made to be fished. If they are to be fished, they should not take enough time to tie to make them art, QED. It seems to go against the grain of some folks for a utilitarian object to be made needlessly beautiful or, even if it is beautiful, to put it in a shadowbox frame and admire it when it should be fishing and its place on the wall taken by *real* art, like a painting of dogs playing poker. Fine. Lots of people hunt with taped-together 870s, but that doesn't mean that beautifully engraved, richly but cleanly stocked Best-grade side-by-sides shouldn't exist. Or that they are not art.

One view is summed up in a definition by John Barsness (quoted by Bodio): "Art relates to the human condition; craft is everything else." I'll buy that, as long as it is granted that part of the human condition is the urge to create unique and beautiful things, and that this urge may be manifested in some pretty utilitarian objects. I've heard it argued very convincingly that the first art was a decorated weapon. The idea of art as the exclusive province of particularly gifted musicians, writers, painters, sculptors, et al.; the cult of artist as hero, art for its own sake—all this blew up as recently as the early nineteenth century. To the extent that it has freed

84

artists as social commentators I think it is good; to the extent that it has encouraged the average person to think of art as something practicable only by a select few, I think it is bad, or at least not helpful. A large part of the effect of much universally acknowledged art is owed to a superlative mastery of craft, and many apparently pedestrian crafts are lifted far above the commonplace by a practitioner with an artistic soul. Art is all around us, and to the degree we recognize and appreciate it, our lives are enriched. Bamboo rods may be too functional, limited, and predetermined to qualify as art in the same majestic sense as Brahms' Fourth Symphony, but there is more to them than mere assembly, or craft, if you prefer. Bamboo rods, in reflecting what you believe is beautiful, become your art.

Again, it's up to you. If you just want to make fishin' poles and feel that to gussy them up with varnish that might make you mad if you scratched it is pointless, that's perfectly fine. If, on the other hand, you see bamboo rod making as an opportunity to push yourself and make something as fine as it can be, thinking of rods as art makes some sense. It makes even more sense to the maker who wishes to sell a few rods, because in today's competitive bamboo market, beauty is synonymous with quality. See, bamboo rods are now collectible. Thanks to the appearance and interest of well-heeled buyers who can't cast, a beautiful rod that casts poorly sells quicker than a great-casting rod that looks like hell. I'm guessing that you don't want to make either, but the question of which rod might constitute a better work of art sounds like an entertaining argument. Please form one line to the left. Throughout this chapter, I'll supplement the instructions for the various finishing operations with tips and ideas for making a rod that is conventionally handsome. You are free to disregard them and follow your muse, of course, but it may be helpful to have a place to start.

Just a general note before we start putting things together. The four main cosmetic elements in a bamboo rod are the quality of its joints, its straightness, color, and finish quality. Straightness and joints have been discussed earlier, and finish quality will be addressed in the section on varnishing. A rod is either perfectly straight or it's not, but color is an element where there are no absolutes. Variables to be considered include cane color (by the time you have a glued-up blank I feel it's too late to change its color, though some past and present makers have stained rods; tempering and flaming give you a wide range of possibilities earlier in the process), hardware color (bright or blued), reel-seat wood variety and finish color, thread color and wrap finish (penetrating varnish or color preserver). The most handsome rods, in my opinion, are those where all of the various materials and colors harmonize. Therefore, most of my thread colors lean toward earth tones, with both thread and reel-seat wood chosen to complement the bamboo color.

Adding the Ferrules

Adding ferrules (assuming that the rod is not a one-piece) is the first step toward making a finished rod. Without ferrules you don't have a functional fly rod, so every effort must be made to ensure that they are properly seated and not likely to come off. This is harder than it sounds, because ferrules are the focus of tremendous stress. Ferrule mounting also is a major contributor to rod straightness (or crookedness). Amplified by the length of the rod sections, even a slight misalignment at the ferrule is visible. The requirements for good ferrule mounting are blank straightness, lathe setup and alignment, proper wood-to-metal fit, a good surface for adhesive bonding, proper adhesive, and patience.

Choice of Size and Type

The Super Z style of ferrule, designed by Louis Feierabend, is the best ferrule style that is commercially available. The ferrules made by Classic Sporting Enterprises are, I believe, the best current realization of this style. The Super Z design rewards rod tapers where there is minimal change in dimension over the ferrule, but with a little design foresight it can be used with tapers where there is a significant drop over the ferrule, meaning that the tip ferrule dimension is smaller than the butt ferrule dimension. See Figure 6.1.

Figure 6.1. The Super Z ferrule style as embodied in the Classic Sporting Enterprises Super Swiss ferrule.

It is always better to have a ferrule that is slightly larger than the blank's diameter (measured across the flats) at the ferrule station, rather than smaller. If your rod measures, say, .194-inch at the ferrule, a 13/64-inch ferrule (.203-inch) will be a better choice than 12/64-inch (.188-inch) even though .188 is numerically closer to .194 than .203. Cutting away .007-inch worth of power fibers just might, under extreme conditions, weaken the rod enough for it to snap off at the ferrule, whereas leaving an extra .009-inch inside the 13/64-inch ferrule will not appreciably diminish the bearing surface of the wood and will provide additional purchase for the epoxy.

Decimal Conversions for Ferrules

10/64 = .156	12/64 = .188
11/64 = .172	13/64 = .203
14/64 = .219	20/64 = .313
15/64 = .234	
16/64 = .250	18/64 = .281
17/64 = .266	19/64 = .297

Marking the Blank

Depending on how your rod blank turned out, you may need to move the cutoff point for the ferrule just a bit either way. After marking your cutoff point on exactly the right measurement, place a male ferrule section alongside the rod as shown in Fig. 6.2 and mark the blank with pencil at the end of the ferrule and at the end of the ferrule serrations. As long as you use Super Z–style ferrules, you can use the male ferrule for all the layout, because the female consists of a sleeve soldered over a male ferrule. The interior dimensions of male and female ferrule sections on the bamboo end are identical.

Figure 6.2. Marking the blank for cutting.

You may wish to saw off the excess bit of rod section before you do the layout, but I prefer to leave it on in case I need to straighten the end after I check straightness in the lathe. In either case, allow a tiny fraction of an inch for the thickness of the ferrule end or waterproofing cap. For a truer cut, I prefer to trim the excess off in the lathe with a jeweler's or

Figure 6.3. I leave the excess on until I have the blank centered in the lathe, because if it's crooked there's nothing to hang on to when straightening. (I also like having several inches of excess at the ferrule ends because if I do have to straighten with heat, I don't want to put too much pressure right at the end—that's about the only way to pop a glue joint.) I trim the blank with the lathe running. That may not be accepted shop practice, but it works for me because I use a very fine Exacto saw. If you use a saw with coarser teeth it could grab and something could break or you could get hurt. If you do this with the lathe off, be sure to rotate from flat to flat every couple of strokes to avoid chipping.

Exacto saw (see Fig. 6.3). I do this with the lathe running, but that may not be accepted shop practice. Certainly it should not be done with a saw that is flexible enough to buckle or break. When cutting with the lathe off, rotate the blank by hand every few strokes to prevent splintering.

Lathe Setup

Another quick safety detour. If you're used to power tools, you know not to wear loose clothing, neckties, jewelry, or long hair when using them. This goes double for a lathe, and if you've never used one before, you should get a book or find someone knowledgeable to help you understand its operation before you turn it on.

Assuming that the blank is straight, it is up to the lathe and your turning setup to hold the blank in the proper alignment so that the ferrule seat will be turned properly. A little checking of the lathe itself is in order.

A dial indicator on a magnetic base is helpful in making sure that your lathe chuck is properly centered on the spindle. Chuck up a drill bit, end mill, or piece of precision-ground round stock and position your indicator so that it reads directly on top of the round piece. Turning the chuck by hand will reveal any eccentricities. If the indicator reads more than a couple of thousandths variance, it's a good idea to loosen the chuck's backing plate and tap it back into true. If your lathe is set up in such a way that you can't do that, you may have to compensate with masking-tape shims on the blank.

When you put the blank in the lathe chuck, it must be protected by a layer of masking tape just below the mark for the end of the ferrule. Given a good-quality tape, one thickness is enough, provided you don't crank the chuck down too tight. You want to make sure that the tape overlaps on only one flat and to place that flat *between* the chuck jaws (see Fig. 6.4). If the extra thickness of the tape overlap is under a jaw, it can throw the blank off center by several thousandths. Of course, if your chuck is off center anyway and you can't fix it, you may want the overlap under a jaw, or you may need to add other small strips as shims to even things out. With the blank mounted in the chuck,

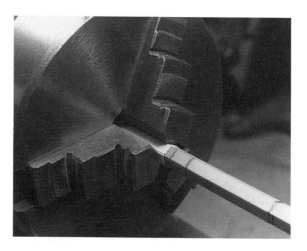

Figure 6.4. A blank protected from the chuck saws by a wrap of masking tape. Note the location of the tape overlap between the jaws.

Transforming the Blank to a Fly Rod

take readings from flat to flat with the mounted dial indicator just as you did with the round stock. Reading right next to the chuck will show you if the blank is centered; I will accept a variance of plus or minus .001-inch from flat to flat at this point (see Fig. 6.5). A significantly egg-shaped rod section might necessitate greater tolerances. Once this measurement is consistent, moving the indicator out to the end of the blank and re-peating the process will tell you whether it is straight or not. If there is a variation of more than plus or minus .002-inch, you should heat the blank up and straighten it. Be very careful. Heating and stressing a section end is your single best chance to pop a glue joint. You can reglue it, of course, but you'd rather not do that. This, by the way, is why you

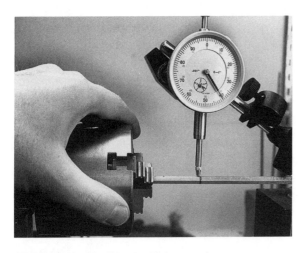

Figure 6.5. Using a dial indicator to check straightness. Measure right at the chuck to center the blank, then move out to the ferrule cutoff point as shown and check each flat again to make sure the blank is straight. If all six numbers are within a couple thousandths of each other and if you cut the ferrule station correctly, the rod will be straight at the ferrule. It's possible that with very light rods the spring pressure of the indicator might flex the section and register the rod's spine instead of measuring straightness, but I've had no problems with rods taking ferrules down to 11/64-inch.

want to work so hard to get this part of the rod straight during gluing.

The long end of the blank that pro-trudes out the back of the headstock needs to be supported as it spins, and it needs to be supported in such a way as to hold it in line with the lathe. The spinning blank provides another acid test of straightness; a straight blank will spin as smoothly and quietly as a driveshaft, but a crooked one will wobble and buck. By all means, take it out and straighten it! It will be necessary to make a little cork insert for the end of your lathe spindle to prevent the blank from banging around inside it (see Fig. 6.6). A wad of masking tape wrapped around the blank would do the job, I suppose, but a selection of three or four cork inserts for different-sized blanks will do the job much better and save a lot of tape. The support for the blank

Figure 6.6. A cork spindle centering and securing the blank in the center of the headstock spindle.

can be pretty simple; mine is embarrassingly so (see Fig. 6.7). I had considered making something better for the book, but my lazi-ness got the upper hand by arguing that some people would be glad to see that a cob-bled-together apparatus will work perfectly well. I intended to make something better years ago, but (and this goes for a lot of my stuff) the hastily improvised rig kept work-ing, so why bother? There were and are rods to be built.

Turning Ferrule Stations

Ready to turn the ferrule station? Well, almost. I prefer to do most of the wood re-moval with a tool bit, but it can't be just any

Figure 6.7. My support for the free end of the blank. It's just a board with a hole drilled through it and a cork ring with a smaller hole glued over the hole for cushioning. If it didn't work I'd have made something better.

Figure 6.8. Note the tool profile. It must be very sharp or you'll catch fibers and tear them instead of cutting cleanly. Just to double-check your alignment, take the very finest possible cut, then check the blank to make sure each corner is being taken down equally.

Figure 6.9. Take very light cuts and try the ferrule often, moving the file and sandpaper sooner rather than later. It's better to quit early and have to spend extra time with the file and sandpaper than to overcut. Measure frequently, and remember that every thousandth you move the tool bit in takes two thousandths off the diameter of the work.

tool bit. The point of the tool bit must be needle sharp or it will catch the bamboo fibers and tear them. A standard tool profile is fine, but remember that you want it razor sharp with a sharp point, no radius at all. The tool also must meet the work right on the centerline (see Fig. 6.8).

The first step in turning the station is to make a very light pass from the end to the first mark, which is where the ferrule serrations end (see Fig. 6.9). You want to take off no more than just the very tips of the corners. Stop the lathe, and make sure that all the corners are being taken down equally (see Fig. 6.10). Inequality in this department means that your blank is not straight after all. It's hard to make yourself tear down the whole setup to straighten the blank at this point, but you'll either be glad you did or sorry you didn't. Assuming everything is okay, make a series of very light cuts taking the wood down until it is .005-inch to .008-inch larger than the desired finished dimension. You need to be careful, because the rod end will spring away from the cutter, making the end larger than the part right next to the

chuck. If you cut with the tool bit until the ferrule will slip over the rod end, it will be too loose. It's much better to stop while the part next to the chuck is still just slightly oversize and do the final fitting with a fine file and sandpaper. Work on the rod end until the ferrule just fits on, then work your way down until the ferrule will go on nearly all the way.

Transforming the Blank to a Fly Rod

Figure 6.10. The station corners after the first light pass.

Figure 6.11. When you get to the point where the ferrule looks like it's about to fit, blend the corners of the blank from sharp where the ferrule starts on the blank to round where the serration cuts begin on the ferrule.

Figure 6.12. Make final reductions with a fine file or sandpaper. The blank will spring away from the cutter and cut less at the end than near the chuck.

Figure 6.13. Using a small, fine file or sandpaper, start at the end and work until the ferrule just slides on.

Figure 6.14. Work your way down the ferrule station until the ferrule slides all the way on. You may have to work on the corner blending a bit more, but take your time.

There needs to be a smooth transition from the sharp corners of the blank to the round ferrule station. Take a small triangular file, and blend the corners from the first mark to the second, as shown in Fig. 6.11. Some guys do this with the lathe running, but I sure wouldn't. Carefully file one corner at a time. After this task is accomplished, finish fitting the ferrule until it slides on with a smooth fit, as shown in the accompanying photo sequence, Figs. 6.12 through 6.14.

These instructions are for gluing on ferrules with epoxy, which is fairly thick and has outstanding toughness and gap-filling ability. One kind that I have used and recommend, Brownell's Acraglas Gel, is used for glass-bedding big-game rifles and exhibits minimal shrinkage and maximum strength. When it sets it is extraordinarily tough but maintains a tiny degree of flexibility. This flexibility helps prevent the epoxy between ferrule and blank from being destroyed by the difference in flex (not to mention the coefficient of expansion) between metal and bamboo.

Acraglas Gel is the type in the green box; the stuff in the red box is too brittle. Acraglas has worked well for me on a number of rods and can be found in almost any sporting goods store, but there's another kind I just started using that seems like it may be even better. It's an epoxy that golf club manufacturers use to secure the club head to the shaft, and if there's any joint that has to take as much stress as a fly rod ferrule, the joint between a golf club head and shaft would be a good candidate. It's called shafting epoxy, oddly enough, and is available from a mail-order place called Golf-Smith (see Appendix B), though a local pro shop might know what you're talking about and be willing to sell you some.

Though you want a close wood-to-metal fit for epoxy, you don't want a pound-it-on-tight fit, as you would if you used Pliobond or the old thermal cement, because the epoxy needs room for a film in order to be strong. Not a lot of room, just enough—.001-inch is plenty. If the ferrule station is perfectly round (no remnant of the flats) I will often score a very fine groove lengthwise down the middle of a couple of flats with the rod stationary in the lathe and the toolbit turned sideways (see Fig. 6.15) to give the air and excess glue an avenue of escape. This groove also gives the epoxy extra purchase, but it need not be deep, and it need not extend past the first mark. You don't have to do this, but it allows you to maintain a nice close fit and still get the ferrule on without causing a hernia.

Figure 6.15. This ferrule station is turned and ready to glue, and an air relief groove is being cut down the center of the flat. You only need two or three of these, and they don't need to be deep enough to cause concern about compromising the integrity of the section.

Figure 6.16. A filed ferrule is on the left, an unfiled one on the right. Note the difference in thickness.

After all your wood removal is done, erase your pencil marks before you forget.

Preparing Ferrules for Gluing

The serrations on the Classic Sporting Enterprises ferrules are pretty fine, but I like to thin them to almost nothing with a file before gluing them on (see Fig. 6.16). I position the serrations in the middle of the flats and find that thinning the tabs considerably not only makes a nice sharp fold over the corners but also reduces or eliminates the crack in the varnish where the ferrule meets the wood. Some makers position the serrations on the corners instead of in the middle of the flats and sand the tabs into pintails. This seems to me to give the serrated portion a less secure grip on the rod, but this objection is probably mostly academic given modern adhesives, and this ferrule treatment under transparent wraps does look nice.

Anyway, back to filing. A drill bit or custom-made metal mandrel supports the ferrule while you file. Thin all the way back to the beginning of the serrations. Care is needed, as the metal gets paper-thin to prevent the teeth of the file from catching a corner and bending or tearing it (see Fig. 6.17). After the serrations are thinned with a file, blend out the file marks with sandpaper strips. I usually start with 240 grit and go down to 600.

I prefer to perform this operation after fitting the ferrule to the wood because after thinning the serrations are very delicate and easily bent. If the ferrule is to be blued, thinning the serrations obviously must be done before bluing, at least if you plan to use penetrating varnish on the wraps. The only other preparation I give ferrules is to score some scratches on the inside of the ferrule with a small burr to give the epoxy something to grip. The zinc in nickel silver makes it slick—that's why it works so well—so even epoxy has a tough time sticking to it. Roughening makes a big difference (Fig. 6.18).

I don't recommend pinning ferrules. A loose ferrule most commonly results from the bamboo shrinking inside the ferrule (assuming that the ferrule was properly fitted to begin with), and a dozen pins won't prevent that. At best, a pin makes it potentially difficult to get the loose ferrule off to reglue it. At worst, it will keep the ferrule on the wood even when it is loose, and if the rod continues in use it will provide a wedge and a weak spot to bust the end of the section into splinters. If a ferrule becomes loose, it's much better to pull it off more or less easily and reglue it before any damage is done. Some

Figure 6.17. With the ferrule braced on a drill bit or a mandrel, use a fine triangular file to thin the serrations. Angle the file downward so you don't catch the corners. A light touch is required to remove as much bulk as possible without tearing or cutting through the tabs; just take it slow. The more the serrations are able to flex, the less chance you have of the varnish cracking where the ferrule meets the wood.

Figure 6.18. I use a small carbide burr to scuff the inside of the ferrule in preparation for gluing.

people fear that a ferrule may come loose from the wood while they are attempting to pull rod sections apart, with the result that the angler is left with a ferrule that is stuck and no way to get it apart. I've never heard of this actually happening, but, as Carl Sagan said, "in an infinite universe, anything that is not specifically prohibited by the laws of nature is mandatory," so I guess it probably has. It has been my experience that loose ferrules start clicking long before they are ready to pull off, and even a ferrule that clicks quite noticeably takes heat and patience to remove. This fear may have been warranted in the days of the old thermal cement, but I think that the best epoxies today are much better, and a properly prepared ferrule glued with a good epoxy should give few problems. Just keep your unfinished sections as dry as possible.

Gluing

The wood is turned, the ferrule fits on just right, the serrations are filed, the surfaces are roughened. Mix equal parts of your epoxy (if that is the correct proportion—it is for both Acraglas Gel and GolfSmith Shafting Epoxy), dab a fair amount around inside the ferrule with a toothpick, and roll the rod end in the remainder. I prefer to work on one ferrule at a time with a fresh batch of epoxy just to keep the panic potential to a minimum. Place the ferrule on the blank and push steadily and firmly against a soft wood block or the edge of your workbench. You want a soft surface to avoid marring or denting the ferrule. Initially, the ferrule will slide on partway and then stop as compressed air and excess glue push back. After a few moments (maybe a few long moments) of continuous pressure, glue will continue to ooze out of

the serrations (see Fig. 6.19), and you will hear a sharp crackling sound as the compressed air escapes. You may need to exert fairly heavy pressure, but avoid an all-out brute-force effort when seating the female ferrule both because it is unnecessary and because it is possible, I hear, to blow out the internal moisture cap. I've never accomplished this even though I've never used supporting ferrule inserts, but keep it in mind when it seems like it's taking forever for the ferrule to seat, your hands are getting tired, and your temper is getting short. Relax, it'll go on. Sometimes I'll heat the ferrule slightly to expand it and make installation a little easier.

Once the ferrule is seated, twist it around on the blank, remove it, reapply epoxy, and repeat the process to make absolutely sure that you have achieved a good glue film.

The next step is to bind the serrations down onto the blank. A thin nylon cord will work fine for this, but I have come to prefer Kevlar thread. Kevlar's extreme strength for its diameter allows it to exert more pressure and results in a sharper, cleaner bend of the serrations over the rod corners, and its small diameter and flosslike flatness means that virtually no excess dried epoxy is left behind after the thread is removed. With one end of a 5- or 6-foot length of thread or cord tied to

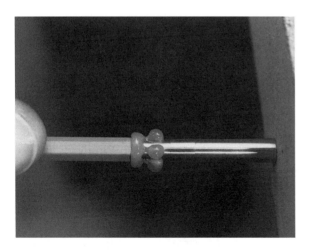

Figure 6.19. Pushing the glued ferrule on against the edge of the workbench.

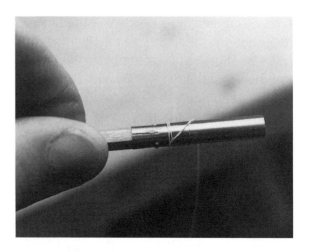

Figure 6.20. Starting the ferrule binding thread.

Transforming the Blank to a Fly Rod

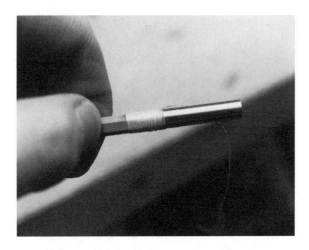

Figure 6.21. The glued ferrule with serrations bound down. Note the sharp fold of the serrations over the corners.

some immovable object, wrap steadily and with increasing pressure from the ferrule shoulder to the end of the serrations (see Fig. 6.20). Remove excess epoxy as you go, and once you have wrapped all the way down and back up (see Fig. 6.21), cut the thread and tie it off with plenty of half hitches, then set the section aside to cure.

Dressing for Fit

Once the epoxy cures—and you really should leave it alone for a couple of days just to be on the safe side—you may need to dress the ferrules for a perfect fit. I've had sets that fit together perfectly right out of the package, and then there have been those that have taken quite a bit of work. If the ferrules do not fit together easily and mate fully, they must be dressed. To accomplish this, cut a 1/4-inch wide strip of 1000 grit sandpaper and rotate the rod while holding the sandpaper wrapped around the portion of the male ferrule that needs reducing. (Never take metal off the inside of the female ferrule.) Determining the location of that portion is the trick and is the reason why you need a reasonably narrow strip of sandpaper. Typically, if there is a problem with fit, it is that the male ferrule will fit into the female only partway. Judging by where the male ferrule

stops and by rub marks on it, work on short sections of the slide, moving progressively closer to the shoulder until the male ferrule will fully seat into the female.

It may take a couple of sessions to get the ferrule fit just right. This may seem obvious, but the tolerance on a well-fitting ferrule is considerably less than a thousandth of an inch, and once the material is gone it stays gone, so it pays to take things easy. There's something else that I almost didn't mention but probably should. I've had ferrules that seemed to fit perfectly when the rod was first finished get tight later. Nickel silver can grow an oxidation film that will affect the fit and should be cleaned off with a little lighter fluid, but I've had ferrules that actually seemed to expand slightly. Keeping the strips and blank dry until the rod is varnished is something I'm pretty careful about (even though it's pretty dang dry here to begin with), so the bamboo certainly could swell a bit and change ferrule fit. There's no such thing as completely impermeable varnish. This may not be a problem in other areas of the country, but if it happens to you, just dress the ferrule again.

Adding the Cork Grip

The process of adding a cork grip would seem pretty straightforward: Just glue the rings on, chuck it in the lathe, and go to town, right? Well, yes, that's basically it. However, there are a few fine points. None of this is new and you'd probably figure it all out yourself, but if you haven't turned a grip before, I might be able to save you some rings.

Nothing stands out on a fly rod more visibly or unfavorably or is more uncomfortable than bad cork or an ill-shaped grip. The primary considerations are the use of good quality cork and the choice and execution of an appropriate grip design. Tastes in cork grips vary, of course, but if you put a full-size 7-inch full wells grip on a 7-foot 3-weight rod, you should have a reason.

Quality

Buy your cork directly from an importer or from someplace that sells a lot of it. The average fly shop that carries a selection of graphite rod–building materials has a box of fifty or a hundred rings. The cork in those little boxes is rarely any good, it's expensive, and such a small sample gets picked to the bone by the first guy to hit it. You'll wind up with trash. The usual minimum order from an importer is one thousand rings. This sounds like a lot, and if you are just starting you probably don't want to tackle such an order alone. You might consider it, though, because cork is not becoming more plentiful, more affordable, or more consistent. Good cork is something that you always can sell. If you can't order a thousand rings yourself, try to find another maker or two to go in with you. Order the very best stuff. If it's not good, you will have the option of sending the shipment back. Chances are you'll have to wait a few months for delivery. The most common dimension for rings is 1 1/4 inches in diameter, 1/2-inch thick with a 1/4-inch hole in the center. However, some suppliers carry 1/4-inch-thick rings. They cost a little more than half what a 1/2-inch ring does, which naturally lowers the price of the minimum order. The skinny rings make a good-looking grip because whatever pits and gaps in the cork show up are only 1/4-inch long.

The next quality consideration is arranging the rings within the grip. Even if you have a bunch of decent rings, they will not be equally good. Given a dozen 1/2-inch rings for a grip that are the best you can get, the objective is to arrange them in such a way that whatever pits are present show as little as possible. Your two very best rings should go at the front, where the grip tapers to meet the blank (see Fig. 6.22). For the rest, the trick is to figure out about what the diameter of your desired grip will be at a given point, then use a ring for that point whose pits are located somewhere other

Figure 6.22. This is a good cork ring, one you'd want to save for a face ring or for one that will have its end grain exposed.

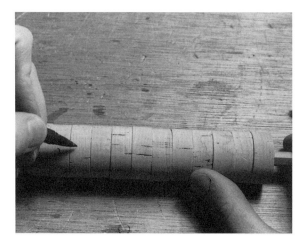

Figure 6.23. Once you arrange your rings to minimize the visibility of pits, number them so they don't get mixed up.

than at that diameter. Arrange the rings as best you can, then number them so they won't get mixed up before you can glue them (see Fig. 6.23).

Grip Design

If you are undecided, the best thing you can do is to look at a bunch of rods and figure out what you like. The grip is an important part of the overall shape and flow of the rod and should harmonize with it. A few broad considerations first. Although you may choose to disregard them, there are a few traditional grip shapes that go with certain rods.

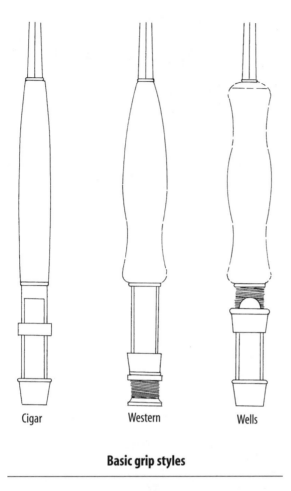

Cigar   Western   Wells

Basic grip styles

You will only occasionally see a full Wells grip on a rod under 8 feet long because the Wells is a power grip: The flare gives your thumb something to push against on a heavy, powerful rod. On a light, delicate rod it is unnecessary, makes the rod feel like a toothpick, and looks funky. There are always exceptions, of course. I've seen a few short light rods with very small and slender wells grips that looked and felt okay and obviously were what their owners wanted. A cigar grip is traditionally associated with downlocking and sliding bands, because the smooth tapered shape blends well with the trim reel seat. Uplocking reels seats work well with a Western or full Wells grip—the flare at the heel of the grip does a nice job of concealing the hood under the cork. Grips on bamboo rods are traditionally shorter than those on graphite rods, which usually have grips in the neighborhood of 7 inches long. (Some don't.

Winston and Thomas & Thomas do a nice job of scaling the grip to the rod. But then, both companies make fine bamboo rods as well.) I agree that slightly shorter grips look trim and compact, and most of my grips run 6 or 6 1/2 inches, but you can take it too far. Some collectors, especially eastern ones, will blanch at the sight of a grip longer than 5 1/2 inches (because that's how long Payne's were). If somebody wants a grip that short they'll get it, but I find it too short for comfort.

A grip should be tailored, to some degree, to the user. The hand should close fully around the grip without being so thin that the hand cramps. A grip that is too large, particularly at the front, is uncomfortable as well and interferes with the perception of control and accuracy. Some people like a palm swell; others like to move their hands around and find a swell disconcerting. If the rod is yours, you know what you like. If it's for someone else, try to establish up front what that someone prefers. Get a tracing of a favorite grip or sketch an agreed-upon design if possible.

Putting It Together

Rings usually have a 1/4-inch bore, which is obviously too small for many bamboo rods. I made a set of Garrison-style cutters to enlarge the holes, only to find that the

Figure 6.24. Using a large (and coarse) rat-tail file and lathe to enlarge the bore. Place a layer of masking tape on the file to prevent it from cutting too large a hole.

easiest way to enlarge the holes was to chuck a large rat-tail file in the lathe (wrap masking tape around it to protect the jaws), wrap masking tape just beyond the desired diameter, and slide the rings up on the file with the lathe running (see Fig. 6.24). You want all of the rings to fit snugly but not squeaky tight, except for the last one, which should be tight enough to form around the blank without gaps.

An optional tuning operation is to sand the gluing surfaces lightly on a flat surface to eliminate any gaps caused by dented or warped rings. This also removes the bleaching, which can leave white lines between rings. String the rings onto the blank just in order to make sure everything fits, and mark off the appropriate distance for your reel seat. Of course, you need to decide on a reel seat. Whatever kind you use, it will probably be a commercially made one, at least to start, so you should buy it ahead of time to make sure of your measurements. I'm partial to downlocking and sliding-band reel seats because they help balance the rod better, the line doesn't get wrapped around the reel seat as easily, and because it makes gluing and turning the grip easier. It's easier to glue the rings, turn the grip, dip the rod, and line up the reel seat with the guides if you put the reel seat on last. If you are using an uplocking reel seat with a hood concealed under the last ring of the grip, it's probably best to glue the reel-seat filler, hood, and covering cork on before you glue the rest of the rings to ensure that the cork and hood are centered on the filler. Turning the grip with the reel-seat filler and hood attached can be awkward because the balance won't be great (before gluing on the filler, you need to gently drill the butt of the rod with a center drill so that you can use a live center). Still, I like to be able to put a fair amount of pressure on the rings while the glue dries, and the other options (gluing the hood ring along with the rest of the rings, gluing the hood and ring after the rest of the grip) seem to encourage a

Figure 6.25. A gluing clamp made of aluminum and threaded rods.

Figure 6.26. Spread the glue right next to the rod shaft. Don't spread it too thick or too far out from the blank or it will seep out and be visible in the surface of the grip.

glue line between the hood ring and the next ring of the grip.

You're nearly ready to glue on the rings. Before you mix the glue, you need a way to clamp the grip together while it dries. A clamp like the one shown in Fig. 6.25 is easy to make, or you can apply your native intelligence to materials at hand. The choice of glue for the grip is not terribly crucial as long as you use it sparingly. Apply the glue in very small doses to the blank, and slide the corks over it. Apply a thin coat to the cork in a circle extending a little more than 1/8-inch from

Transforming the Blank to a Fly Rod

the blank, as shown in Fig. 6.26. The idea is to apply enough glue to secure the ring to the blank and to glue the rings together, but not enough to squeeze out to where the surface of the grip will be.

I use Nyatex for this as well, because I like the blank to be sealed off with epoxy under the cork even though moisture shouldn't get in there and because it cures slowly and allows plenty of time for any excess glue (if you apply it right, there won't be any) to squeeze out, resulting in virtually no glue lines, and because I have to order it by the quart and I might as well use it up. I don't like over-the-counter 2-ton or five-minute epoxies for this job because they are too thick and can set before any accidental excess has a chance to squeeze out.

One final thing before you glue. Make sure the butt end of the rod is straight, or the grip will not be centered on the blank, the reel seat will not align with the grip, and it will be obvious that something is wrong with the rod.

When you glue the grip, increase the clamp pressure until the gaps between rings disappear. The rings will compress slightly. This is fine, but you have to be careful where you start the rings at the butt end, or you could wind up with a little extra blank sticking out for the reel seat, making the butt section that much shorter than you'd intended. Plan for the rings to scoot up 1/16-inch or so, and if they slide more or less, remove the clamp, readjust the rings, and resume clamping. Allow the glue sufficient time to dry, because sanding the grip generates plenty of heat, which could disturb a partial bond.

Turning

Chuck the blank in your lathe after protecting it with masking tape, as you did when turning ferrule stations. A cover of masking tape should protect the wood right up to the cork, so that if you slip you won't sand away at the blank. Because the rings

Figure 6.27. Establishing the cylinder with coarse sandpaper backed by a small board and braced against the lathe ways.

Figure 6.28. Bob Widgren using his grip-shaping lathe. The follower—the rod directly below the unshaped grip—is guided by a template that can be changed or adjusted to make grips of different sizes and tapers.

will not all be perfectly centered on the blank, it helps to begin by establishing a centered cylinder. Backing a strip of 50 or 100 grit sandpaper with a small board, start at the front of the grip as shown in Fig. 6.27 and brace the board against the ways of the lathe and hold it firmly so that it first just hits the high spots, then gradually increase contact until the sandpaper makes full con-

Figure 6.29. A rough cylinder, ready for shaping.

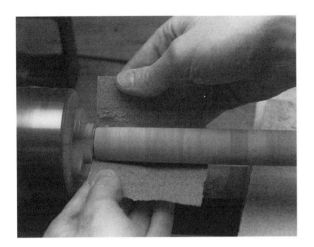

Figure 6.30. Starting to shape the grip with coarse sandpaper.

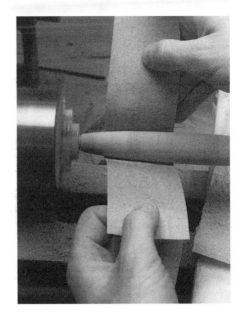

Figure 6.31. Continue shaping, and finish the grip with fine sandpaper.

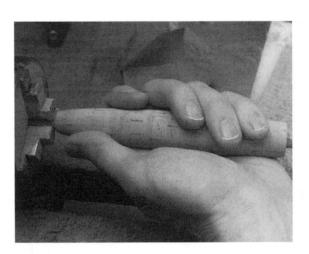

Figure 6.32. The finished grip. Check to see how it feels in your hand before you call it done.

tact with each rotation. If you push too hard too soon, the sanding rig will bounce off the high spots and you will wind up with an oval cross section. The same sort of thing, only worse, will occur if you start right off wrapping sandpaper around the grip freehand. The off-center rings will influence the cut and the grip will be oval or off center.

The ultimate rig for establishing the cylinder (and for roughing the grip) is a high-speed tool-post grinder on your lathe, using a coarse abrasive disc or cutoff wheel. Bob Widgren (Los Pinos Custom Rods) has a really slick air grinder mounted on a wood lathe, with the grinder on a sliding pivot that follows a template. Unless you make lots of grips you probably don't need something like that, but you might be interested just to know about it (see Fig. 6.28).

Once you have established your cylinder (see Fig. 6.29), use strips of sandpaper to remove everything that doesn't look like the grip you want. I do most of the cork removal with 100 grit production paper, then move to 240 grit wet or dry, and finally to 400 grit. You can go as fine as you want, but I find a 600 grit finish a little too slick when wet. See the accompanying photo sequence, Figs. 6.30

to 6.32. I try to use cork that is good enough that no filler is needed. If some sort of filler is needed, however, the best stuff I have found is Fix brand Wood Patch in Light Mahogany. It matches cork very well, and it seems to change color with dirt and use at the same rate as cork. To fill pits in the cork grip, pick out any glue that remains in a pit while the rod is still in the lathe, press in a little Wood Patch, allow to dry, then sand the grip smooth again by turning it. If you want to add a nickel silver winding check, do so after the grip is turned.

Locating the Spine

Before you think too much about guides, you need to decide on which flat they will go. Let's take the tip section first. Place the ferrule on a flat smooth surface, support the rod toward the tip with one hand, and push downward with the other hand (see Fig. 6.33). Roll the rod gently back and forth under pressure, and there will be a more or less discernible "kick" at a certain point in the revolution, and another more or less discernible point when the rod seems to come to rest, to bend easily and resist rolling. This

Figure 6.33. Locating the spine. This is a little harder with the butt section—an alternate method is to roll the section on your thigh, pressing down on both ends, but I think that using the smooth ferrule as a bearing against the bench gives the best result. The flat that is facing up when the blank is trying to hold its bend and is resisting rolling is the one the guides go on.

rolling process reveals the location of the rod's "spine," which is usually taken to mean the plane in which the rod resists bending the most. The spine is so called because it is usually assumed that a spline (strip) that is stronger than the others asserts itself. This may be the case, or it may be that one spline is weaker than the others, or that two strong splines or two weak ones oppose one another. So, where do the guides go? Bear with me.

The subject of a rod's spine actually starts way back with splitting, and I hope you'll forgive me for waiting this long to complicate things. If you checked all your strips for weaknesses or flaws, and if your planing was normally accurate, the differences between one spline and another should be really quite small, but we are talking about a natural material, so differences probably will exist no matter how careful you are. Even a small difference in strength between splines can result in a spine.

Can this spine be reduced or eliminated, and is that desirable? Maybe and maybe. Let's start with the material itself. There's a theory that bamboo, growing tall and straight despite pressure from prevailing winds, naturally grows in such a way as to be more resistant to bending in the plane described by the path of the wind. Therefore, if you initially split your culm into six strips and take one narrow strip from each large strip to make your rod section and preserve each strip's position relative to its neighbors in the culm, the finished section should have some of the same bending characteristics as the whole culm, including extra resistance to bending in a particular plane (the spine). And, for better or worse, each rod section will have the same characteristics. Following this theory, if you build a section from narrow strips that were immediately adjacent in the culm, the rod's tendency to have a pronounced spine would be reduced. Following it still further, though, it could lead to a variance between tips, if one came from a "strong" side and the other from a "weak" side of the culm.

Does this theory hold water? It's hard (some would say impossible) to tell, because the differences between strips resulting in a spine are very slight, and with bamboo, slight variations in virtually every parameter are the norm. I'll leave you to make up your own mind. For what it's worth, I usually start with six large strips and take one narrow strip for each section because that's what makes the most sense to me and because it seems the method most likely to result in uniform action between tips, but the variations are endless. According to the Stein and Schaaf book on Dickerson, he (Dickerson) used two culms for each rod, selecting culms with an oval cross section, taking cane from the peaks of the oval, and alternating strips from both culms in the rod section. Wow.

I don't think that a spine in a rod is a particular defect, so long as it is properly dealt with. Which brings us back, at long last, to the question of which flat to use for positioning the guides. When you roll the rod section as described earlier, there will be a tendency for the section to jump or kick at a certain point in the revolution, and a tendency for it to come to rest at a certain point in the revolution. The flat that is facing up when the rod kicks marks the plane in which the rod is strongest under compression in that plane. The flat that is facing down when the rod tends to come to rest marks the plane in which the rod is weakest under compression. A common assumption is that these two flats oppose each other, but that is only sometimes the case. Garrison recommended placing the guides on the flat that was weakest under compression, and I agree, though perhaps not for the same reasons. Locating the spine has to do with accuracy, not power. When you put the guides on the flat that is facing up when the rod wants to bend, the rod seems better at tracking straight during a cast and, consequently, more accurate.

Don't take my word for it, though. Once you have the ferrules in place and a grip turned, install a tip-top with thermal ferrule cement (so you can move it), tape guides on with narrow strips of masking tape, and try casting the rod with the guides on the weak flat, then on the flat that kicks. See which you like better.

The Tip-Top

Before you install a tip-top you must trim the tip(s) to length. Remember that the ends of the wire loop on a Perfection-style tip-top take up a bit of the length inside the tube, and you need to figure that into the precise cutoff point. To cut off the excess at the tip, roll the tip on a hard wooden surface under a very sharp knife (see Fig. 6.34). Mark the length of the inside of the tube on the tip and use a scraper or a fine file to round the corners just a bit. Theoretically, you know what size tip-top to use by virtue of the tip measurement, but I prefer simply to have a bunch of them on hand in different sizes and see which fits best with the corners of the tip taken down just slightly (see Fig. 6.35). There aren't a lot of fibers left by the time you get to the tip, so I don't

Figure 6.34. Cutting off excess tip with a sharp knife. Roll the tip with pressure on the knife, and angle the knife slightly so the edge is toward the part you want to remove and the back of the knife is toward the ferrule. This will ensure that any splintering that occurs will be in the cut-off piece, not in the part you want to keep.

Transforming the Blank to a Fly Rod

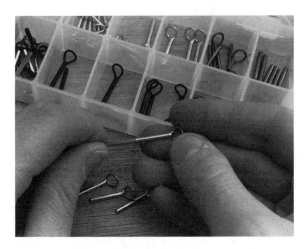

Figure 6.35. Selecting the correct tip-top.

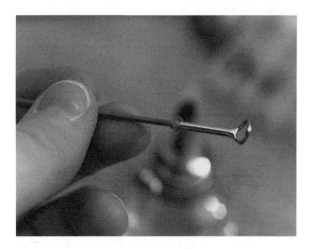

Figure 6.36. Push the tip-top onto the tip, aligning it carefully. Pull off the excess cement after it cools enough to touch but before it sets completely.

approach fitting the tip-top like fitting a ferrule. You want to take off a little so the cement will have more bonding area, but this is a very delicate area, so don't try to make it perfectly round. Also, tip-tops vary a bit even within a given size. One 4 1/2 may be too tight, whereas the next 4 1/2 fits perfectly. Sometimes a tip-top will have a burr inside the lip of the tube that needs to be removed.

I prefer to use a thermal ferrule cement, the kind that comes in a stick and is available at any fly shop. This cement is plenty strong for the task, makes last-minute alignment adjustments possible, and if it comes loose in the field, a few seconds' heat from a match or lighter will reflow the cement and renew the bond. Also, if you break off an inch or so of the tip while fishing, you may be able to use the same tip-top for a field repair if the break is short enough not to increase the size of the tip-top needed and if you carry a little stick of cement and a lighter in your vest. An alcohol lamp works best as a heat source for this task in the shop because it doesn't throw soot.

To install a tip-top once the blank is trimmed and a good fit is accomplished, heat the end of the ferrule cement stick with your lamp, then dab a bit of it on the rod tip by rolling the rod tip in it. Before it cools, rake

off a little into the end of the tip-top tube. Briefly heat the tip-top so that the cement flows into the tube, reheat the cement on the rod tip (don't burn the rod!) and tube, and push the tip-top onto the tip (see Fig. 6.36). Wait a few seconds for the cement to cool, then pull away any excess. If you catch it just right, the excess will be the consistency of semi-dried pizza cheese and will come off easily. Wait too long and it will be tough; act too soon and it will stick to your fingers and burn. It's the sort of thing you learn pretty quickly.

Adding and Wrapping the Guides

There are two main considerations about guides on a bamboo fly rod: how many and where. Actually, there is another: quality. Plain stainless snake guides can be soft and easily grooved, so buy the best hard-chromed guides you can find. Whether they are chromed, bronzed, or black-chromed, the snake guide and the double-foot "boat style" stripping guide are still the only choices that satisfy the traditional requirements of the bamboo rod. That's not to say that you can't experiment with single-foot ceramic guides in place of snakes, only that you should realize that most bamboo rod enthusiasts are traditionalists of one sort or another and are not likely to appreciate your innovation. Tastes may change, but don't count on it. Most enthusiasts shun the ceramic-insert stripping guides as well, preferring the plain Mildrum Carbaloy boat guides. The ultimate stripping guide for a bamboo

Figure 6.37. Agate stripping guides by Daryll Whitehead. These are beautifully made and finished.

rod is of course the boat guide with agate or agateen (synthetic agate) insert. For a long time, the only source of these guides was the remnants that survived stuck back in some corner of a rod repair shop, or old broken rods. Just recently, Daryll Whitehead started making them (see Fig. 6.37), so for the time being we're saved.

Back to our two main considerations—how many and where. There must be enough guides to distribute the pull of the line over the length of the rod. Too few guides and the line will slap the blank, and excessive strain on sections of the rod between guides may occur. A heavy rod for big fish may have proportionately more guides than a smaller, more delicate rod, but too many guides add unnecessary weight to the rod. Guides play a vital role in maximizing the ability of the rod

to shoot line. Too many or too-small guides create unnecessary friction, and too few or too-large guides allow the line to flap around and bunch up at the guides. A fairly useful rule of thumb is that a rod should have a guide for every foot of rod length, excluding the tip-top, plus two. A 7- or 7 1/2-foot rod, therefore, will have nine guides, commonly eight snakes and one stripper. I would not hesitate to add a guide or two to a heavy rod.

The size of snake guides will naturally increase from the tip to the butt. The size you begin with at the tip is the most important choice. Smaller guides are lighter, and weight at the tip is crucial, so if you're in doubt, choose the smaller size. It is almost impossible to get hard-chromed commercial guides smaller than 2/0 these days. 1/0 is the smallest commonly available size, which will work well for line weights from 6 to 4. Smaller than 4 and you'll be glad to have size 2/0, and for rods larger than 6 you might consider starting with size 1 guides. Most rods will use three sizes of snake guides. If you start with size 1/0 you might go up to size 2 before the stripping guide. I'll use a couple of the largest size on the butt section, then split the remaining guides between the two smaller sizes.

The size of the stripping guide is up to you, within limits. If it looks too big or too small for the rod, it is. A larger guide is better for shooting line, but a big guide that looks fine on a graphite rod looks goofy on a bamboo rod. Because they were intended for silk lines, many stripping guides on classic bamboo rods are really far too small for today's plastic lines, but they're still part of the classic look. I try to split the difference and use a guide that is large enough to shoot line reasonably well but is not any more than large enough. In Mildrum boat guides I'll usually use an 8 on lines 4 and smaller, and a 10 for lines 5 and 6. For the rare 7-weight or higher, it just depends. A 10 is probably big enough for a 7, but I may go a little larger, particularly for something like a steelhead rod where long casts are the regular fare.

Now for the consideration of where the guides go. They are not spaced equidistant along the blank, of course. They must be closer together at the tip, where the bend is greatest, and should become farther apart by regular intervals toward the butt. I try not to have my first interval between tip-top and guide larger than 5 1/2 inches, though I have seen some larger. A small rod or a large rod with extra guides might have a first interval as short as 4 inches. An interval increase of 1/2- to 3/4-inch is about right, meaning, with the 1/2-inch scheme, that if your first interval is 5 1/2 inches, the second will be 6 inches, the third 6 1/2 inches, and so on. It is a good idea to have a guide right next to the ferrule in order to put the ferrule at the end of an arc rather than at the center. The stripping guide should be placed far enough up the rod so that the angle of the line when hauling and shooting line is not too acute. Too far up, though, and the line will flop around and wrap around the blank. A good compromise for people with average-length arms is between 25 and 26 inches. Most of mine are around 26 inches, but I'm six foot four and have long arms.

What you need, therefore, is a guide-spacing scheme that satisfies the above requirements. The stripping guide should be somewhere around 25 to 26 inches from the butt, and there should be a snake guide next to the ferrule(s) (it doesn't matter much whether above or below). You should have two more guides total, excluding the tip-top, than the rod is long in feet, give or take a guide, and the intervals between the guides should grow in a regular progression (1/2-inch or 9/16-inch, for instance). The interval between tip-top and first snake guide should be between 4 1/2 to 5 1/2 inches.

That sounds difficult, perhaps, but it's not. Even with an unusual rod length or configuration, it has never taken me more than fifteen or twenty minutes of messing around with a tape measure and pencil to lay out guides. Starting with a tip-top to first snake guide interval that seems about right for the rod, say, 5 1/2 inches, I'll mark off intervals that increase by half an inch and see where the guides fall. If the closest guide to a ferrule is 2 inches away and six guides from the tip, I know that if I increase the 1/2-inch increment to 9/16-inch, it will put a guide just about where I want it. For standard-length rods I usually just use Garrison's guide spacings, which satisfy all of the above requirements beautifully, provided you increase his guide sizes a bit to account for fatter modern fly lines. Wayne Cattanach's book also contains a program that will lay out guides given various parameters. Here are a few standard guide spacing layouts for common two-piece rod lengths:

6 1/2-foot
Tip-Top

1st snake guide	5 inches
2nd snake guide	10 1/2 inches
3rd snake guide	16 1/2 inches
4th snake guide	23 1/4 inches
5th snake guide	30 1/4 inches
6th snake guide	38 inches (above ferrule, on tip joint)
7th snake guide	46 1/2 inches
Stripping guide	55 1/2 inches

7-foot
Tip-Top

1st snake guide	4 1/2 inches
2nd snake guide	9 3/4 inches
3rd snake guide	15 3/4 inches
4th snake guide	22 3/8 inches
5th snake guide	29 1/8 inches
6th snake guide	36 3/8 inches
7th snake guide	44 inches (below ferrule)
8th snake guide	51 inches
Stripping guide	59 inches

7 1/2-foot

Tip-Top

1st snake guide	4 7/8 inches
2nd snake guide	10 3/8 inches
3rd snake guide	16 5/8 inches
4th snake guide	23 7/8 inches
5th snake guide	31 3/8 inches
6th snake guide	39 inches
7th snake guide	47 1/4 inches (below ferrule)
8th snake guide	55 3/8 inches
Stripping guide	64 inches inches

8-foot

Tip-Top

1st snake guide	4 3/8 inches
2nd snake guide	9 1/2 inches
3rd snake guide	15 1/4 inches
4th snake guide	21 1/2 inches
5th snake guide	28 1/4 inches
6th snake guide	35 1/4 inches
7th snake guide	42 3/4 inches
8th snake guide	50 1/2 inches (below ferrule)
9th snake guide	59 inches
Stripping guide	68 3/8 inches

Figure 6.39. The little grinding wheel I use in the lathe. It's slower than a bench grinder, but that's the point. Safer, too, if you insist on holding the guides in your fingers.

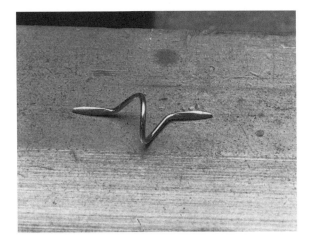

Figure 6.38. Nicely ground guide feet. I know, lots of guides come preground, but they're all burned and look like hell. You can see the feet under transparent wraps, of course, and sooner or later you'll run into someone who will notice this little detail and appreciate it.

Grinding and Wrapping Guides

The first thing you need to do when you're ready to wrap on guides is to prepare the guides themselves. Even "preground" guide feet are usually very coarsely done, and a few minutes with a grinding wheel are needed to even them up. Especially on rods with chrome guides and transparent wraps, I like to grind the guide feet to a nice leaf shape (see Fig. 6.38). I try to thin the feet some as well. If you leave them too stubby they won't flex with the blank, and you can wind up with little cracks in the varnish at the ends of the feet after a while. Some sort of grinding wheel is recommended, but a regular grinder is a bit too fast and scary for me, so I use a little grinding wheel chucked in the lathe (see Fig. 6.39). After grinding the tops, smooth any burrs of the bottom of the feet with sandpaper or a fine stone.

Once your guide set is ready to go, tape them to the blank with thin strips of masking tape and check for alignment. This is completely counterintuitive to me, but some snake guides will set off to one side, and if you swap ends they will stand up straight. If you think the way I do, that will seem like the strangest thing you've ever heard, but you'll see what I mean.

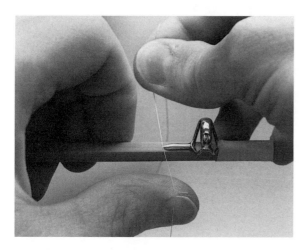

Figure 6.40. To start the wrap, lay the thread from the spool over the loose end and continue wrapping over it to bind the tag end down. Some builders trim this tag end off after a few wraps; I like to leave it in and lay it alongside the guide foot. That way I can snug it up after the wrap is completely finished and trim it right at the guide. Either way is fine, but if you trim the tag and then wrap over it, it helps to fray the end after you cut it so that it won't make a bump.

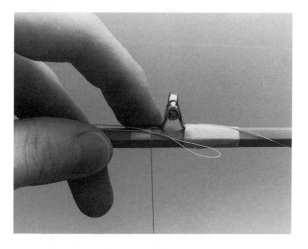

Figure 6.41. Continue wrapping. About one-third of the way from the end of the wrap, lay in the loop you will use to pull the second tag through. Keep the thread tension constant so the wrap stays smooth; if you let the tension lapse there will be a dark line in the wrap if you use penetrating varnish.

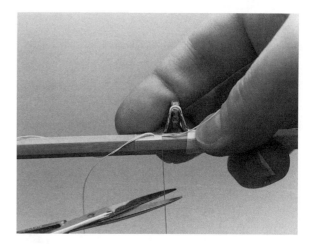

Figure 6.42. When you get to the end of the wrap, cut the thread, leaving an inch or two to pull through.

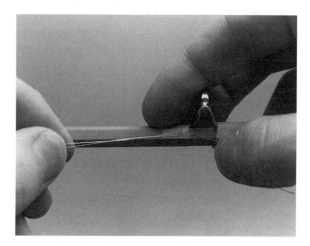

Figure 6.43. Pull the tag through. Using Gudebrod's G String, it's unusual for the pull loop to break, but sometimes, especially if you've wrapped too tightly, the silk can break before you get the tag all the way through. If you can't salvage it cleanly, start over. If you've done it enough it won't take that long, and if it takes you a long time you need the practice anyway. No need to settle for an inferior wrap.

Wrapping on the guides is pretty straightforward. The accompanying photo sequence (Figs. 6.40 through 6.44) shows the common method of wrapping the thread first over the loose end, then wrapping in a loop that will be used to pull the second end back under the wrap. Thread doesn't work all that well as a pull loop. Monofilament is better, but what really works is a product by Gudebrod called G String. It is a fine, braided poly string, like kite string only thinner. It compresses as you wrap over it, doesn't twist much, and never breaks. A spool may last you the rest of your life.

While we're on the subject of tag ends, something I've fallen into the habit of doing is leaving the starting tag on, laying it against the guide foot after it's initially bound down

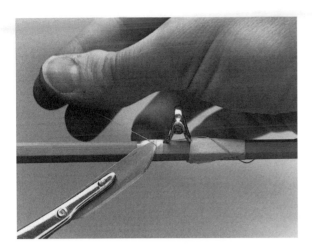

Figure 6.44. When the wrap is complete, trim the tag ends as close as possible with as sharp a knife as you can find. A razor blade is a little tough to handle, but a scalpel with a standard curved blade is perfect. Using the belly of the curve, you can catch the thread right at the wrap. If you leave a tiny stub, you can sand it off when you varnish wraps if you're using penetrating varnish. If you plan to use color preserver, the wrap has to be perfect, because if you so much as scuff the wrap with sandpaper after you put the preserver on, the varnish will bleed through.

and trimming it under the guide foot after the wrap is complete. It saves time, makes a smoother wrap, and allows me to snug up the starting end of the wrap if I accidentally bump it while wrapping.

To wrap a guide, tape one foot down with masking tape and wrap the other. I usually wrap one foot on all the guides on a section, turn around and wrap the second foot on all of them, then check to make sure none of the guides are goofy before I add trim wraps. This is faster than doing all the wraps and trim for each guide one at a time. Also, I leave the tag ends for the trim wraps hanging out and trim them only just before the wraps are varnished. That way, if a trim wrap accidentally gets nudged, it doesn't just fall off and can be snugged back into place.

A trim wrap is just like any other wrap, only shorter, so the pull-through loop has to go in right away. Most of the instructions I've seen for making trim wraps call for making the very first turn of thread over the pull-through loop. However, trim wraps done this

way are very fragile. They stay put better if you make one turn of thread, then insert the loop. That way the tag end is locked between two turns of thread instead of between the thread and the slick blank.

On bamboo rods it is pretty standard to make the wraps no longer than the guide feet. The spare, minimalistic look is in, and if you put on trim wraps, use fine thread and make them very thin, five or six wraps at most.

The main points to consider in wrapping guides are maintaining an even thread tension, wrapping as closely and evenly as possible without a lot of nudging and rubbing, and touching the thread as little as possible. The use of some sort of jig is optional, of course, but I'm so accustomed to mine (Cabela's Rod Wrapping Stand) that I'd hate to try to do without it.

Wrapping the Ferrules

One wrap that calls for a little more discussion is the wrap at the ferrule that binds down the serrations and reinforces the bamboo at the transition. Although some fine makers have wrapped the ferrule serrations and put only a trim wrap on the bamboo, I'm a little more cautious and prefer to put a quarter-inch wrap on the bamboo. This is an area of great stress, and although an argument could be made that if a stress is great enough to break the bamboo at this point it will do so, wrap or no wrap, a little reinforcement here makes me feel better, regardless of what it does for the rod.

This wrap actually consists of two separate wraps—one over the serrations and one over the bamboo, divided exactly where one ends and the other begins. The reason for this is the crack in the varnish that often appears at this point. You want to do your best to keep this crack from occurring by thinning the ferrule serrations, but most rods that have been fished hard show it. If your ferrule wrap consists of one continuous length of thread from ferrule to bamboo, this crack, should it occur, will break the thread and the wrap will unravel. So you make two wraps so that the crack—again, should it occur—will lie between them.

The trick to making this double wrap look good is to make the wraps meet perfectly. The best way I have found to accomplish this is to make the juncture the starting point and to wrap the bamboo first, nudging the wraps right up to the ferrule serrations. After this wrap is complete, I turn the rod around and wrap the serrations starting at the bamboo end and nudging the wraps right up against the bamboo wrap. On the serration wrap, you can wrap up the ferrule as far as you like. I've seen some rods where the entire ferrule is covered right up to the welt or the slide. I usually just wrap up to the shoulder because the thread has little to add except weight once the serrations are covered.

There are a couple of ways to put a guide at the ferrule. One is to wrap the guide like any other, with the guide foot nearly butting against the ferrule serrations. If you wish to add more reinforcement, you may make the ferrule wrap as though there were no guide there, varnish the wrap, and then, once the varnish is dry, wrap the guide with one foot sitting over the varnished wrap. The trade-off for this extra reinforcement is that the underlying wrap is softer than bamboo. If there's any danger of the guide feet working loose it would probably happen here first. That hasn't happened on any of the rods I've done that way, and some of them get fished pretty hard. But if the guide does work loose, the bamboo at the ferrule is still reinforced. This latter wrapping method is usually reserved for heavy rods, and I wouldn't call it a necessity even for them, but there it is, for whatever it's worth.

Wrapping the Hookkeeper

I don't like hookkeepers and hardly ever put them on rods. To me they clutter up the rod, are an invitation to hook yourself,

and are less effective than simply running the leader around the reel and hooking the fly in the stripping or first snake guide. Some people must have them, though, and if you're going to put one on a rod it's a nice touch to do so with a continuous wrap. Start the wrap at the grip, and wrap the near end of the hookkeeper. When you get to the shoulder, remove the tape from the other foot and pass the thread under the free foot for each turn. When you get to the opposite shoulder start wrapping over the foot again and finish the wrap. Easy. If it's a strap-and-

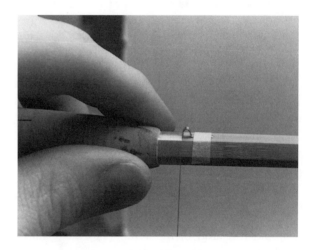

Figure 6.45. Start the wrap just as you would for a single guide, and wrap until you reach the shoulder of the strap.

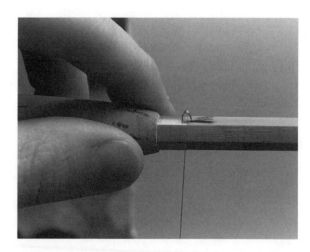

Figure 6.46. Remove the tape that held the strap down and bend the strap up slightly so that you can slide each wrap of thread under the end. Continue wrapping until you get to the second shoulder.

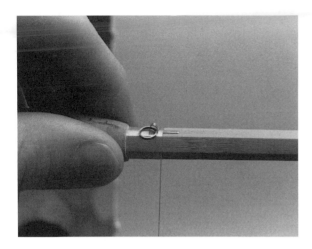

Figure 6.47. Slide the ring under the strap and wrap over the re-mainder of the strap, finishing it just as you would a guide.

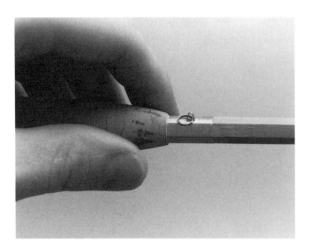

Figure 6.48. The completed wrap.

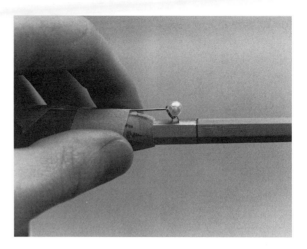

Figure 6.49. When you have the wrap finished and are ready to var-nish, tape a pin with a large round head to the grip to hold the ring away from the blank. Or you can secure the ring in the upright posi-tion with a tiny dab of glue. I like the pin because I don't have to worry about varnish collecting in the ring when I dip, and when I'm done varnishing and I pull the pin away it automatically removes a lot of the varnish I would otherwise have to chip away.

ring hookkeeper, pass the ring under the free foot just before you start wrapping over it. Strap-and-ring keepers are a little tricky to varnish. The way I've dealt with them is to use a large round-headed pin taped by the point to the grip to hold the ring out from the rod and to keep it from filling with varnish. (See the accompanying photo sequence, Figs. 6.45 through 6.49.)

Using Silk Thread

The search for the perfect thread is just one more of those interesting little twists that makes this craft so fascinating. A fly tier who spends what may seem to the uninitiated like an inordinate amount of time looking for a patch of deer hide from just the right part of the deer, or for the perfect cree dry-fly neck, makes a good comparison. Materials are im-portant, even down to the ones that might at first seem pretty basic.

The color, quality, evenness, and trans-lucency of your guide wraps is one of the first things anyone will notice about a rod, and the right thread makes a difference. If you want transparent wraps, some colors or brands will work better with a certain kind of varnish than others.

Silk thread is not as easy to work with as nylon, but it's the right stuff for a bamboo rod. There are a few companies still making silk thread, but all I can say is, if you find a color and brand that you really, really like, lay in a pretty good store of it. Fine thread (OO or smaller) is great stuff, because it lies flat and close to the blank and goes transparent with varnish better than thicker thread. Pearsall's Gossamer fly-tying silk is lovely stuff, though the color selection is limited. Kinkame is a Japanese silk that comes in very fine sizes and in a rainbow of colors, but the dyes can be inconsistent. Belding Corticelli is still available, though not in many of the old favorite colors. Utica is an American company that sells silk thread for a very reasonable price, but their finest silk seems to me still too heavy for a light rod. Same with Gudebrod, though they make good threads in about twelve colors and their products are widely available through rod builders' supply houses. Sources for silk are listed in Appendix B.

It seems as though there's always something keeping a thread from being absolutely perfect, but that's not to say you won't get good results from any given thread. Just try different kinds and see what you like.

The Delicate Art of Varnishing

Before dipping, it is important to seal the wraps with three or four coats of varnish. What you use to seal the wraps depends on what you want. If you want transparent (translucent, at least) wraps, you will probably use a penetrating, slow-drying spar varnish for the first coat. Don't worry if you use urethane for subsequent coats. You will need to allow plenty of time for the spar varnish to dry (I allow a week, but that's just to be safe), but the thread surface with one coat of spar in it will still be very rough, so just about anything will stick to it.

If you want to keep the color in the thread and not have transparent wraps, you need to use some kind of color preserver. I really don't like the commercial color preservers much. They don't do a great job of gluing the thread and guide to the blank, and they are very susceptible to varnish seeping in under the guide feet and making transparent splotches. What has worked well for me is Varathane 900. This is a very fast drying urethane varnish (there are doubtless others like it on the market), and its effect is similar to that of the usual color preservers except that it glues the thread down better and produces a color perhaps a shade darker than color preserver. U40 Rod Varnish (in the small glass bottle) makes the wraps slightly more translucent, but it works well also. If you use Varathane or a similar varnish as a color preserver, you still need to be careful to get plenty of it under the guide feet or the varnish you use to dip can soak in there from underneath and make dark splotches.

My varnishing treatment for guide wraps goes like this: either a coat of spar or three coats of Varathane to fix the color I want, then three or four thin coats of Varmor urethane. If I use Varathane, I'm careful to let the last coat dry for a couple of days so the first coat of Varmor doesn't soak into it and mottle the thread. Then I lightly sand the wraps with 1000 grit sandpaper, and I'm ready to dip. You want to be sure that you have the thread well covered before you sand, particularly if you use color preserver, or you will break through the varnish and sand the thread, and that looks like hell if you try to finish over it. In fact, if I'm using Varathane as a color preserver, I often will not even touch the wraps with sandpaper until the first coat of dipped varnish is dry.

I use a small artist's brush to apply the varnish to the wraps. I've heard some makers recommend using the fuzzy end of a paper match, but I've tried it and don't think it works all that well. A good brush will minimize bubbles and hold the amount of varnish you need and apply it evenly. Use a good-quality brush and take care of it, and it will last for a couple of rods. Don't bother with the little disposable brushes sold with model paints—they throw bubbles like crazy.

The wraps don't have to be perfectly smooth before you dip, because you will sand them between coats along with the rest of the rod; however, the smoother they are the less work that sanding will be, so try to make thin, even coats and apply enough coats to fully cover and embed the thread.

Finishing

Varnishing can be as easy or as tough as you want it to be. If all you want to do is get some varnish on the rod so that the water won't hurt it, that's easy. Just read this section and forget everything that sounds like too much trouble. On the other hand, if you have a desire to create something remarkable, you will probably wind up pursuing the fabled flawless coat of varnish, and everything I could possibly tell you won't seem like nearly enough information.

For the sake of discussion, let's assume that you will be dipping your rods. "Dip" is really too short a word for this process. You lower the rod into a long tube filled with varnish, then, with agonizing slowness, withdraw the section so that the surface tension of the varnish pulls away all but a very thin, perfectly even coat from the rod. There are other ways, of course. You can brush the varnish on, squeegee it on with a finger, or, perhaps, if you already have expertise in the area, you could spray it on. For results per hour of time invested, however, I really feel that dip varnishing is the best way to go.

Creating a dipping apparatus is discussed in Chapter 12. Speaking from experience, I would just say that it is possible to get good results from a crude and hastily improvised setup. There are only three major requirements your apparatus must satisfy in order to produce a flawless coat of varnish: 1. you must be able to control airborne dust, 2. you must be able to control temperature, and 3. you must use an electric motor to withdraw the rod section from the varnish. It helps to be able to see what you're doing, of course, and it helps if you can be in a fairly comfortable posture while dipping, but these requirements are for you, not the varnish.

Before we go on, one final point of emphasis about the apparatus. Use an electric motor. Though you may rig up whatever variable-speed DC motor or gear-reduction transmission your heart desires, a common rod-turning motor works very well for pulling. These may cost as much as twelve dollars, but I found mine at a surplus store for a buck. The results produced by an electric motor's perfectly steady withdrawal rate are so strikingly superior to those produced by the commonly offered alternative of an old fly reel, and the motors themselves are so cheap, that you will do yourself a serious disservice by not using the electric motor. If you use a reel you will have runs. Rig your motor with a switch so that you can easily turn it on and off while you're watching the section being withdrawn.

On to varnishing. There are two main areas in which your varnish job can be good or bad. One is varnish application, and the other is surface preparation. The varnish application might be considered bad if it has drips and runs, or if it is either thick and goopy-looking or too thin to allow you to sand it without breaking through. There are only three things the varnish cares about as the rod is being pulled: 1. how thick or thin it is, which varies with temperature, 2. how quickly it dries once it is exposed to the air, which varies with both temperature and humidity, and 3. how slowly the rod section is withdrawn, which, along with viscosity, governs the thickness of the varnish coat. The rod section should be pulled out slowly enough that any excess varnish that might sag or run has time to be sucked off by gravity and the surface tension. It's all interrelated. If the varnish is too thick, you can't pull the sections slow enough. Conversely, if you pull the sections too fast, the varnish can't be thin enough to prevent runs. With my varnish and setup, I pull sections at about 2 1/2 inches per minute. Most makers seem to use a rate between 2 and 6 inches per minute, but it's best to err on the slow side if there's any doubt.

How the factors of varnish thickness and withdrawal time work for you will be the subject of some experimentation, because varnishes vary somewhat with respect to thickness out of the can, and it may be that one varnish requires an ambient temperature of 80 degrees and humidity lower than 60 percent to work well, while another is perfectly happy at a lower temperature and higher humidity. In general, though, a higher temperature will give you greater latitude and insurance against runs or sags.

This brings up the topic of what varnish to use. The first question is the larger one: spar or urethane? The question isn't really a matter of purity anymore, because most "spar" varnishes these days probably have some urethane in them anyway. The real difference, as far as we are concerned, is that spar varnishes like McCloskey's Man o' War or Pratt & Lambert 61 are predominantly oil-based, which means, among other things, that once dry they can be polished with a mixture of very fine abrasives and solvent to remove dust or scratches. On the down side, over the long haul spar can become brittle and crack, or turn gummy due to long storage in the rod tube. Urethanes are varnishes formulated with plastic, and the resultant coat of varnish on a rod has all the virtues of plastic. It is very tough, very flexible, and, compared to spar varnish, permanent. It takes about a month to fully harden, but beyond that time it is essentially neutral. It is also more tractable than spar when dipping, being less finicky about temperature and humidity and more consistent in its formulation. Its downside is that it is much more difficult to polish than spar, and scratches cannot be filled in and rubbed out as undetectably as with spar.

I prefer urethanes, and I have had the best luck with Pratt & Lambert Varmor (R10), though I have played around some with spar varnish and probably will continue to do so in the future. The choice really is yours, because whatever finish you choose, you will have to learn how it responds to your environment, what thickness is too thick for your temperature and humidity, what rate of withdrawal gives an optimum coat, and so forth. The question of thickness leads to the matter of thinning or reducing your varnish. Some varnishes may need it. One of the things I like about Varmor is that its consistency is perfect

right out of the can. Eventually, though, the varnish in the tube will thicken, and its life can be extended by adding a teaspoon or so of the appropriate thinner from time to time. There comes a time, however, when the whole batch will need to be replaced. With a tightly capped tube, the varnish should be good for one to two years, depending on how many rods you dip. The time the varnish is exposed to air is what matters.

I use an aluminum rod tube with a screw cap to hold the varnish. Varnish that sits in your tube for longer than a week will need to be mixed. I used to pour it from the tube back into a can and mix it with a stirrer, but that's too much exposure to air. Just drop a couple of clean half-inch ball bearings into the tube and turn the capped tube from end to end ten or twenty times before dipping.

Any finish will be only as smooth as the surface it covers. Varnish actually will exaggerate flaws by making them shiny, so be aware that the quality of your finish is affected when you remove the enamel, and again when you sand off the dried glue. Your objective at every stage is to create and maintain the smoothest, flattest surface possible without touching the power fibers. This work continues even after the first coat of varnish is on. Even if you have a perfectly prepared blank and guide wraps, it will take more than one coat to achieve an attractive finish, and what you do to the varnish between coats also has a great impact on the final finish quality.

It is necessary with most varnishes, certainly with all urethanes, to scuff or degloss each coat before subsequent coats are applied. The most common abrasives for this task have long been #0000 steel wool or powdered abrasives like pumice or rottenstone. The problems with these abrasives are that they conform to the tiniest contour of the surface and tend to produce a rounded appearance to the finished rod. 1000 or 1500 grit sandpaper applied with a small, hard sanding block will produce rod flats that are truly flat and perfectly smooth. If there is a secret to a crisp, clean, flawless varnish job, this is it.

That's the theory. If your dipping apparatus is complete, if your rod has all the guides done and well sealed with several coats of varnish, you're almost ready to go. Mask off the ferrules with Scotch Magic tape, starting with one complete wrap just a fraction beyond the end of the ferrule wrap and spiraling up the length of the ferrule. To keep varnish out of the female ferrule, you can insert a dowel or some other plug and tape over it, or just spiral the tape over itself past the end of the ferrule, then fold it over.

There is obviously only one way to dip the butt sections, but there are two ways to go with the tips. I feel that the best is to mask off the ferrule and hang the section from the tip-top. The increasing diameter of the rod when you pull it out tip first helps to prevent runs. If you leave your ferrules bright, you will do well to leave the masking on until the rod is fully varnished. If your ferrules are blued, you will probably want to put a coat of varnish on them to protect the bluing. If you put two or three coats on them, the varnish will obscure the lines of the welt and shoulder and look funky, so the best thing to do is to mask them on all but the last coat, then remove the masking for the final coat.

Now you're ready to dip. From now on, everything you do will have one overriding aim: to stir up no dust. Dust that is on the rod before it goes into the tank and airborne dust both will get you. To get dust and fingerprints off the rod, you need to rub it down with a lint-free cloth and a little thinner. For a lint-free cloth, I use an optics cleaning cloth (from Edmund Scientific, listed in Appendix B) that does an outstanding job of catching and holding dust in its weave. The thinner will soak into the wood a little bit, so after wiping it down you should hang it up in your drying cabinet for twenty or thirty minutes to allow all the thinner to evaporate.

Otherwise it will bubble up through the varnish as it dries.

After the rod has been cleaned off with a cloth and thinner, be very careful not to touch it with your bare hands other than at the points that either will be above the varnish line or are covered by tape. With a strong backlight, examine each flat of the rod for dust. If you have an air compressor, it is an outstanding idea to take the rod into a separate room (or outside) and blow it off with compressed air. Outside probably is better, or you will stir up more dust with the compressed air than you will remove from the rod. In any event, you must carefully examine the rod immediately before it goes into the varnish. When you are satisfied that it is free of dust, lower it into the varnish immediately, before any dust lands on it.

Leave it in the varnish without disturbing it for a couple of minutes to allow any bubbles that might have formed in the immersion to detach, and to allow any dust around your apparatus to settle. Actually, the largest single source of dust is you. Your clothes, skin, and hair are constantly sloughing a veritable cloud of particles. Before pulling a crucial final coat of varnish, I will often take a shower to dislodge the most recent accumulation of dead skin cells, then do my work wearing nylon (no lint) running shorts. It may sound weird, but just wait. If you get sucked into the pursuit of a perfect finish, you'll be doing it too.

Having waited a few minutes, you're ready to start pulling. However, you don't withdraw the section with one steady pull. You must stop the motor occasionally to allow the varnish that collects at various points on the rod to be pulled down by surface tension. The varnish that forms a skin within the circle of the guides must be allowed (or encouraged) to pop, and time must be allowed for that minute surplus of varnish to run back into the tube. With a constant pull, that varnish would make a run on the wrap. The same sort of situation occurs whenever the varnish must negotiate a step from a larger-diameter surface to a smaller one. The step from winding check to wrap, for instance, can produce a run if a pause of a minute or two is not allowed. Going from a wrap to the bare blank is a similar step down, and I usually wait twenty or thirty seconds with the bottom of the wrap just barely clearing the surface of the varnish before resuming the pull.

If you're pulling a butt section, here's how it will go:

1. Immerse the section until the varnish is just touching the winding check or tip of the grip. Wait for a couple of minutes.
2. Start the motor for the briefest of seconds and wait at least a minute for excess varnish to clear the winding check (if you use one).
3. Start the motor and stop it again just as the end of the grip wrap clears the varnish. Wait another full minute. The relatively large diameter of the rod at the butt, the swell that often occurs on rods just ahead of the grip, and the step down from wrap to blank often combine to cause a run here.
4. Starting the motor again, pull until the bottom of the first wrap of the stripping guide (or any intermediate decorative wrap) clears, then stop and wait twenty or thirty seconds.
5. Pull until the top of the second wrap of stripping guide appears, then wait another twenty or thirty seconds. If the varnish bubbles in the guide ring and frame do not pop of their own accord, you may need to encourage them. I use a piece of stiff, heavy cotton string, which acts as a wick as well as a poker.
6. Pull again until the bottom of the second wrap just clears, and wait again. Repeat the process with each guide.

When you have pulled the complete section, you may remove it from your dip-

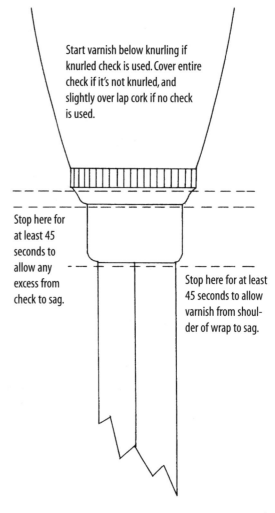

Start varnish below knurling if knurled check is used. Cover entire check if it's not knurled, and slightly over lap cork if no check is used.

Stop here for at least 45 seconds to allow any excess from check to sag.

Stop here for at least 45 seconds to allow varnish from shoulder of wrap to sag.

Dip varnishing sequence at grip

ping apparatus and hang it in your drying cabinet. Unless this is your final coat, you will not need to worry too much about a little airborne dust because you'll sand it out anyway. For your final coat, however, you want to avoid exposing the blank to dust until the varnish is tack-free, so if your apparatus is enclosed in some sort of cabinet or plastic sheath, it's best to leave it in there for a couple of hours before moving it.

After the first coat has had time to dry for a day or two (perhaps longer with spar), lightly sand the whole rod, wraps included, with 1500 grit sandpaper. This operation takes a delicate touch, for too much sanding or pressure (or insufficient drying time) and you will break through the finish, and the

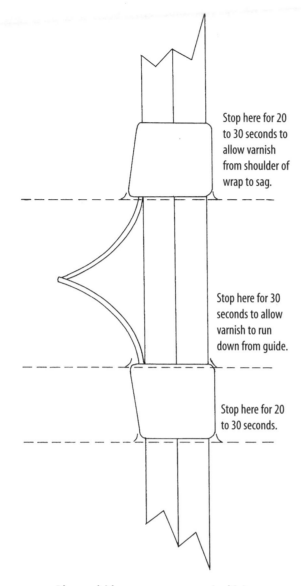

Stop here for 20 to 30 seconds to allow varnish from shoulder of wrap to sag.

Stop here for 30 seconds to allow varnish to run down from guide.

Stop here for 20 to 30 seconds.

Dip varnishing pause sequence (guide)

The first coat will look pretty shaggy because the varnish will soak in at the nodes, and tiny pores, fissures, and scratches will be visible because they'll be shiny, but sanding and a second coat will take out most of the rough spots. A third coat and the rod will look great.

In case you were wondering, I don't try to chip the varnish off the guides. After a few hours of fishing the varnish wears off where it should and protects where it doesn't wear off.

Signing the Rod

If you wish to add an inscription to your rod, the best tool is a very fine technical pen. I used a Rapidograph for a while, but I didn't use it enough to keep it from getting clogged with dry ink, and emptying and cleaning it after every use was a drag. I wasn't happy with the results from anything else, so I suffered along for a while until I bought a Rotring Rapidoliner—essentially a disposable technical pen. I don't know if the ink is formulated differently or what, but I have used the same pen for nearly three years exclusively for rod inscriptions. It may take a few minutes of shaking, point downward, to get the ink flowing after the pen has sat idle (point upward) for a couple of weeks, but it has never clogged and has yet to run out of ink. Of course, this experience has been limited to one sample, but I wouldn't expect there to be any variation from one pen to another.

For inscriptions, the finer the line the better, in my opinion. My pen is marked .25, which I assume means .25-millimeter. Whatever, it's plenty fine. This particular pen (in my climate) will mark on unvarnished bamboo (sanded smooth to 1000 grit) without spreading, but try yours on a piece of scrap first. If you have problems, use a sealer or make your inscription after the first coat of varnish has dried and has been sanded. If you screw up and act fast you can take the ink off with a pencil eraser. If that doesn't

feathered edge where you broke through will always be slightly visible through subsequent coats. It also takes time and a fair amount of sandpaper. The sandpaper is designed to be used wet, but I have to see what I'm doing, so I just accept the fact that it will load up fairly quickly. I've had some luck cleaning the sandpaper with one of those big sanding belt erasers, but that takes time.

How many coats? It depends on the rod's size and how well the most recent coat of varnish turned out. I normally put two or three coats on the tips and three or four on the butts.

Transforming the Blank to a Fly Rod

seem to work, use 1000 grit sandpaper. There may be other marking methods, but that's what works for me. What does *not* work is a so-called "permanent" fine-line felt-tip marker. These things are solvent-based, and varnish will make them blur.

Affixing the Reel Seat

You're almost done, but be patient still. Gluing the reel seat is about the easiest part of rod making, but it's still possible to get in a hurry and do it poorly. The main things to think about here are getting the seat on straight and applying glue in such a way that it doesn't gush out all over your cork and everything. I use a regular old rod-building epoxy for this task.

If you're using a sliding-band reel seat there are only four parts to worry about: filler, trim ring, band, and cap. First, glue the filler and trim ring on the rod by spreading glue around inside the filler starting from the end that will be next to the cork. This way, the excess glue will run out the butt end. If you put the glue on the blank, the filler will push it out all over the cork. A tiny bit of glue on the trim ring will secure it to the filler and the cork. Emphasis on tiny. Twist the filler around as you slide it up to ensure even distribution of the glue. Line the reel seat up with the guides and allow the glue to dry.

That's assuming you are using a filler with a bore that matches the end of the blank, in which case you will either have a good wood-to-wood contact if the corners of the blank are turned down a little, or the space afforded by the flats will hold the glue. If you need to build up the blank with string, you may have to apply a little extra glue to the shaft as you slide on the filler. If the shaft gets too round, it will simply form a seal and push all the glue out.

Next, slide the band onto the filler over a strip of paper so that it won't go anywhere while you glue on the cap. The butt caps for sliding-band reel seats are regularly tempted

to fall off, so make sure you have a good epoxy joint by scoring the surface of the wood filler and the inside of the cap with a file or scribe where it will meet the wood. This cap is one area where I would consider using a pin for security, but with good scoring on the mating surfaces I haven't had a cap pop off yet. I know, I'll be punished for saying that.

When gluing the cap, particularly if it is the round type that fits on a mortised filler (as opposed to the type with a hood), I put a piece of masking tape on the outside and mark the side that will be the bottom before roughening or gluing. Once the surface is prepared, dab epoxy into the bottom and back of the cap. You want to use enough so that a good film will result, but not so much that it squeezes up into the pocket where the reel foot will sit. If it does squeeze up there, remove the cap and clean the excess off the filler and the inside top of the cap, then replace it. Removing excess glue from the filler around the bottom of the cap is easy; just do it before the glue sets. If you're using a commercial reel seat and filler set, it is fairly likely that the fit between filler and cap will be somewhat loose. If the fit is extremely loose, you should make or obtain a new filler or not use the set, but if it is only moderately loose, you can take care of it with a little creative clamping. Once you have the cap in place and it is evident that you don't have glue where it isn't supposed to be, you can hold the cap in place with an old reel foot until it at least achieves a decent tack. You shouldn't leave the foot there until the glue dries hard, because a little excess might seep in at the edges, and you know what that would mean. Leaving it for ten or fifteen minutes usually is enough to make sure the cap stays in the right place.

For other reel-seat types, the process is essentially the same. Common sense dictates what part to glue first. You always want the excess glue to squeeze out where it won't be a hassle to clean off. If a little epoxy does get on the filler, a rag or cotton swab moistened with rubbing alcohol will remove it.

Accessories for the Finished Rod

Finally, your rod is done. Since you're probably kind of proud of it, you won't want to take it anywhere without a bag and tube. There are a few good suppliers of tubes (Appendix B). You can make a tube yourself if you have a big enough lathe, of course, but I'll just assume for now that you'll buy one. The bag is a little different, because almost all of the commercially available rod bags are for graphite rods that have only one tip. Rod bags are fairly easy to make, as sewing projects go.

Rod Bags

The material for your bags should be 100 percent cotton of one sort or another so that it will absorb any moisture that happens to adhere to the rod when it is put away (the rod should be dried *before* it is put away, but maybe *you* won't be using it). Most of my bags have been made from a light denim, but a cotton duck or flannel would work equally well. Whatever you use, it's a good idea to cut it into slightly oversize pieces, then wash and dry them a couple of times to shrink the fabric and soften it. You'll get the best price by buying fabric by the entire bolt and by watching for sales. Fabric stores are almost always having sales, so you should be able to find something suitable for a couple of bucks a yard.

I've seen lots of different bags, ranging in complexity from simple sleeves to copies of the old Hardy bags with snaps *and* zippers. All of my bags have been of the sleeve style described in the Garrison and Carmichael book, and I've never found any reason to complicate things. If the tube is the right length you don't have to worry about the tips slamming into the lid with enough force to do any damage, and it seems to me that friction keeps them in the bag just fine anyway.

Making the sleeve-type of bag is pretty simple. Iron the fabric first to make it easier to handle. Cut a piece of fabric 1 1/4 inches longer than your rod sections, marking the outline with chalk. About 3/4-inch will be used in the rolled-over hem at the mouth of the bag, and 1/2-inch in the seam at the bottom of the bag. If your cloth is very heavy, you may need to add another fraction. The width of the piece, for most rods, should taper from 10 inches at the mouth to 9 inches at the end. This will allow pockets 1 inch wide plus a fraction for the tips and 2 inches plus a fraction for the butt. A step that isn't absolutely necessary but that will make things a little easier and may add durability to the bag is to bind the edges of your trimmed piece with a zigzag stitch. Then you won't have to deal with loose threads getting in the way when you sew or with snagged guides when the bag is finished.

A trick just to make sure the bag comes out the right length is to cut it a little long, then test for length once the side and bottom seams are sewn but before it's turned right side out and the divisions sewn. The sections should sit down inside the bag about 3/8-inch at this point, since you'll lose 1/4-inch in finishing the seam. If the sections sit too far inside, run another line of stitching across the bottom and trim off the excess. And if the bag still turns out a little too long that's just fine; you can run a line of stitching the necessary fraction of an inch up from the bottom of the finished bag. The only thing you can't fix is a bag that's too short.

The first step in making the bag is to fold over the hem at the mouth of the bag. This hem will be 3/8-inch wide; fold over 1/4-inch of the edge and iron, holding with pins if necessary, then fold it over again to make the 3/8-inch hem. Secure this hem with pins and run a line of stitching down its middle, or two lines at the edges of the hem, 1/4-inch apart. Your best friend in keeping everything neat and straight is the iron. Iron the seams when you get them rolled but be-

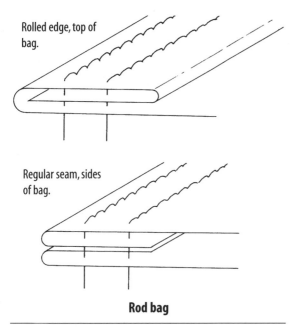

Rolled edge, top of bag.

Regular seam, sides of bag.

Rod bag

reference because it'll be straight, whereas the stitched edge may not be. Run a second line of stitching parallel to the first line and 1 1/4 inches over. Before you finish this line, insert a short length of piping doubled over to serve as a loop to be used to pull the bag from the tube or to hang the bag up for storage.

The Ferrule Plug

The final thing you should consider as an accessory is a ferrule plug. It's not absolutely necessary, but it is a very nice touch and helps keep dust and crud out of the female ferrule. Ferrule plugs are easily made with cork, brazing rod, and whatever hardwood strikes your fancy, or they can be turned from aluminum or nickel silver with cork added. The only trick to making ferrule plugs is making the cork cylinder. You will need to make a cork cutter from steel tubing. I usually cut a cork plug with the cutter held in the lathe chuck and the lathe either turning at the slowest speed or being turned by hand. A really fine wine cork may be a suitable source for the cork cylinder, but I usually just glue two flawless rings together and can get five or six plugs out of them. You really need good cork for this, because the finished cylinder will be very thin. Then I use a small rat-tail file chucked in the tailstock to drill and size a hole through the center of the plug. The hole should be just large enough to provide a tight fit onto whatever you are using for a plug body. I use 1/8-inch brazing rod for most of my plugs, with either a bamboo or hardwood knob on the end.

Once the cork plug is made and centered with a hole, slide the cylinder onto a short section of brazing rod and turn it down slightly oversize in the lathe (or by chucking it in an electric drill). The hole should be large enough that the cork won't split, but small enough that the friction of its fit will keep it from spinning on the rod. You'll need to apply the same principles that are used in turning the cork grip—use the gentle appli-

fore you sew, iron a crease when you fold the cloth in half. The closer and flatter the parts being sewn lie, the easier it will be for them to pass through the machine, the less the work will bunch, and the easier it will be to see the straight edge of your work and keep your stitch running parallel to it.

Next, stitch the edge of the bag. The first stitch will be made with the bag turned inside out. Make sure that the hem at the mouth of the bag is inside the bag at this point—you want the rolled edge to be outside on the finished bag so it doesn't snag the guides. So, fold the piece in half, match the edges carefully, secure with pins and iron, then run a line of stitching 1/4-inch from the edge all the way around the side and bottom, or two lines like a jeans seam.

Turn the bag right side out using a dowel or brush handle or something similar to poke out the corners. Run another line of stitching 1/4-inch from the edge. Now you're ready to divide the bag into pockets. It's a good idea to iron the bag again and insert a few pins in the bag to prevent the two sides from crawling out of alignment. Run a line of stitching 1 1/4 inches from the folded edge. It's important to use the folded edge as your cation of solidly backed sandpaper to even and true the cylinder. You want to leave the cork cylinder long; you'll trim it to length after you glue it onto the shaft. To make the rest of the ferrule plug, drill a 1/8-inch hole partway through whatever you want to use for a knob, then glue a short piece of brazing rod into the knob. After the glue is dry, chuck the rod end in the lathe to turn or dress the knob. Cut the rod to length, file the cut end smooth, glue on the cork cylinder, and after the glue is dry on the cylinder, trim the cork flush with the rod end and size it with 320 grit sandpaper.

The ferrule plug offers one more opportunity for you to add a unique touch to your rod. Bamboo, ebony, horn, tagua nut, nickel silver . . . as with every other aspect of bamboo rod building, the possibilities are endless.

. . . conquered by the skillful manipulation of the slender rod, which curves to the pressure as gracefully as the tall pine to the blast of the tempest. —George Dawson

7. CARE OF THE BAMBOO ROD

The most common and implacable enemy of the bamboo rod is the door. I would go so far as to say that 98 percent of rod breakage occurs because of carelessness or abuse, and the remaining 2 percent is the result of faulty materials or workmanship. Although it is a commonly held belief that bamboo is fragile and requires special care, this is only true in the sense that it is somewhat less tolerant of abuse than graphite and requires some care, as opposed to graphite, which requires practically none. A few simple rules should suffice to keep a bamboo rod intact and useful for many years. Most of the same rules apply to graphite rods, by the way. They are just as vulnerable to doors, falls, and hook digs as bamboo; the main difference is that if you tick a graphite rod's tip with a streamer and then it "mysteriously" breaks on your next big fish (or snag), you can ship the graphite rod off to a factory where they will just shove on a replacement tip.

1. When a rod goes through a door, it's broken down and in its tube. This means *any* door, beginning with car doors and on up to and including commercial aircraft hangar doors. If this rule were followed re-

ligiously, 90 percent of all broken rods could be avoided.

2. When walking through brush or trees, break the rod down and carry it with the tip pointing behind you. Too much trouble? Don't expect loads of sympathy when you run the tip into a tree and snap it off.

3. Be especially careful when casting large streamers, beadheads, weighted nymphs, or split shot. These rigs travel lower than dry flies, and it's easy to slam one into the rod (or your scalp) if you aren't paying attention. If a hook dig into the power fibers occurs, reinforce it with a wrap of white thread and coat the thread with a penetrating spar varnish. If you don't fix the dig, the next long cast or heavy fish could snap the tip at the gouge. This happens all the time with graphite rods, but the owners simply blame the manufacturer and ship it off. Someone at the factory sighs, and grabs a replacement tip out of a barrel.

4. When playing a fish, don't "give the fish the butt" and bend the rod tip into a sharp J. This may not immediately break the rod, but it will encourage it to take a set, will shorten its life, and is arguably the least effective way to apply pressure to and tire out a fish.

5. Buy a chamois and use it. Never put a rod in its tube wet. Never, never, ever.

6. Never store a rod in a damp place. If extended storage is required, hang the rod up in its bag in a warm, dry place.

7. If your fly or line becomes snagged, don't try to free it by jerking with the rod. Duh. There's a great story about Pinky Gillum recounted in Martin Keane's book, *Classic Rods and Rodmakers.* It seems Gillum was fishing one day when he saw a recent purchaser of one of his rods a short distance upstream. As Gillum moved closer, the man got snagged on the bottom and began yanking sharply with the rod. Gillum waded out, took the rod, snapped the leader, removed the reel and handed it to the man along with his money, turned, and waded away without a word. Apocryphal, perhaps, but if anybody can beat that story, I'd like to hear from you.

8. Cast maximum distances with the rod when you need to, but not regularly just for the hell of it. A bamboo rod has a long life only when used sensibly.

9. Rotate tips. Evening out use and fatigue is the best reason for having two tips. I suppose you could argue that the rod will last just as long if you use one tip until it's a noodle and then switch to the second one, but making the rod last for at least your lifetime with a consistent action is the idea.

10. When you disassemble the rod, place one hand on each side of the ferrule and pull straight away from yourself (see Fig. 7.1). Do not twist. If you can't get the ferrule off that way, get a friend to face you and take the same grip. I've never seen a stuck ferrule that this two-person pull wouldn't unstick. Or place the rod behind your knees and use pressure from your legs against your hands (see Fig. 7.2).

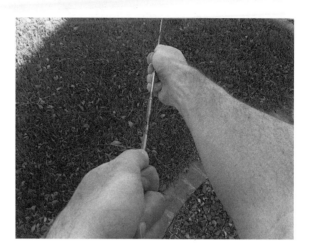

Figure 7.1. Separating rod sections by the normal method. Pull straight away, and make sure you're not pointing the tip at anything you could ram it into when the sections come apart. For a two-person pull, your partner will face you and take the same grip.

Figure 7.2. Separating rod sections with leg pressure against the hands. This is more powerful than the straight-ahead pull but not as powerful as the two-person pull. Again, watch where the tip is going to go.

Care of the Bamboo Rod

PART 2

EQUIPMENT, SKILLS, AND TECHNIQUE

8. Building Planing Forms

Making rough planing forms is easy, particularly if you have a table saw, or access to one. The forms can be made out of wood, and because they will have a straight groove with no taper, they can be made in practically any length. Four feet is a nice length. I built mine from a single 8-foot piece of 2 x 2, but shorter is fine. The choice of 2 x 2 (the nominal size, of course) was somewhat arbitrary. I would think that any stock 1 inch square or larger would be fine. No, it doesn't have to be square—it can be rectangular.

The first step is to procure the wood. Forms made of hard maple or some other hardwood are great, but I just went down to the nearest builder's supply store and picked out the straightest fir 2 x 2 I could find. Unless you have access to a jointer, you will need to get a straight piece of wood and work with it before it warps. If you can get to a jointer, use it to square up your stock. If you can't, select the best stock you can or, if necessary, use a smooth plane to even it up.

The rough planing forms will have two different types of groove. The groove on one side will be a straight 60-degree groove, or two 30-degree bevels placed together. The other side will have a 90-degree groove, or a 30-degree and a 60-degree bevel placed

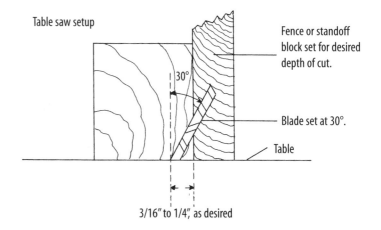

Table saw setup

Fence or standoff block set for desired depth of cut.

30°

Blade set at 30°.

Table

3/16″ to 1/4″, as desired

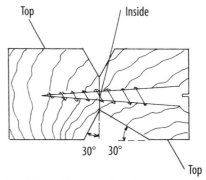

Top

Inside

30°   30°

Top

Finished rough forms. You can see from the 90° groove how the 30° table saw or router table setup is used. Simply bump the fence over a touch and place the inside surface (instead of the top) against the table and the top (instead of the inside) against the fence.

Rough planing form construction

together. You can make both grooves with one table-saw setup or jig. This is one of those things that is easy when you can see it; please refer to the accompanying illustration.

You're beveling a 90-degree corner, so if you rotate a stick with a 30-degree bevel a half-turn, you will have a 60-degree bevel. You're simply calling what was the inside the bottom.

After cutting the wood into two 4-foot (or whatever) lengths, you will be ready to cut the groove. With a table saw, all you need to do is set the blade for a 30-degree cut and set the fence so that the blade barely nicks the corner of the wood. Or you can use a 60-degree grooving bit in a router table. If you don't have a router table, one can be improvised (if you're careful) using nothing more than a piece of plywood clamped to your workbench with the router fastened underneath. Or you can just use a router freehand with a 30-degree chamfering bit. This type of bit has a bearing at the tip that keeps the depth of cut constant.

Bevel one edge of each piece so that when placed together a 60-degree groove is formed, then place them together and check the depth either by measuring across the gap or using a dial depth gauge. The 60-degree groove depth you want in your rough forms depends to some extent on what sort of rods you want to build and how closely you want to pay attention to what you're doing. A good general-purpose form might have a groove that measures around .190-inch deep. You may want to build two sets of wooden forms: one with a 90-degree roughing groove and a deep 60-degree groove (.200- to .250-inch) to make the initial handling of strips easier and for really big rods; and one with medium 60-degree grooves (.140- to .170-inch) for taking the strips for smaller rods down closer to the largest finished dimension. You want the dimensions to be in the ballpark for this step, but you don't need to sweat it too much. The forms, being made of wood, are easily adjusted.

Once you have the 60-degree side of the form done, nudge your table saw (or router table) fence over 1/32-inch and run the 30-degree bevel for the other side, the side that consists of a 30-degree and a 60-degree bevel. You will want this groove to be just a little deeper because you will be working with the rough strips and will need some extra room. To make the 90-degree groove, use the same saw-blade angle (or router bit), but orient the wood as shown. When you cut the bevels for the 60-degree groove, you always placed the "inside" of the forms against the table-saw fence. To cut the 60-degree side of the 90-degree groove, place the *top* of the stick against the fence. This 60-degree side will have to be deeper than the corresponding 30-degree bevel in order to meet it at the corner, so once you have the correct setup, nudge the fence over just a tiny bit and make another pass if necessary.

A jig that holds a plane at a 30-degree angle to the wood is very easy to make, so don't despair if you don't have a table saw or router. With your block plane and a protractor you can create a jig using scrap pieces of wood with a minimal investment of time.

Once your bevels are cut, clamp the pieces together side to side and on the top and bottom, and fasten them with wood screws. Then, plane the top surfaces to remove any irregularities. The 60-degree groove can be cleaned out with a triangular file or a 60-degree center gauge. If the groove is too deep, plane off some of the top. If it's too shallow, deepen it with the center gauge. Easy, no?

It would be easy to make wooden forms with a fixed taper by planing the inside surfaces of the forms before fastening them together, or by planing the tops afterwards. And if you added a push-pull bolt setup every 5 inches, you would have adjustable forms. There's a way to do this for every budget and taste.

Adjustable Planing Forms

Planing forms are the heart of this craft. If you want to make six-strip rods with no gaps and good internal joints, your forms must create a 60-degree angle. You cannot bargain with geometry—any other angle will produce results that are at best unpredictable and most likely unacceptable.

Creating this angle at a precise taper over a 6-foot length of twin steel bars presents serious difficulties for a machinist. Cold-rolled steel, relatively straight as it comes from the mill, contains residual stresses resulting from its manufacture, and machining can allow the stresses to manifest themselves, causing the bar to warp. Using hot-rolled steel solves the problem of skin stress but requires expensive surface grinding to square up the stock.

Making a good set of planing forms is a serious pain for a machinist who truly understands what you need. Speaking from experience, I would advise those seeking a set of planing forms to plan either on spending a pile of money or on making their own. It actually would be easier for you to make forms well than for a machinist to do so because you can afford to use simple tools and take your time.

I built my forms using essentially the same process outlined in Wayne Cattanach's book, but with some variations. There is an easier way to cut the 60-degree groove in the forms, and for drilling the holes it's worth some extra time and trouble to find a milling/drilling machine, if at all possible. A doweling jig will work fine, and if you absolutely can't get on a milling machine, you should not let that stop you from building your own forms.

The first step is to procure materials and tools. You will need:

- A 12-foot-long section of 3/4-inch square cold-rolled steel (cut in half), as well as a few short pieces for drilling practice.

- A couple of new India stones, and a little diesel fuel for washing and lubricating them. Most hardware stores sell large combination India stones with a coarse and fine side. These work well. You will want a fairly large stone, both because it is easier to grip and therefore less fatiguing to the hand, and because a larger abrasive surface cuts faster than a smaller one.

- Access to a Bridgeport or similar mill (don't be discouraged if you have no experience with machine tools—investigate!); or an "Improved Dowl-It" self-centering doweling jig and an electric drill.

- 1/4-inch, 3/8-inch, and center drill bits

- A 5/16-18 tap and handle

- Fourteen 3/8- x 1-inch shoulder bolts, fourteen 5/16-18 x 1-inch set screws. There are two methods outlined in the accompanying illustration (Ill. 8). This list is for the method that uses shoulder bolts. If you use dowels, all you need are fourteen dowels and twenty-eight 1/4-inch bolts, and only two drill bits and one tap: 1/4- and 5/16-inch bits, and 1/4-20 tap.

- A preground 60-degree lathe threading tool

- A jig to hold the threading tool. You may improvise on this. For instance, a Veritas sharpening jig (described in Chapter 9) would work pretty well.

- Eight C-clamps

- A pair of heavy-duty rubber gloves. Diesel fuel gives me a rash, and God only knows what else it does that we don't know about. If there's not a decent breeze outside, a respirator wouldn't hurt, either.

Cut the 12-foot steel bar exactly in half (you or the supplier will probably have to do this before you can easily transport it). The main priority in building forms is alignment. The two steel bars that constitute the form must be in perfect alignment, and they must stay in alignment throughout their range of adjustment. In order for this to be so, the holes for screws and dowels must be drilled straight, meaning that they must be perpen-

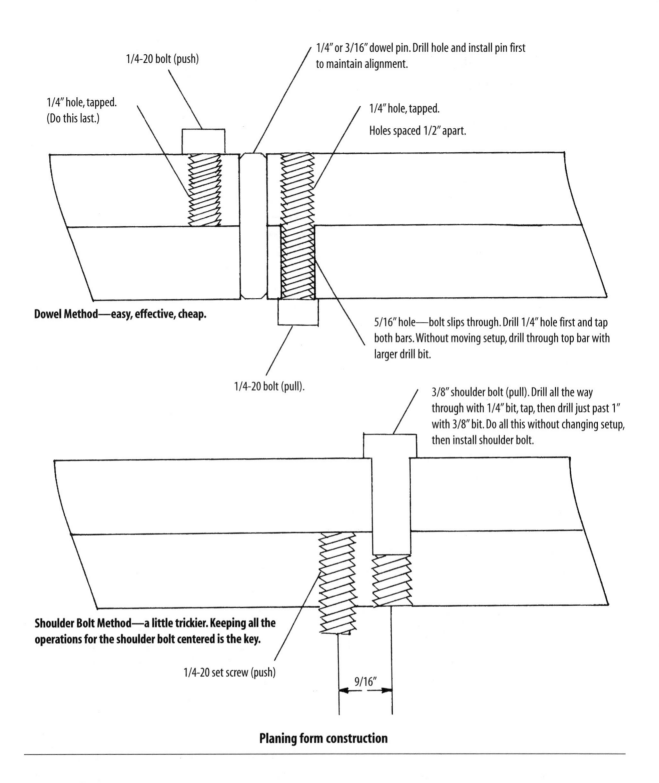

1/4-20 bolt (push)

1/4" or 3/16" dowel pin. Drill hole and install pin first to maintain alignment.

1/4" hole, tapped. (Do this last.)

1/4" hole, tapped.

Holes spaced 1/2" apart.

Dowel Method—easy, effective, cheap.

5/16" hole—bolt slips through. Drill 1/4" hole first and tap both bars. Without moving setup, drill through top bar with larger drill bit.

1/4-20 bolt (pull).

3/8" shoulder bolt (pull). Drill all the way through with 1/4" bit, tap, then drill just past 1" with 3/8" bit. Do all this without changing setup, then install shoulder bolt.

Shoulder Bolt Method—a little trickier. Keeping all the operations for the shoulder bolt centered is the key.

1/4-20 set screw (push)

9/16"

Planing form construction

dicular to the bar, and holes that go through both bars must be drilled while the bars are clamped in alignment. It is virtually impossible to drill each bar separately and then expect them to match and align properly. To provide a good mating surface, place the bars side by side about an inch apart on a flat surface, preferably outdoors, like a deck or patio. Put down some newspaper or plastic, because this will be messy. Wear rubber gloves. Wet your India stone with diesel fuel and gently stone both bars simultaneously with long strokes until you have removed any nicks, burrs, or protrusions. You don't need a perfectly smooth, shiny surface, you just need to make sure that the bars will fit together flush. In fact, you should be careful not to take too much metal off at this stage, because if you take the "skin" off a cold-rolled bar, it will warp. Use a stone, not a file, and take it easy.

The smooth sides are to go together. On the side of one bar opposite the smoothed side, mark lines every 5 inches, beginning 1 inch from the end of the bar. You can coat the bar with layout die and use a scribe, or you can make the marks with a fine permanent marker and scribe in the center of those lines. This is the layout for the shoulder-bolt holes, and you should mark each location exactly with a center punch. (The accompanying drawing of the station layout shows two different ways of doing it, so the center line could as easily be for the dowel. I'll discuss the operation as though shoulder bolts are to be used because it's the more complex method.)

One of the advantages to making your forms 6 feet long is that there will be stations 1 inch from each end. This controls the ends, keeping them from springing apart or closing together more than you wish because of the setting at the penultimate station, and allows you to plane all the way to the ends of your forms. If you make your forms some other length, it's worth the extra work to put stations on the ends even if the interval between stations is only 3 or 4 inches.

Next, place the dressed sides of the bars together and clamp them for drilling. The more C-clamps you use, the better, up to a point. You will want at least four C-clamps holding the bars together from side to side, and at least four more holding them in alignment at the top and bottom. Use a punch to mark each at one end so that the two can always be placed together in the same relationship. You're now ready to drill some holes, but don't just grab the Black & Decker and go for it.

The importance of drilling all the holes

perfectly straight through the stock cannot be overemphasized: Both bars must move on the same plane in order to preserve the 60-degree angle. There are a few different ways to make perfectly perpendicular holes. The surest way is to use a milling/boring machine. If you have access to a Bridgeport or similar mill, you can tram the head into perfect perpendicularity with the table, which means that you use a dial indicator mounted on a beam that is fastened by a collet at a right angle to the head. As you swing the indicator around, variations in the reading will tell you whether the head is perpendicular or not. Once you have this adjustment made, install the table vise and check it as well. Shim it if necessary. Now you have a setup that is square to the world.

Clamp the bars in the table vise and support both ends at the maximum distance from the vise with jacks. Using a dial indicator in the head, run the table back and forth and make adjustments with the jacks to level the bars horizontally in the vise. When this setup is perfect, clamp the vise down hard and then double-check the alignment. Once the bed has centered a hole location, lock it so that it will move only up and down and perform all the drilling and tapping necessary for that hole without unlocking it. A spring-loaded tap handle that uses a center in the drilling head to position it is invaluable in keeping the tap running square. Go slow and use plenty of fluid for all drilling and tapping. Too much pressure can mean a rough hole or a broken tap. You don't want a broken tap.

With the bars clamped securely together, drill and tap one hole every 5 inches using the layout lines and punch marks you made earlier. These holes will be for the shoulder bolts, to be installed in each hole as soon as it is drilled. (In the alternate method, this step would consist of drilling two holes: One for the dowel, which would be installed as soon as the hole was finished, and one, set 1/2-inch to the side, which would be for the 1/4-inch pulling bolt. The drilling-tapping-drilling process for this bolt is similar to that for the shoulder bolt.)

To continue, drill and tap the holes for the shoulder bolts first. The process for the shoulder bolts goes like this: Start the hole with a center drill. Drill a 1/4-inch hole through both bars. Tap the hole with your 5/16-18 tap. With a 3/8-inch bit, drill just past 1 inch, or through one bar and a touch more than 1/4-inch into the one below. Do all of this without disturbing your setup, whether you are using a milling machine or a doweling jig. It is vital that each step, each different bit or operation be centered on the same axis, or your shoulder bolt will bind. Once a hole is drilled and tapped, install a shoulder bolt and tighten it.

I suppose you can do more or less the same thing with a drill press if it is big enough, though you would have to make a different setup for every hole. There's no real substitute for a massive rigid machine, though, and most drill presses are not adjustable for perpendicularity. The next best alternative to a mill is the least expensive method: A doweling jig with removable inserts will perform the same function of keeping the holes perpendicular and centered, though with slightly less precision. If you use a doweling jig, you will need to experiment on scrap stock until the jig is drilling holes straight through. Drill a 1/4-inch hole, then stick a precision-ground dowel through it. Using your dial calipers as a depth gauge, check the dowel's distance from the top of one side of the stock, then from the other. Use a square to scribe entrance and exit lines that match exactly, and check entrance and exit holes. Once everything looks good there, use the dowel, a square, and a strong backlight to check once more. Drill, check, and shim, drill, check, and shim until your holes are consistently good. Patience should bring you to the point where your entrance and exit holes are within .010-inch or less (less is better) of one another. When your doweling jig

is shimmed just right, the operation is virtually the same as with the mill: Drill, tap, drill, insert shoulder bolt, tighten, and move on.

After the shoulder bolts are all done, remove them and lay out marks for the set-screw holes 1/2-inch to the sides of the shoulder bolt holes. I prefer to have the heads for the set screws and shoulder bolts on opposite sides of the forms, but I don't suppose it matters much which bar you put the set screws in. Drill and tap the holes for the set screws. Once this is done, you are ready to go back to the India stone and diesel fuel. With the bars fastened securely together, stone each side until you have a smooth, even surface. You don't have to stone down to a mirror finish, but you do need a true, burr-free surface in order to accurately shave out the groove.

An alternate method of making stations uses a dowel for alignment and two 1/4-inch bolts for push-pull. It's easier, requires fewer drill bits and only one tap, and should work as well.

Making the Groove

After this round of stoning you will be ready to make the groove. I got this idea from Joe Saracione, but a similar method is mentioned in Perry Frazer's *Amateur Rodmaking*, so the basic notion has been around for a while. In order to form the 60-degree bevel in your forms, shave out the groove using a 60-degree thread-cutting lathe tool held in a block or jig. It's very elegant and effective.

Thread-cutting lathe tools can be had for a couple of dollars at a machine-shop-supply house. Carbide-tipped ones are available and that's what I use, but the high-speed steel version might be better because it is keener and not likely to wear in this application. At any rate, you need a tool that is already precision ground, and you should double check the angle and make sure that the point is centered on the vertical axis of the tool. The idea is to hold the tool perpendicular to the forms, and to pull the

Set up ahead of time

This sketch is what I would build if I were to do it again. It is based on a jig Ed Hartzell built to hold a 60° center gauge for scraping wooden forms. It's just a suggestion, and anything that holds the tool perpendicular to the bottom of the block will work. A simpler version (inset) would be to mill a slot a little more than halfway through the side of the block and hold the tool with three or four set screws.

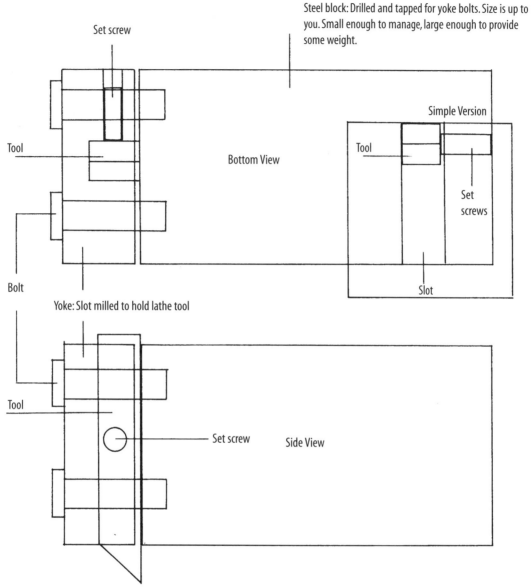

Set screw

Steel block: Drilled and tapped for yoke bolts. Size is up to you. Small enough to manage, large enough to provide some weight.

Tool

Bottom View

Simple Version

Tool

Set screws

Bolt

Slot

Yoke: Slot milled to hold lathe tool

Tool

Set screw

Side View

Suggested Construction: Drill four holes for yoke mounting bolts; cut off portion of block that will serve as yoke; mill slot for lathe tool. Drill and tap set screw hole, ream bolt holes in yoke, tap yoke holes in block. If slot is milled square, no shimming should be necessary.

Jig for Scraping Groove in Steel Forms

tool along the groove, taking a 30-degree cut from each side. Just like the stylus on a record player (remember those?).

In order to hold the tool, you can apply your own ingenuity to materials at hand. I made a "mouse" that holds the tool in a block of steel with set screws so that the depth of cut is adjustable, and a tool epoxied into a block of wood would work. Just make sure that the tool is mounted straight. If it's canted to one side, or forward or backward, it will not make a perfect 60-degree angle.

Once your forms are set up with shoulder bolts and set screws and are stoned flat on each side, use a dial indicator depth gauge with a 60-degree point to set a reverse taper in the forms. What you do is set the bars farther apart where you want the groove to be shallow and closer together where you want it to be deep.

The actual taper in your forms is open for discussion. I made my forms 72 inches long, with the tip-side taper from .025- to .095-inch and the butt-side taper from .075- to .145-inch, or a taper of .001-inch per inch. Since machine capacity wasn't an issue, I figured I might as well use the whole 12-foot bar. Other than drilling a few more holes, it was no more work than making 62-inch forms, and the extra stations help keep the forms as nearly closed as possible for a variety of tapers, which takes advantage of the alignment virtues provided by the shoulder bolts.

Regardless of form length, I think it is helpful to overlap the butt and tip tapers slightly, particularly if you intend to build any one-piece rods longer than 6 feet. Then again, you may feel that any overlap you may need is provided for by the fact that the forms are adjustable. As I wrote, it's open for discussion.

As an aside, you could make 8-foot or even longer forms if you really wanted to build one-piecers. When I visited Ed Hartzell in Portland, Oregon, he showed me a hunk of maple that he intends to turn into a set of forms for one-piece 8-footers. I haven't described it much, but making forms from hardwood is an option. Aluminum or brass work, too, and are less cantankerous than cold-rolled steel, though they are stickier and might tend to grab the plane on final passes. Ed Hartzell has applied the scraping method in making his own forms from hard rock maple, and his rods confirm the viability both of the method and the material.

Back to setting the reverse taper in your forms. For a groove at the 70-inches station on the tip side of .095-inch, setting your cutting tool to a depth of .095-inch and keeping the

forms completely closed at that station would give you the desired depth. Opening the forms to a "depth" of .005-inch would give you a groove of .090-inch, and so on. That's how it works. What you should do is start with a depth in the forms of .030-inch or so in order to give the tool room to cut, also adding .030-inch to the final depth of your cutting tool. Therefore, if you follow my taper you will set your cutter to a depth of .120-inch, use your dial indicator depth gauge to set a measurement of .025-inch at the 70-inches station, .030-inch at the 65-inches station, and so on, to a measurement of .095-inch at the 0-inches station. Your cutter will be set to a depth of .120-inch, though if your block is adjustable it is easier to start with a lighter cut and gradually increase the depth. Let's check: .120-inch cutter depth less .095-inch equals .025-inch, which is the desired form depth at the small end of the tip groove. Easy.

Once the reverse taper in your forms is set, pull your cutting tool assembly straight down the groove, being careful not to put more pressure on one side than on the other or to angle the tool. If your block or holder is fairly heavy, you won't have to apply pressure at all—just pull. The tool will chatter a bit at first, but you can reduce this by cleaning up the groove with a fine-toothed triangular file from time to time. If you use a Veritas jig, you'll need to clean off the shavings and run a file across the top of the forms fairly frequently to deburr them so the jig will keep rolling smoothly. Take your time, don't try to do it all in one night, and that's all there is to it.

When your cutter is set at the final depth and no longer cuts, your depth gauge should show an equal depth all along the forms. Take a couple of careful final passes with your file or a triangular stone, vacuum the chips out, and adjust the forms back to the completely closed position. If you did everything carefully, your forms should show nearly exactly the desired taper, with no bellies or tight spots. If your tool was accurately ground and correctly secured, your groove will be a clean 60 degrees for the entire length of the forms.

Don't get too excited if the stations don't measure within a thousandth or so of your intended taper. They probably will, but the forms are adjustable, and what's really crucial is that the taper is gradual, with no discontinuities, and also that the tip bevel is shallow enough to make rods as light as you want. As long as you work gradually toward the final depth with an adjustable cutter you should be fine.

In conclusion, making your own forms is easier than you probably thought and about as time-consuming as you probably expected. I didn't keep close track of my time, but my forms took a minimum of forty hours to complete, and probably more. That's a long time, but no longer than it takes to build a rod, and my materials only cost about forty dollars.

If you figure you've got the time and skill to make a bamboo rod but not to make your most critical rod-building tool, you might want to ask yourself if you're not in just a little bit too much of a hurry. I wish I'd asked myself that question earlier. I've bought forms and made my own, and it won't take a Rhodes scholar to guess which I did first, or which I now recommend. You might figure on saving some time by buying forms, but they don't make these things like pickups, and I could have built several sets of forms in the weeks I spent waiting for my "boughten" forms to be delivered.

The choice is the same as it has always been: You can spend money or time. Making your own forms results in intimate knowledge of your most important tool, and that's worth a lot.

9. SHARPENING THE PLANE BLADE

Perhaps the most important factor in successfully hand-planing a rod is having a plane blade that is not only surgically sharp but also correctly sharpened. Of course, exactly what constitutes correct sharpening may be the subject of some disagreement.

The first thing to consider is what type of stone to use. When I was growing up, one of the things men did while on a fishing trip or standing around in a hardware store was to compare knives, debate the merits of the steel in a Case versus a Camillus, shave hair off their arms and argue about how to best sharpen a knife, axe, or whatever. You'd get the occasional proponent of India stones, but, day in and day out, a good Arkansas stone was the undisputed champion. Well, things change. Today you still have Arkansas stones and man-made India stones, but you also have ceramics, diamond stones, and man-made water stones, also called Japanese water stones.

Although you are perfectly welcome to use any sort of stone you choose, I would have to say that you can't beat a good selection of Japanese water stones. (Actually, the term "Japanese water stone" is almost generic. Norton is now making a line of water stones that are manufactured right here in the U.S. of A.) When sharpening a plane blade, you need an edge that is not only razor sharp but also perfectly straight. In order to produce that straight edge, you need a perfectly flat stone. All stones become cupped with use, because tiny particles of the stone break away as you sharpen with them. This is desirable (the particles breaking away, not the cupping) because it continuously exposes fresh sharp particles and prevents the stone from clogging. Ceramic and diamond stones are an exception, because the whole idea behind them is that their abrasive particles are so hard and sharp that they don't need to wear away. However, if they aren't perfectly flat to begin with (and many are not), you can't flatten them. That's why I have found them unsuitable for this type of sharpening.

That leaves us with India, Arkansas, and Japanese water stones. Japanese water stones are the fastest-cutting of these three because they are relatively soft. The action of sharpening creates an abrasive paste on top of the stone, and new sharp particles are exposed at a faster rate than with other stones. Does this mean that they become cupped faster than other stones? Well, yes. However, they are also much easier to flatten once they do become cupped than other stones. To me, the water stone's combination of faster cutting and easier flattening more than makes up for the need to flatten it regularly.

You can flatten water stones by rubbing them in a circular motion on a piece of plate glass sprinkled with a little 400 grit Carborundum powder and water. Or you can affix a piece of 320 grit wet or dry sandpaper to the same glass with an even coat of spray adhesive on the back of the sandpaper and accomplish the same thing (see Fig. 9.1). I prefer the latter, for what it's worth. Once you have flattened the stones with the glass and abrasive, finish by lapping them together under running water (see Fig. 9.2).

Figure 9.2. Lapping stones under running water. Actually, it's wasteful to have the water running all the time; you should let a little paste build up between the stones and wash it out at intervals.

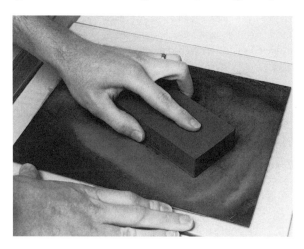

Figure 9.1. Flattening a water stone. A sheet of 320 grit wet or dry sandpaper is affixed to a plate glass with spray adhesive (just spray it on the sandpaper), and a little water is added for lubrication. Be sure water stones are well soaked before you do any work with them.

Now that you have flat stones, it's time to turn your attention to the blades. A sharp edge can be (and probably has been) defined as the intersection, at an acute angle, of two perfectly smooth surfaces, both occurring on the exterior of a single object. For our purposes, both smooth surfaces should be flat. It is implicit that an edge cannot be sharper than either surface is smooth, which explains why it is very important that your first act, when you unwrap a new plane blade, should be to flatten and polish its back, meaning the surface opposite the bevel, or the surface that, on a block plane, will face downward.

Unless the back of the blade is extremely uneven, waterstones will work as well as anything else for flattening. Work the blade down to an even sheen with an 800 grit stone, then to another even sheen with about a 1200 grit, then polish with your finest stone, at least 6000 grit. This may take a while, but you only have to do it once.

Once the back of the blade is flat and polished (see Fig. 9.3), start with the bevel. I've become a big fan of sharpening jigs for plane blades. The critical skill in sharpening

Figure 9.3. Polishing the back of the blade. You'll need to start with an 800 stone to get the manufacturing scratches out, but be sure to get all the 800 grit scratches out with a 1200 grit stone, finishing with your polishing stone. Your blade can be only as sharp as the back is smooth.

Sharpening the Plane Blade

Figure 9.4. The Veritas sharpening jig.

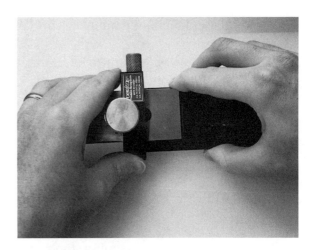

Figure 9.5. The little angle mechanism on the Veritas jig doesn't go high enough for me, so I scribed a line on the aluminum extrusion and use it as a guide to set the amount of blade that protrudes from this jig, which establishes the initial sharpening angle. This works only with the jig turned around backwards, which also makes it easier to get the required high angle.

Figure 9.6. The sharpening angle I use most is about 45 degrees.

is the ability to "hold a flat," or to take repeated passes at exactly the same angle. Any deviation from stroke to stroke produces a rounded bevel and a less keen edge. I used to think I could hold a flat pretty well freehand, but my first use of a jig produced a result superior to my most concentrated freehand effort.

Although I'm partial to the Veritas jig (see Fig. 9.4), I don't suppose it matters much what kind you use, as long as it allows you to create a sufficiently steep bevel. Some jigs assume that you will sharpen everything at a 30-degree angle—come to think of it, the Veritas jig has to be turned around "backwards" to get sufficient clearance. Back in Chapter 3, the angle at which block-plane blades should be sharpened for use on bamboo was discussed. Experience has convinced me that the standard grind of 30 degrees is too shallow and that smooth, chip-free cutting starts with a bevel of about 40 degrees. You can go as high as 55 degrees and still have a keen, reasonably easy-cutting edge if you sharpen it well enough, but I sharpen most of my blades at about 45 degrees (see Figs. 9.5 and 9.6).

There are two schools of thought, if that doesn't sound too grandiose, regarding the proper way to sharpen the bevel. One way is to employ successively finer stones with the blade held at exactly the same angle for each stone, with the result that the entire face of the bevel is honed with the 800, 1200, and 6000 grit stones, for instance. Known as "single-angle" sharpening, it produces as good an edge as you could wish for. A second method is to steepen the angle of the blade by a degree or two for each finer stone. This is somewhat faster, since you don't have to remove as much metal overall to get the desired edge. Some have said that the edge thus produced is not as durable as a single-angle edge, but I haven't found that to be the case. It seems to me that as long as the final "angle" surface on the bevel is sufficiently wide, say, at least 1/16-inch, there is no practical difference. I suppose an exaggerated multiple-angle edge could adversely affect the way the shavings break and perhaps lead to lifts, but I haven't had that problem.

Whichever method you choose, the process requires little explanation. You should sharpen with your coarse stone until a definite burr forms all along the back of the blade (see Fig. 9.7). Don't remove the burr yet. Your medium or fine stone should be employed until that heavy burr is replaced by a much finer burr, and your polishing stone should be used *on the bevel* until that burr is almost imperceptible. Only after your bevel is in perfect shape will you lay the blade perfectly flat on the polishing stone and take a few strokes on the back, never lifting the blade from its flat alignment. I saw a PBS show one Saturday morning not long ago where the host, explaining how to sharpen a plane blade, got all but done, and then said to lift the blade and take a few angled strokes on the back. Arrrgh! No! That may work for pine and oak, but not for bamboo.

Your final edge should easily shave hair off your arm. In an age where auto sunshades carry the warning "Do not operate automobile with this shield in place," I'm a little hesitant to actually recommend that you test your blades that way, but it's the time-honored method. And if the blade *won't* shave hair off your arm effortlessly, then it's not sharp enough. When you look directly at the edge under a strong light, there should be no glints or sparkles (see Fig. 9.8).

If you desire more information on sharpening, the wrapper that comes on a Hock blade is very good; and you shouldn't waste your time sharpening anything other

Figure 9.7. Sharpening on the 800 grit stone. Note the cutting paste that builds on the surface of the stone.

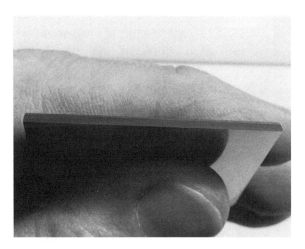

Figure 9.8. The final edge should have no glints or sparkles visible when viewed head-on. It also should easily shave hair off your arm, but that's your business.

than a Hock blade, by the way. There was an excellent article on sharpening by Ernie Conover in issue 5 of *The Planing Form,* and most woodworking texts contain discussions of greater or lesser completeness and clarity. And, if you think I'm all wet with my fancy imported stones and jigs, meaning that you can produce a perfect edge freehand on Grandpappy's old Arkansas oilstone, my hat's off to you.

10. How to Build and Use a Binder

The need for a binder is not absolute: Many rods have been made without one. If you get a couple of bobbins for two spools of 16/4 cotton thread, all you really need is the patience to cross-wrap the thread with a spool in each hand, moving hand over hand all the way down the rod. If you keep the tension the same for both threads you won't have any twist, and you will straighten the blank by rolling and pressing it on a flat surface as discussed in Chapter 5. In issue 14 of *The Planing Form* there is an article on building that discusses lacing by hand in greater detail.

A binder is a very nice thing to have, however, and it's easy enough to make that you shouldn't be without one if you plan to make more than a few rods. There are two basic types of binders: the kind that uses a driving belt and wraps one thread at a time, and the kind that wraps two or four threads simultaneously using counterrotating wheels. Both types have their good and bad points, and if you get used to using one kind you might not see the need for the other. The single-thread or Garrison-type binder is easier to make and, properly adjusted, works very well. The four-thread binder is a little more involved to make but can be adjusted to do maybe a better job of eliminating twist in the glued-up sections.

My suggestion would be to start with a single-thread binder because it will work well and because you can slap one together in a weekend. The accompanying drawings show a machine made of metal, but you could just as easily use wood. A scrap piece of 2 x 8, some empty thread spools for pulleys, an old sewing machine tensioner, a wooden disk for a crank, and a few aluminum or brass scraps and you could be in business.

Many of the dimensions on this type of binder are not critical, but there are a few fine points. What will determine how well the machine works is the alignment of the guides for the rod blank and the support cradles. If the rod is held straight while the thread is spun on, there is a certain nonzero probability that it will come out straight. Don't make the guides too wide, or the rolling action of the rod will pull it out of line with the support cradles. Your driving belt (80-pound poly kite string) will wrap twice around the driving wheel for traction, and it helps for the ingoing and outgoing guide pulleys to be offset slightly so that the belt will not catch on itself.

It's probably a good idea to save the job of notching the thread guide for last. You want the thread to hang more or less straight down from the guide to the center of the rod,

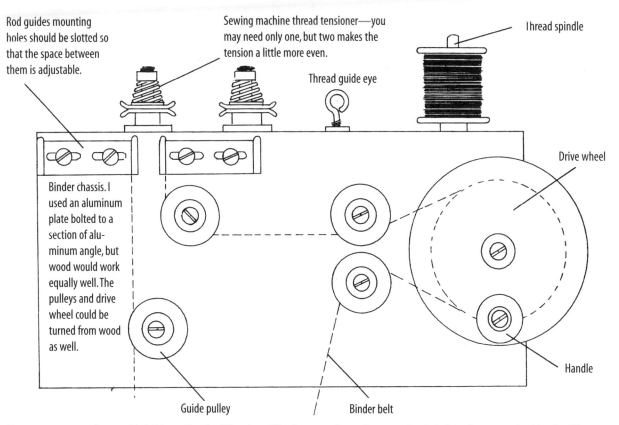

Rod guides mounting holes should be slotted so that the space between them is adjustable.

Sewing machine thread tensioner—you may need only one, but two makes the tension a little more even.

Thread guide eye

Thread spindle

Drive wheel

Binder chassis. I used an aluminum plate bolted to a section of aluminum angle, but wood would work equally well. The pulleys and drive wheel could be turned from wood as well.

Handle

Guide pulley

Binder belt

Measurements are really not critical. Drive pulley should be about 4" in diameter; other pulleys around an inch. Space between rod guides should be about 3/8", and the thread guide should position the thread between loops of drive belt on the blank. While my binder is about a foot long, 6" high and 4" wide, I've seen several others and all are different.

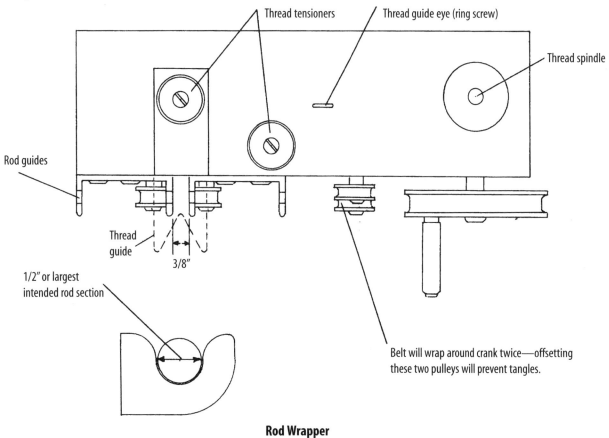

Thread tensioners

Thread guide eye (ring screw)

Thread spindle

Rod guides

Thread guide

3/8"

1/2" or largest intended rod section

Belt will wrap around crank twice—offsetting these two pulleys will prevent tangles.

Rod Wrapper

and you will need a couple of different notches to put the thread right between the driving belt loops for different diameter rods.

You'll need a few weights, but not many. If you have a 1/2-pound, a 3/4-pound, a 1-pound, and maybe a 2- or 3-pound weight (the last for binding before heat treating, not for gluing), you'll be covered. You can use just about anything heavy for weights. I turned my weights out of an old axle I found, but people have made them out of lead or concrete poured into cans, and lead shot or BBs sealed inside short sections of PVC pipe. Improvise as needed.

The weights have small hooks so they can be hung on the ring of a small pulley, which in turn hangs on the drive belt that passes under its wheel. The belt itself, as already mentioned, is 80-lb poly kite string. Cut off five feet or so, pass one end under the pulley wheel, and fasten the ends with a square knot. Add a drop of super glue to the knot, trim the ends close with nail clippers, and the belt is ready to use. You will need to watch for the knot as you bind and occasionally help the binding thread over it. If you use epoxy or a similar glue, you will have to discard the belt after gluing, but they are easily made.

Issues 3 and 26 of *The Planing Form* include articles on building counterrotating wheel binders. The machine designed and drawn up by Bob Milward (Issue 3), a maker in British Columbia, is one that shows just how easy it is to build something that works. For what it's worth, I would recommend that any binder you build either be powered by a hand crank or incorporate some sort of clutch. This recommendation was first made to me by Daryll Whitehead, who has one of the most impressive power binding machines I have ever seen. The problem with an electric motor is that it can't tell when there's a problem. If a tangle or knot in the thread occurs, or a thread tensioner binds or a spool falls off, or any of another half dozen things that conceivably could happen does, you could easily have a broken blank.

11. OVENS FOR HEAT-TREATING CANE

There are several different apparatuses that will achieve the temperatures necessary to heat-treat cane that might qualify as "ovens." One of the simplest is the method outlined in Claude Kreider's book whereby a steel pipe is hung from the ceiling by wires and heated by passing back and forth over it with a blowtorch while rotating it. This makes me nervous, but I know people who have done it with good results recently. Also, I know people who simply flame their cane in the culm and perform no other heat treatment, so if the job of building an oven seems like too much for you right now, don't let it deter you from building rods.

Garrison, of course, had an oven consisting of a big hunk of steel pipe fired by a row of propane jets underneath. Even if duplicating this setup appeals to you, I'm not sure, in this age of unlimited liability, if I would recommend that anyone try that. Mike Clark uses a piece of stovepipe fixed like a chimney on a kerosene heater for an oven. The sections hang from a crossbar at the top and are switched end for end to even out the heating. I've heard of makers bumming time on pizza ovens, and various industries use ovens for annealing and other purposes that could work if you know the right people.

What seems to me like a modern, economical, and practical solution for the individual maker is a small, narrow electric oven based on a long mica strip heating element. I built mine according to Wayne Cattanach's instructions a few years ago. He originated the design and writes about building it in his book, so if you have that book the following may be redundant. However, because sometimes the same thing explained another way is helpful, and for those who don't yet have a copy of Wayne's book, I'll describe the construction of this type of oven as I did it.

The basic idea of an oven like this is two pieces of metal ductwork, one 4 x 8 x 59 inches and the other 6 x 10 x 60 inches, both capped on one end, with the smaller fitting inside the larger and separated by a layer of fiberboard insulation. A long heating element runs along the bottom, and the rod sections are held by a rack made of 1/4-inch wire mesh. The heating element is controlled by a universal electric oven thermostat, available at any appliance repair store.

Your list of materials and tools runs as follows:

- 54-inch-long mica strip heater. Available from HiWatt, listed in Appendix B. These heaters are much less expensive when several are ordered at one time, so it would be a good idea to put several orders together. *The Planing Form* is a good clearing house for this kind of thing. The staff might know if anyone is already putting an order together, or can at least run a small ad for you to attract others.

- Two short (3 3/4-inch) pieces of 1/2-inch conduit.
- Universal oven thermostat; Robertshaw is a common brand.
- High-temperature wire and connectors for thermostat. (Get them along with your thermostat at an appliance repair shop.)
- Metal junction box or similar to house thermostat. Radio Shack has small metal project boxes that would work well.
- One 59-inch length of 4 x 8-inch steel duct with plain cap. Find a local heating–air conditioning company that makes their own ductwork.
- One 60-inch length of 6 x 10-inch steel duct with plain cap
- One 6 x 10-inch cap with an inside lip for a 4 x 8-inch opening
- One sheet of 1-inch fiberboard insulation (4 x 8 feet). You only need about half a sheet, but most places only sell it by the sheet. From this sheet you will cut two strips 6 inches wide by 60 inches long, two strips 8 inches wide by 60 inches long, and two 4 x 8-inch rectangles, one of which will insulate the end space between the two boxes, the other of which will serve as a door for the oven.
- 1/4-inch mesh heavy wire screen, 60 inches long and 12 inches wide
- Pop rivets and hand-riveting tool. These tools are cheap and very useful.
- Power drill for making rivet holes and vise grips for clamping

Once your tools and materials are assembled, your first task is to cut the fiberboard insulation into strips to fit your ductwork. I don't suppose it matters much which way the strips overlap, but I made my strips 6 and 8 inches wide and overlapped that way. You need to be careful cutting the stuff, because getting fiberglass dust in your lungs can be dangerous. Wear some sort of mask or respirator. Cutting is best achieved by placing the fiberboard, foil backing up, on a piece of plywood or similar material, then using a straightedge to guide a sharp knife. When you install the insulation, you will do so with the foil side out.

The best assembly, I think, is to attach the plain cap to the inner box first. Then, slide the inner box along with the insulation (foil side out) into the larger box before you attach its cap. Cut a 4 x 8-inch piece of insulation for the end and install it, then attach the cap on the larger box. Attach the caps by clamping them on with vise grips, drilling holes, and installing pop rivets.

Make a rack for the oven out of the wire screen. If you can get a sheet metal brake, by all means use it. In fact, the place that makes your ductwork would probably make your rack for a few bucks at the same time if you provide the screen. If you can't, use a couple of pieces of plywood to get a straight edge and sandwich the screen so it won't twist or warp while bending.

Use a nibbler or hacksaw to cut a narrow notch about 1 inch deep into both boxes so that the thermostat tube and element wires will have someplace to go (see Fig. 11.1). Drill whatever holes will be necessary in your thermostat housing to mount the unit and its wires, and attach it to the side or top of the oven in a spot where you will be able to see and reach it when the oven is in its intended location. Slide the rack in, attaching the bulb for the thermostat about halfway (or wherever the length of the metal tube allows). Make feet for the heating element out of conduit, drilling holes just to either side of the element for the screws that will secure the element to the conduit. Do not drill into the element itself!

Attach high-temperature-wire leads to

Figure 11.1. A view of the end of my oven, with the cap removed to show the insulation and passage of wires. Be sure to use high-temperature wire from an appliance repair supplier. The insulation on normal wire will disintegrate and bad things will follow. My oven lies on the long side of the rectangle because that's how I interpreted the drawing in Wayne Cattanach's article in *The Planing Form*. I've since learned from Wayne that the oven should be rotated 90 degrees—tall rather than wide. Mine works fine the way it is, but you might wish to set yours up the other way.

the element, and slide it in. Wire the leads and a heavy-duty three-prong power cord to the thermostat, and install it in its housing. Don't cut corners and ignore that green wire. Ground this sucker. After everything is hooked up and working fine, attach the cap that covers the end gap between inner and outer boxes. Cut a 4 x 8-inch piece of fiberboard for a door, and you're set.

To fine-tune my oven I drilled a small hole more or less in its center to insert a dial-face thermometer that reads up to 500 degrees Fahrenheit. I also drilled a couple of small vent holes in the far end to allow steam to escape and to keep the heat from building up too much in the closed end. There are lots of things you could do with this oven if you have an urge to experiment. I've considered building a convection oven using more or less the same sort of construction and heating elements, and using two elements instead of one and a more advanced thermostat to help control the temperature a little more tightly.

The reason I haven't done that yet is that my oven, as it is currently designed and constructed, works just fine. My one complaint is that it doesn't have enough thermal inertia or power to prevent a drop in temperature when the sticks are put in it. I've tried putting pieces of steel rebar inside to capture and hold the heat, but the best solution would be to make it large enough to accommodate a layer of brick or ceramic tile inside. Like a pizza stone in your kitchen oven, these would help maintain a steady temperature and even out the heat. This probably would necessitate a beefier heating element, or an extra one. Still, the oven I have works well, and it's small and light enough to move easily, and that's worth a lot to me. If your oven is likely to stay in one spot, you might think about making some modifications like these.

Ovens for Heat-Treating Cane

12. DEVISING YOUR OWN DIPPING APPARATUS

Your dipping apparatus can be quite simple. I varnished rods for a while with nothing more than a rod wrapping motor and spool clamped to my workbench, a length of kite string passing through a pulley hung from the ceiling in the center of the garage, and a tank standing upright on the floor. Because my garage ceiling is only 8 feet 3 inches high, this limited the length of sections I could dip, and eventually I broke down and punched a hole through the garage floor and built a permanent installation for dipping. Drilling a hole through concrete seemed like a major project at first, but I rented a 3/4-inch impact drill and drilled closely spaced holes all around the perimeter of the desired hole, then knocked out the center and dug as deep as I could into the soil below. Easy. Although I installed lights and built an enclosure for the dipping apparatus consisting of a 2 x 4 frame and a plastic sheath, I didn't bother to upgrade the admittedly crude motor and pulley arrangement, and it has so far worked flawlessly. The only weakness to this setup is that the kite string, even though it is braided and has virtually no inherent twist, will eventually work itself into a bias where it will cause the section to rotate perhaps once or twice (depending on the length of the section) over

the course of its withdrawal. This has not posed a problem, it just means that I may have to reach around the rod to pop a bubble in a guide ring once in a while.

One thing you must do without fail is to use some sort of termination on your string that will close securely and that has a little bit of weight. A small swivel snap such as you find at any hardware store will work well. Whatever you use, make very sure there is absolutely no way that the section you are dipping can disengage from the string without a deliberate, specific manipulation on your part. If you do not take this precaution, someday you will wind up fishing a rod section off the bottom of the dip tank. Actually, if it's the butt section, it will bob and float about halfway up the grip. It's the sort of mistake you make only once, but I'd like to save you the trouble.

If you want a really good finish, the main requirements of your dipping apparatus, as explained in the text, are that 1. you must be able to control airborne dust, 2. you must be able to control temperature, and 3. you should use an electric motor to withdraw the rod section from the varnish. The control of dust and temperature depend very much upon your situation. It is possible to control dust within a room to a certain extent

144

by keeping things clean and by moving as little as possible while varnishing. This is pretty tough, however, and the creation of a much smaller, sealed environment makes dust control much easier. You have options. You could, as I did, build a small booth encased in plastic. This is easy and cheap, and the plastic itself will hold a static charge and attract dust. Wayne Cattanach encased his entire dipping apparatus in a large (36-inch diameter) PVC pipe. If you have access to this sort of pipe as a freebie, it might be attractive, but the pipe and caps of this size are very expensive if you walk into a supply house and buy them. An existing closet could be converted into a booth as well, or if you have (or can create) a hatch that leads up into an attic you could build a box that extends up into the attic and hang a plastic curtain down into the room below, as shown in Fig. 12.1.

Once you have a small controllable area for dipping, controlling dust is fairly easy. If the enclosure is more or less airtight and you keep it sealed between uses, no dust will get in, and an occasional vacuuming or the installation of a small air filter will keep things clean. You can install free-hanging plexiglass panels as static attractors. Joe Saracione told me about this, and I think he credited Jim Schaaf with the idea. Whoever the author was, it works, and you can use it whether you have a booth or not. Rub the panels with a piece of silk ten or fifteen minutes before you dip, and they will attract any free-floating dust. Their charge diminishes over time but is effective for a surprisingly long while. Carpet, especially modern plastic-fiber stuff, is good for catching and holding dust, too.

Just as with dust, temperature is easier to control in a smaller space. I have two lights in my booth: a 48-inch twin-tube fluorescent light that serves as both illumination and a heat source, and a 60-watt clip-on incandescent lamp that serves primarily to boost the temperature. I try to dip at temperatures between 80 and 90 degrees Fahrenheit. The fluorescent light seems to add between 5 and 8 degrees to the surrounding room temperature, and the incandescent bulb will add another 5. So if the ambient temperature is 70 degrees or above, both lights go on. If it is 75 degrees or above, the fluorescent light alone tends to suffice. If I were in a colder climate, I might find a small lamp at the bottom of my PVC casing necessary to warm the varnish. Your heating requirements may vary, but I would strongly caution you against using any source of heat that might prove to be a source of ignition, either to the booth or the varnish, and against making an enclosure so small that the exposure of an open varnish tube could possibly result in flammable vapor concentrations. I and several other makers I know have used electric lamps inside dipping booths with no ill effects, but you are on your own and it pays to be cautious. In other words, if someone were to put a 1,500-watt ceramic heater inside a tiny plastic booth along with a gallon of highly flammable varnish in an open container, that would be just plain dumb.

What do you use for a varnish tube? Frankly, it doesn't matter all that much. I use an aluminum rod tube with a solid bottom plug and the vent hole in the cap plugged, but you can use PVC pipe or copper or steel or anything else that is unaffected by solvents and can be made airtight. Obviously, the tube needs to be as long as the longest section you intend to dip and should be about 2 inches wide (or a little wider) at least at the top, so that the varnish the rod section displaces will not run out over the top of the tube. And there should be adequate room to dip a section without the guides scraping the rim of the tube, and so that you can see what's going on. Also, assuming that your tube can be tightly capped, drop in one or two clean half-inch ball bearings so that you can mix the varnish up without pouring it out. Just tilt the tube (tightly capped) back and forth.

Something that might be helpful to talk about is the spool. The spool on my motor is just epoxied on, though it would be easy to add a simple clutch. You can't reverse an AC rod-turning motor or change its speed, so far as I know, but with the power off and with the mechanical advantage of a spool to hang onto, you can lower or raise the section fairly rapidly just by turning the spool. Providing a clutch by spring-loading the spool on a spindle might make things a little easier, but I've done enough rods just cranking the motor that I feel no real desire to change. However you arrange it, the diameter of the spool will govern your withdrawal rate (assuming that you use a rod-turning or similar fixed-speed motor). The spool should be wide enough and positioned at the proper angle so that the string that will be required to dip your longest typical section will wind across it evenly in a single layer. If the string overlaps, or slips and bumps, that will create small jarring bounces in the string that can result in runs or sags on the rod.

Obviously, it would be impractical to include descriptions of every possible dipping setup, but the photos of mine (Figs. 12.1 and 12.2) should give you an idea of how easy it is to whack something together. Be creative, and remember that you can get good results with an improvised setup, so try the least-destructive route first.

Figure 12.1. The overall view, showing the plastic booth and tube sunk in the floor.

Figure 12.2. A closer view inside the booth, showing the motor with spool, finish tube, and air cleaner.

13. SELECTING A REEL SEAT

There are lots of different ways to look at reel seats. At its most prosaic, a reel seat is just a clamp, and lots of them, even on some classic rods, are little more than that. At the other extreme, a reel seat can seem more like jewelry than anything else, and given a graceful shape, careful machining and finishing, fancy knurling, maybe even engraving. You have plenty of choices among commercially available components, from simple aluminum screw–locking seats to engraved nickel silver ones. And, if you have or acquire some machine-tool skills, you can make your own, which increases your options still further.

The first question is, What sort of reel seat should you use? The answer is that it depends. The size and type of rod is one consideration. Traditionally, smaller, lighter rods carry sliding-band reel seats, while larger, heavier ones carry screw-locking ones of one sort or another. Another consideration is what you like (or what the customer likes). I like sliding-band reel seats a lot, but some people don't because the band tends to wear a groove in the wood filler and the reel foot. On the other hand, I don't particularly care for uplocking seats of any kind, but they seem almost mandatory on big western-style

rods. Get some catalogs and find something that appeals to you.

If you're satisfied with what you can buy, you could stop right here. However, I'd like to bring up at least the possibility that you might want to make some of your own components, at least eventually. There is a school of thought among rod makers that you really haven't actually *made* a rod unless you have personally created every single piece of it out of a piece of wood or a bar of metal. I respect makers who can do that, and I suppose that, in a way, I aspire to it, but it's not gospel. Even if a maker raised caterpillars and spun his own silk, dug and smelted his own ore, and drew his own wire for guides, would all that accumulated virtue result in a better rod? It's an interesting question.

It seems to me that there are two main reasons to make your own components. One is that you may be able to do a better job than the commercial suppliers. I say "may" because a lot of commercial stuff these days is gorgeous. Another would be that you want to add a unique touch to your rods and have the time to do it. For the record, I think using commercial components is just fine, but let's talk about the latter possibility.

The easiest starting point for adding an

extra personal touch is the wood filler for the reel seat. If you have a lathe, you can make fillers for any reel seat that uses a simple cylindrical filler. If you have a router, you can make mortised fillers for sliding-band or other kinds of seats. There are a couple of good reasons to make your own fillers, other than just for the hell of it. First, if there is one area where commercial component makers can fall down, it's in the quality of the woodworking and finish on fillers. Off-center holes, insufficient sanding, and inconsistent varnish are common, as of this writing. I don't really blame the makers, because the fillers retail for, what, five bucks, ten for something fancy? If you spend an hour or two making and finishing a reel-seat filler, you can do better, even counting off for the inefficiency of making one at a time, and when you spend fifty hours on a rod, what's another one or two?

Second, you can be more individualistic and selective in your choice of wood. Third, you can make the center hole in the filler exactly the right size. Sure, you can always shim an oversize hole with masking tape or thread on the blank and no one will ever know, but maybe you don't want to do that. Also, in making mortised fillers, especially mortised fillers for sliding bands, you can make the reel seat fit exactly the foot of the reel that will be used with the rod. An Orvis CFO (my personal favorite), for instance, has a much thinner foot than a Lamson, and the difference is great enough that a reel seat that fits one well will fit the other poorly. I hear rumblings from time to time that the industry is going to standardize reel feet and seat dimensions, but I'll believe it when I see it. (I hear that something of this sort actually occurred, at least in principle, at the latest Fly Tackle Dealer Show. I repeat, I'll believe it when I see it.)

The first step in making a filler is to reduce your hunk of wood to rectangular blanks (1-inch x 1-inch x 4 inches will cover most applications). A friend with a bandsaw is worth keeping for this alone, though a woodworking shop would probably saw a hunk of wood into strips for a small fee. The blanks are then center-marked (Fig. 13.1) and reduced to cylinders by turning them in a lathe with a spur (Fig. 13.2) on one end and a live center on the other (see Figs 13.3 through 13.5). The cylinders are chucked in the lathe and drilled (Fig. 13.6), then mounted on a mandrel and turned and sanded to the final diameter (Figs. 13.7, 13.8, 13.9), which is of course determined by your hardware. (You can drill the hole through the blank with a drill press or doweling jig and go straight to the mandrel if you wish. I feel like I get a truer bore with the lathe, which is why I take the extra step, but that certainly doesn't obligate you.) I usually stop cutting with the toolbit and switch to sandpaper when the blank is .010-inch to .015-inch oversize. (When figuring your dimensions, be sure to take your finish thickness into account.) A brad point drill will have a lesser tendency to wander than a regular one, and a mandrel can be made very easily by turning a very slight taper (.002- to .004-inch) on a piece of steel stock the same size as the hole or a little bigger and drilling one end with a center drill to create a recess for a live center. If you don't take heavy cuts, just the wood-to-metal friction will hold the blank. For a more secure fit, lightly knurl an inch or so of the mandrel right where the end of the blank snugs up. It's perfectly acceptable to use a section of threaded rod for a mandrel, securing the blank with nuts on each end. I use a solid mandrel because it seems more accurate and quicker, but plenty of folks do it the other way.

For a filler that does not require a mortise, turning a shoulder may be the only other step necessary.

Cutting a mortise is easy with a router table, and a router table is in turn fairly easy to make if you don't wish to buy one. Some reel-seat fillers are made with wide, rounded mortises that probably could be achieved freehand with a rasp or a belt sander. Others

Figure 13.1. Center-mark the 1 x 1 x 4-inch blank.

Figure 13.2. A turning spur.

Figure 13.3. A blank mounted in the lathe between the spur and live center. Most woods are soft enough that there's no need to drill a center hole for the live center; you can simply press the bit into the end grain with pressure from the tailstock far enough to hold it.

Figure 13.4. Turning the cylinder.

Figure 13.5. The completed rough cylinder. You can trim off the remaining square stub with a saw either in the lathe or out.

are made with sharp-shouldered mortises that are only a little wider than the reel seat. I prefer the latter, at least partly because it's easier to line it up perfectly. This type is best cut with a jig (Fig. 13.10) to hold the filler and fingernail bit in the router table (Fig. 13.11). I use a fingernail bit with a 1/2-inch diameter and a 3/4-inch cutting length. The bit works fine for sliding-band seats the way it is, but I had a sharpening shop modify one for me by cutting a sharp relief to the sides for a cleaner, sharper mortise (see Figs. 13.12 and 13.13). Backing up a couple of sentences, I

Selecting a Reel Seat

Figure 13.6. Drilling the hole. A brad point drill is really necessary—a regular bit will wander too much.

Figure 13.7. A drilled cylinder mounted on the mandrel and being turned to its final diameter.

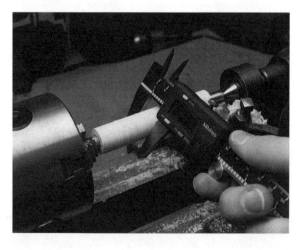

Figure 13.8. Check the cylinder regularly, and leave .005-inch to .010-inch for sanding.

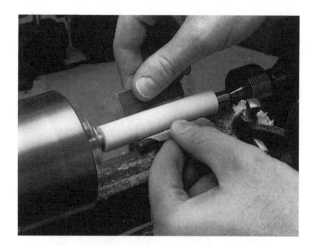

Figure 13.9. Sanding out machining marks. I usually start with 240 grit and go up to 600 grit sandpaper.

Figure 13.10. A mortising jig pretty much as described in Wayne Cattanach's book. Drill a hole through one block of wood with a doweling jig, then saw the block in half exactly. The size of the hole and the bolt depends on the size of the rods you intend to make. I've found 3/8-inch to be a pretty good all-around size, though if you mostly make light rods you might want to go with 5/16-inch. The bolt is epoxied into the block half on the left, and the short section of reel seat for relief could be cut out of the block itself.

write "best cut" meaning, to some extent, "more cheaply." The shop safety theme may be getting old by now, but if you work with a sharp exposed power-tool bit spinning at 15,000 RPM, you must be very, very careful. If this makes you nervous, that's good, you'll probably be fine. If you are accident-prone, however, you should strongly consider just buying your wood fillers.

If you make your own filler, it naturally

Figure 13.11. Cutting the mortise on a router table. My router table is simply an aluminum plate on a 2 x 4 frame with a plastic fence secured to the plate with C-clamps. Because I only make one kind of reel-seat filler I never need to move it much, but when I do need to make adjustments for different reel feet I just tap it a bit one way or the other. Commercial router tables are nice and have the advantage of safety shields, but a couple of boards will work.

Figure 13.12. An unmodified fingernail bit.

follows that you will need to put some sort of finish on it. The same sort of varnish that you use on the rod will work fine on the reel-seat filler, particularly if the filler is for a screw-locking reel seat. Application by dipping works very well, and the process is just the same as when you dip a rod. Just hang the filler on a short section of dowel with a little masking tape on one end of the dowel for a stop and a screw eye threaded into the

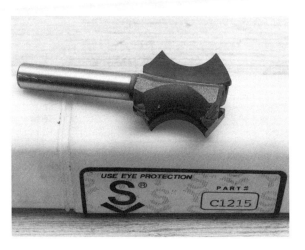

Figure 13.13. A fingernail bit with the sides trimmed back for relief. If you take a bit to a good sharpening shop and show them this photo they should be able to fix you up.

other to suspend it. A sliding-band reel seat filler is a little different, since the band puts quite a bit of stress on the finish. I've used a rubbed-oil-type finish for sliding-band fillers, such as Birchwood Casey's Tru-Oil. This sort of finish is more in the wood than on it, so although it will wear, it is less vulnerable to big ugly chips and is easily touched up or repaired if damage does occur. Probably the very best finish would be some sort of impregnation similar to what you'll see on Winston reel seats of recent vintage, but I haven't gotten around to figuring out how to do that yet.

If you've gotten this far, it's only another step or two up in difficulty to make your own sliding-band reel seat hardware. It doesn't strike me as a particularly good use of space to deliver a whole machinist's primer, but I'll run through the process in broad terms. If you have some machining skills, or acquire them, the process will be obvious.

The first thing to consider is whether you are going to make the hardware out of tubing or solid stock. There is less waste when you use tubing, so your stock costs less, and you can get by with a smaller lathe because you don't need to hog out an 11/16-inch or similar-sized hole. Though you certainly have your choice of sizes, all of my

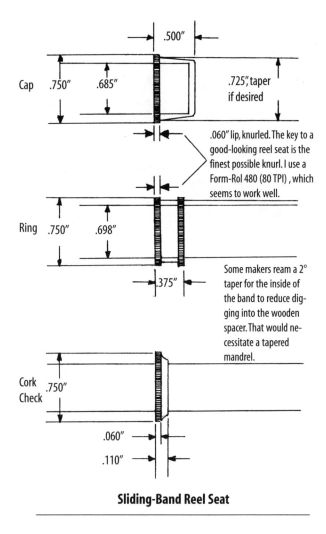

Cap   .750"   .685"   .500"   .725" taper if desired

.060" lip, knurled. The key to a good-looking reel seat is the finest possible knurl. I use a Form-Rol 480 (80 TPI) , which seems to work well.

Ring   .750"   .698"

.375"

Some makers ream a 2° taper for the inside of the band to reduce digging into the wooden spacer. That would necessitate a tapered mandrel.

Cork Check   .750"

.060"

.110"

Sliding-Band Reel Seat

reel seats are based on an 11/16-inch filler, and I'll use this measurement for consistency. This is helped along by the fact that I have about 20 feet of 11/16-inch-internal-diameter nickel silver tubing on hand. Solid stock requires no soldering and may be a little easier to obtain in small quantities.

Let's take the cap first. To make the blank for the cap, you will either drill a big hole in a piece of solid stock or solder a flat piece of nickel silver over the end of a short piece of tubing. I like soldering because there's less waste and, properly done, the solder joint isn't even slightly visible, but other makers prefer machining. To solder a cap blank together, cut and flatten a little square of flat stock that is just larger than the outside diameter of the round stock, place the round stock on the flat stock (the mating

surface must be faced-off clean and square), place both on top of a piece of jeweler's charcoal, drop a couple of drops of liquid flux inside the round stock so they flow around the perimeter, then place three 1/16-inch snips of solder around the inside of the round stock. Heat the assembly with a propane torch until the solder flows. Once the solder cools, snip off the corners of the square with tin snips. The remaining excess will be trimmed off in the lathe.

Once you have the blank, it will be mounted on a stud for machining the exterior. This stud may be split and tightened (expanded) by a set screw, or it may be plain and the cap held on by a little jeweler's shellac. Either way, the stud should be only a thousandth or two smaller than the inside diameter of the cap.

A common cap design has a raised knurled lip, so the machining sequence will be to turn the cap blank down to the diameter of the lip, square off the lip, then knurl the end. The rest of the cap is then turned down to the exterior diameter and the end is faced off. A little attention with emery cloth and the cap is done, save for polishing.

The band is made almost exactly the same way, only the inside diameter of the band is .005 to .007-inch larger than that of the cap. This will mean enlarging the hole either by expanding the tubing by pressing it over a die, or enlarging the hole in either the tubing or a drilled-out piece of solid stock with a reamer or boring bar. It will also mean a correspondingly larger stud. Once you get to this point, however, the process is very similar. Turn to the diameter of the lip, knurl, and shape the center as you wish.

The cork check may seem a little harder just because it's so little, but it's not, really. I think the easiest way to handle the wood-to-metal fit here is to make the inside diameter of the cork check slightly smaller than the outside diameter of the filler, and to turn a slight shoulder on the filler. Either a short section of tubing (I expand a short piece of

Figure 13.14. A sliding-band reel seat filler from start to finish. Note the grain on the finished filler. It's a nice touch to align the grain in a pleasing manner and to make sure that any prominent symmetric features are centered relative to the mortise.

Figure 13.15. A finished filler with superb hardware made by Ed Hartzell. This is my favorite look for a rod—light, clean, elegant.

11/16-inch-outside-diameter tubing with a die to get the smaller inside diameter) or a drilled-out section of stock will go on a steel mandrel. The largest outside diameter will be knurled, the shoulder will be formed, and the check will be parted off, and so on down the line. Making five or six checks at a time like this is the way to go.

There you have it. With the exception of the accompanying drawing (which is more for the sake of illustration than anything else), I purposely have been vague regarding dimensions and designs, because if you're going to go to the trouble to machine your own reel seat it might as well be your own design. With all the different knurls available and with virtually unlimited possibilities, you should be able to come up with something as individual as a signature. Have fun!

Bluing Nickel Silver

Nickel silver is difficult stuff to oxidize, or "blue." Let me rephrase that. There are a few agents that will darken nickel silver more or less satisfactorily; commercial "cold bluing" preparations like Birchwood Casey's Perma Blue or Aluma Black work well

enough—not a real deep black like the old arsenic stuff, but serviceable. The problem is that almost anything you use on nickel silver will wear off fairly quickly with regular use and should be protected by a layer of varnish.

This is easy with ferrules. Mask them off as you normally would for all but the last coat, then remove the masking for the final coat. Leave the masking on the slide of male ferrules, of course, and use a wooden plug to keep varnish out of the female ferrule. Reel seats are tougher to varnish, and locking seats are poor candidates for oxidizing anyway due to the metal-to-metal contact of the threads.

There are other preparations that may give a deeper blue or black, but I'm not sure having really black ferrules is worth the risks involved in using arsenic. Whatever you use, the first priority is that the surface be perfectly clean and free of oil or grease. A good wipe-down with rubbing alcohol or a commercial degreaser should suffice—just don't touch the metal after you've cleaned it.

Most of the bluing agents I've used work best if you brush them on. Perma Blue, for instance, will erode and pit the surface if you immerse the metal and let it sit.

     Selecting a Reel Seat

14. REPAIRING AND REFINISHING BAMBOO RODS

There are quite a few bad things that can happen to a bamboo fly rod, and the longer you make rods, the more of them will come back to you for repair. Repairing your own rods is, I think, quite a bit easier than repairing someone else's (though I intend to include instructions that will do for both). For one thing, if worst comes to worst, you can simply make a new section with every confidence that it will match the original.

It seems to make sense to divide most repairs into two major categories: those that are the result of age and honorable use, and those that are the result of neglect or catastrophe. With time, varnish may get scratched, ferrules may become loose, the cork may get dingy, the guides may become worn and the rod may take a fishing or casting set. In fact, if the rod is used more than occasionally, it's inevitable. All of these conditions are relatively easy to fix during the course of a complete refinishing, and there is a certain satisfaction to giving a well-used rod a new youth.

Having to fix a rod that has been shut in a door, knocked over and stepped on, or snapped off in a tree or at a hook dig is not nearly as satisfying, but it must be done. Most of these problems are breaks of one

kind or another. Tips, being in many ways the most fragile part of the rod, are frequent victims. If a tip is broken no more than an inch or two from the tip, it makes little sense to replace it or try to scarf on a piece. However, if the break is farther down, as in 4 inches or more, the missing piece will most likely have a noticeable effect on the rod's action. In such an instance, you are faced with the choice of repairing or replacing the section.

If the break is not complete—if the problem is a partial fracture rather than a clean break, it may be possible to lace and glue the broken fibers back in place and reinforce them with a clear wrap. Unless we're talking about a very minor fracture, though, I'm not sure gluing and wrapping is a very good fix. By the time a rod is bent severely enough to cause a fracture like the one shown (Fig. 14.1), a whole lot of damage has occurred. The fibers on the concave (compression) side of the bend are damaged too, and the rod will probably never be quite the same.

Except for repairing breaks with scarf joints or removing loose ferrules, there really isn't any repair job that is terribly different from the processes involved in making the rod in the first place.

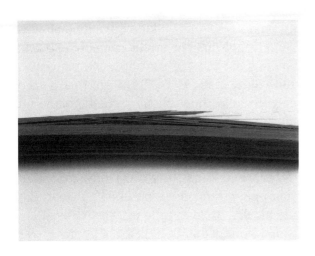

Figure 14.1. A severely fractured rod. You could weave this one back and glue it, but there's probably not much point and there'll always be a kink at the point of repair.

Scarf Joints

A scarf joint is made by planing two sections with matching tapers at identical and complementary angles. A scarf block, which is a wooden clamping form with an angled notch, holds each piece at the proper angle for planing. A scarf joint can join a new section to the end of the old one, or you can use two scarf joints to install a new piece in the middle of a broken section. The latter sort of repair seems to me to be getting close to the "more trouble than it's worth" line, but I suppose it all depends on the rod.

A scarf block is made sort of the same way as your wooden rough planing forms.

The idea is that the two sides of the block, both containing grooves that correspond to 120-degree corners of the hexagonal rod section, clamp together to hold the rod section securely with a flat upward. The face of the block is cut at an angle, which, in turn, exposes the end of the rod section at an angle.

You can make the scarf block out of just about any scrap wood you have around, but something like 4-foot-long pieces of 1 x 1-inch maple would be ideal. A table saw lets you make this easily, but it certainly would be possible to make it with hand tools. After squaring up the stock, the next step is to cut identical 30-degree bevels on one corner of each of the four pieces. The pieces will then be glued together so that two 120-degree V-grooves are formed. How deep the bevels (and consequently the grooves) should be depends on the diameter of the rod section you're repairing. Of course, you can always make the grooves shallower later on, so make sure that they are of adequate depth to support the rod section.

When you've glued up the pieces so that you have both sides of the block done, clamp them together groove to groove in perfect alignment and drill three 1/4-inch holes completely through from side to side. These are for the dowels that will keep the sides of the block in alignment. Install said dowels, which should be just 1/4-inch shorter than the width of the block, and you're ready to

Single Scarf Joint

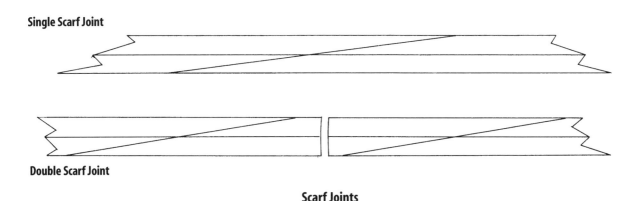

Double Scarf Joint

Scarf Joints

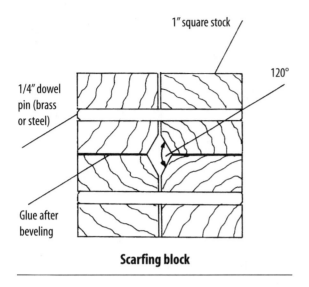

Scarfing block

1" square stock

120°

1/4" dowel
pin (brass
or steel)

Glue after
beveling

through it), so that a skinny diamond-shaped window appears toward the front of the block. Smooth the cut with sandpaper or a plane, and you're ready to go. If the grooves are too deep to hold the sections securely, plane off the inside surfaces of the block until all is well.

This block is essentially the same as the one described in the Garrison and Carmichael book (there's really no other clamping arrangement possible), except that the block is held in a bench vise rather than squeezed together by bolts. The more or less parallel jaws of the bench vise and the dowel guides keep everything square better than bolts. If you don't have a bench vise, simply substitute bolts for the dowels. Whichever you use, don't apply too much pressure to the section, just enough to hold it securely.

Making the scarf joint itself is simple, if time-consuming. Make a section for the repair that matches the taper and color of the broken part and extends for several inches

taper the block in the table saw. If you don't have a tapering jig, you could improvise one with shims, but be sure to use push blocks and all that. You need your fingers.

Cut the taper at a very shallow angle, only 2 or 3 degrees, and you will cut away most of the top piece (the part with no dowels

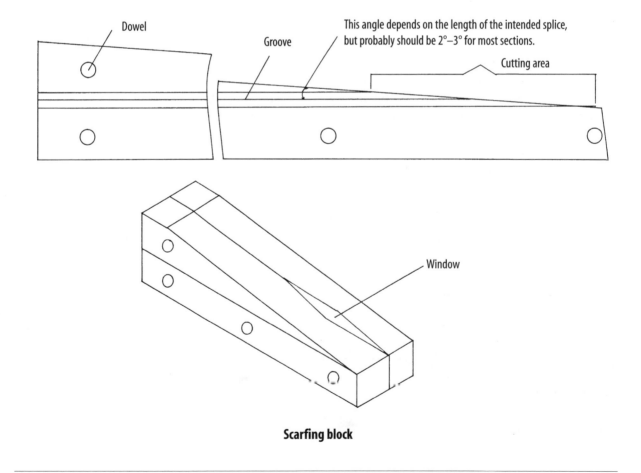

Dowel

Groove

This angle depends on the length of the intended splice, but probably should be 2°–3° for most sections.

Cutting area

Window

Scarfing block

156

beyond the point where the joint will occur. You need to figure out how long the scarf joint will be and mark the two points on the rod where the end of one taper will meet the beginning of the other. Mark the old section and the new section at the point where they are exactly the same diameter. This point should wind up at or about the center of the joint. Position each piece in the block in turn, so that the scarf will begin at the correct spot. Determine the exact point where the piece emerges by laying a straightedge across the block. Plane away the ends of the sections flush with the forms. Mate the tapered ends and make a pencil mark across the joint for reference. Apply glue, and bind securely with thread. When you remove the thread and sand off the glue, you should have a joint whose detectability depends mostly on how well the bamboo colors match.

Ferrule Removal and Gluing

I think you'll find that loose ferrules, even those that click quite noticeably when the rod is cast or wiggled, can take a pretty careful and determined effort to remove. If the ferrules are pinned, naturally the pin must be removed before any further action can be taken. Push firmly or take a light stroke with a spring-loaded center punch in the center of the pin. (You may have to make your own punch for this. Broken drill bits or old dental tools with the burrs removed make good blanks.) This should drift it out a little bit, and, more importantly, it will establish a center so that you will run less of a risk of slipping and scratching the ferrule with subsequent work. Work the pin out until you can grip it with pliers and pull it out the rest of the way. Don't worry about screwing the pin up; you'll replace it anyway.

However the ferrule is glued on, you'll need to apply heat to remove it. Older rods with thermal ferrule cement will take less heat to free a ferrule than will rods using epoxy, but it's still possible to apply too much heat too fast and either burn the bamboo or melt the solder holding the ferrule together (or both). Especially if you are removing an epoxy-glued ferrule, you need to be careful and apply a little heat at a time, gradually building the temperature until the adhesive releases. Heat and test, heat and test. A standard alcohol lamp is probably the best heat source for this purpose.

If you haven't already done it, you need to make a ferrule pulling block. Essentially a split and hinged strip of wood with appropriate-sized holes drilled in it, the pulling block allows you to apply a fair degree of force to a ferrule without marring it or burning yourself. To make the puller, mark a center line on a piece of wood (a fairly hard wood like maple works best) and drill holes on that line corresponding to the outside diameters of the ferrule sizes you will use. The holes should be drilled a half-inch apart or so. After the holes are drilled, saw the block in half along the centerline with a bandsaw or with a narrow blade on a table saw. A strip of heavy leather fastened across the end of the blocks will make a good hinge.

Once you have your lamp and puller all ready, it's up to you to learn the right amount of heat and pressure to apply, and, if at all possible, it's a good idea to practice on junk sections. This is one of those things that can't be adequately described in words; it's a matter of experience, and I'd be lying if I said that the first ferrule or two you remove won't be nerve-wracking.

This is another instance where working on your own rods is considerably easier than working on a classic. If you destroy a ferrule on your own rod, chances are excellent that you can replace it, even if it means replacing an entire set. If worst comes to worst with a monumentally obstinate ferrule, you can simply file it off. If you destroy a ferrule on a Payne or Dickerson, replacing it will not be quite so easy.

Once the ferrule is removed, gluing it back on is about the same as gluing the ferrule on a new rod. If the ferrule was loose due to normal shrinkage, it was probably only by a couple of thousandths and a new gluing job with epoxy will fill the gap better than any shimming you could do.

If the ferrule was very loose, it may be because the bamboo under the ferrule was damaged, and you will need to evaluate the damage and decide whether it can be fixed with glue, whether the damaged portion can be cut off and a new ferrule station turned, or whether an entire new section should be made. Losing an inch or so at the ferrule from either butt or tip is not a big deal. If any change is noted, it may even be positive, because the practical effect will be to increase the drop over the ferrule, which will make the rod feel faster.

If the ferrule you removed was pinned, you may elect to repin it when you reinstall it. I don't like pins, but on a "collectible" rod that was pinned to begin with you certainly should use them, and who can say what will be collectible a few years down the road? To replace the pin, obtain nickel silver wire of the same diameter as the pin you removed. The pin is normally a thousandth or two larger than its hole, and you will need a drill bit of the appropriate size as well. When you reglue the ferrule, do your best to line the ferrule holes up with the original hole through the blank, and run a piece of thread or something through the hole to remove excess glue before it sets up. If you do a good job of alignment and glue removal, you may not need to touch the hole before you drive in a new pin, but otherwise you will need to run the drill through once to clear it. If you are installing an originally pinned ferrule on a new seat, you will naturally need to drill through, using the original holes in the ferrule as a guide.

To reinstall a pin, cut off a short length of your wire and gently taper one end with a fine file. Drive the pin through with soft taps from a small mallet until equal parts are sticking out on both sides. Cut off the excess

as close as you can to the ferrule, and blend down the stubs with a very fine small file: Put masking tape over the projecting stubs (push the stubs through the tape) and file down to the tape. Then remove the tape and finish with a fine stone. If the ferrule is blued, it will certainly need to be re-blued after this.

Once the ferrule is reglued or replaced, if the finish on the rod is otherwise in good shape, you don't necessarily have to strip and refinish the entire section. All you really need to do is replace the ferrule wrap, strip the varnish up to the adjacent guide, and dip from the top of the near wrap of that guide.

Stripping a Rod

It will happen, either because guides are worn or damaged or because wraps have frayed or the finish itself is extensively compromised, that a rod must be stripped entirely. The first step in stripping a rod is to measure everything—guide spacing, wrap length, trim wraps, guide-foot length, ferrule length, *everything*. Next, remove the guides. A sharp knife is used to cut the wraps, but you must be careful to cut only over a guide foot (see Figs. 14.2 through 14.5) so that any slip or gouge will come to rest on the metal rather than the rod. If you're going to discard the guides, cut directly over the foot with a whittling motion. If you intend to reuse the guides, employ a sharp razor blade carefully to slice the wrap at the side of the foot. Once the wraps over the guide foot have been cut away, the rest of the wrap can be unwound with ease. Decorative wraps that do not occur over a guide or hookkeeper require a more painstaking approach. You may start the unraveling with some very cautious knife work, or you may wish to apply a little varnish remover to the wrap alone. Once the varnish is soft you can wipe it off and pick out the end of the wrap with a fingernail or a small piece of bamboo.

Once the guides have been removed,

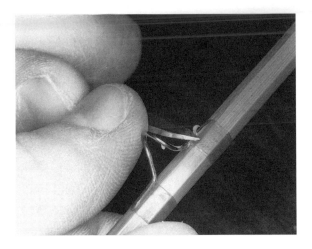

Figure 14.2. Cut away wrap over guide foot.

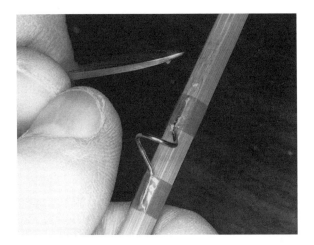

Figure 14.3. Wrap cut from one foot.

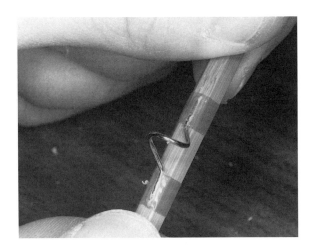

Figure 14.4. Wrap cut from both feet.

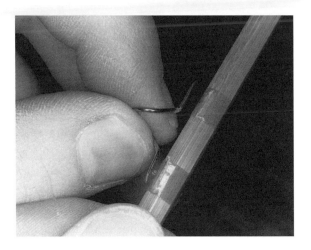

Figure 14.5. Carefully remove guide.

carefully mask off the cork grip and the ferrules and apply varnish remover. You can use whatever you want, but my preference is for the really nasty volatile kinds because they work fast and are solvent-based. I hate to say it, but water-based "safe" strippers take longer to work and can swell the wood. Wait until the finish begins to wrinkle and curdle, then wipe the whole mess off with a rag. If you need to scrape, use a wooden implement. Once the finish has been removed, apply whatever neutralizer is recommended, then hang the rod in your drying cabinet for several days to allow and encourage any lingering solvents to evaporate.

Cork Damage

Among the many virtues of cork is its wear-resistance. Unless a cork has been used for a hookkeeper or stepped on or otherwise damaged, it is usually just dirty. After masking off the reel seat and rod shaft, washing with a mildly abrasive cleaner like Soft Scrub will usually fix it up. There's a Soft Scrub with bleach that does a great job on cork, but keep it the hell away from the rest of the rod. A gentle sanding may help blend in scratches and dings but probably should be avoided on collectible rods. Some grips acquire indentations from a strong grip, and exposing these and other dents to a jet of steam from a kettle will often relieve the dent to some extent. If the grip is extensively damaged, it may be best to incorporate a new grip into a complete refinishing. Once the rod is stripped, peel off the old grip and glue new cork rings down against the reel seat and shape it on the lathe just as with a new rod. You may need to make some sort of jig to center the reel seat and prevent it from flopping around.

I've heard that it is possible in some instances to replace a single cork ring that has broken or come loose by splitting a ring and gluing the two halves together on the shaft, but I've never had the opportunity to attempt such a fix.

Sets

It's not a foregone conclusion that a rod will take a set, but if it is fished regularly for a matter of years it probably will, to some degree. Any constant strain in one direction can produce a set in a rod. Probably the worst set I have ever seen was in a tip section that had been propped up by itself in a corner of a closet and forgotten for a few years. The most common sets that occur in normal use are "fishing sets" and "casting sets." A right-handed person will spend most of his or her time hanging the rod out to the right and will eventually find that the rod has a slight curve to the right. Yanking on many big fish or drifting lots of weighted nymphs may give the rod a downward set, and so on. Casting sets are more often noticed on fairly fast or tip-action rods. A casting set occurs in the tip where the taper thins down and the acceleration is greatest, and it looks like the tip is bent backwards slightly.

The good news is that sets are fairly easy to correct. They can be taken out with heat with the varnish on, though you naturally must be careful to avoid applying so much heat that you damage the finish. You also must avoid touching the areas that have been heated, just in case the varnish has gotten a little soft. If you are refinishing a rod anyway, though, there is no better time than when the guides and varnish are gone to get the rod back to perfect straightness.

The same heat gun that you use for everything else works fine for correcting sets. I have found that sets are sometimes easier to correct with a wider, more diffuse heat source, like an electric stove burner turned up to high.

15. BUILDING–METHOD VARIATIONS OF THE BAMBOO ROD

This book is about making one kind of rod, namely a straight-ahead, no-tricks six-sided rod. I feel that I would fall short of my aim, however, if I didn't talk just a little about the whole world out there of different things you can try if and when you wish for a greater challenge or change of pace.

One possible variation is in the number of strips that make up the rod. In the course of the history of split-cane rods, people have tried virtually every conceivable arrangement and number of strips. Even though six-sided rods have become the norm because they represent the best combination of performance, durability, and simplicity of construction, five-sided and four-sided rods have proven themselves as viable options, and each type of rod has its devotees. Because we're not talking about equilateral triangles anymore, hand-planing these rods obviously would involve making a different type of form—one that has two grooves. Charles Kreider's book has some information on five-sided rods, and there's a nice article about them in issue 29 of *The Planing Form*.

You don't need to stop there. I've seen eight- and even seven-sided rods, and you can do whatever the hell you want. A while ago I was shown a *two*-sided rod. It was a very short one-piece (or was spliced and wrapped, I can't remember which) 2-weight, and the maker had simply planed off the pith side of two strips to form one taper, glued the strips together, and planed the sides of that blank to get the final taper. I can't imagine a very large rod being made this way or any rod like this being very durable. On the other hand, personal incredulity is a poor argument against anything, and the rod was actually sort of cool and didn't cast half badly. The maker needed no planing forms and was able to adjust the taper by trial and error. Too stiff for a 3-weight? Take some more off the sides. Remove too much? Oops, guess it's a 2-weight.

George and Jacques Herter's rod-building book contains a section on rod construction that details a number of different lamination arrangements that seem to have been more popular for trolling or deep-sea rods than for fly rods. Glancing through the section, I see the Shaver Trussbuilt–type of construction that uses a sandwich of bamboo strips with a spruce core. Also included is the notation that, in 1933, a 348-pound marlin was caught on a Trussbuilt rod with a 6-ounce tip. So who knows, the two-strip rod may be due for a revival.

Speaking of one-piece rods, there's another faction of bamboo freaks (as a bamboo freak, I use the term affectionately) made up of people who are hooked on the feel and performance of one-piece rods. It is possible to make a one-piece rod as long as you could possibly want by overlapping two or more setups on your forms. Given enough shop space, the problem is not making an 8- or 9-foot one-piece rod, it's transporting it. Well, you could have a tough time dip-varnishing it, too.

Another set of variations has to do with modifications in the strips that go into a rod of otherwise common construction. Hollow-building is one such variation. It is evident that when you decrease a rod's weight without a proportionate decrease in its stiffness, you increase its power. (Hollow-building does decrease stiffness to a degree, but a slight compensating increase in diameter still yields a lighter section, so the net effect is more power. A hollow rod section should be increased in diameter .002 to .003-inch over a solid section of the same strength.) Hollow-building, in its various forms, is intended to do just that by removing portions of the center of the rod. E. C. Powell, who originated hollow-building, removed all but the outer .070-inch of power fibers, glued cedar strips to the inside, then beveled the triangular strips from these composites. He learned to leave solid cane at the ferrules for strength, but the cedar strips that formed the core of the rod were further reduced in weight by scalloping, leaving internal voids in the finished section with "diaphragms" at intervals. This was revolutionary, and Powell's tournament rods established a number of distance-casting records in their day.

The same sort of effect can be achieved without Powell's cedar lamination by scalloping away the cane itself, and some makers do so. If there is a problem with this sort of construction, it is that the gluing surface in the scalloped sections is greatly diminished. Lew Stoner of the Winston Rod Com-

pany solved this problem with his fluted hollow construction. This patented technique involved (and still involves) cutting a U-shaped groove down the center of each strip, removing material (and thus weight) from the center of each strip, but leaving much of the sides for gluing surface. The finished rod thus has a flower-shaped cavity in the cross section. Hollow-building obviously is limited by the point of diminishing returns to the butt and the occasional midsection. There's plenty of room for experimentation here, but the one thing you'll need to be extra-careful about is the application of glue. Filling up a hollow-built rod with excess glue would pretty much defeat the whole purpose.

Another variation I'd like to call to your attention is the "nodeless" rod. To make such a rod, you cut the nodes out of a rectangular strip and splice the ends back together with a scarf joint. This strikes me as primarily a cosmetic treatment, though I suppose the argument would be made that the scarf joint has greater strength and integrity than the node it replaces. On the other hand, I've never seen a rod break because of a node. Nodeless construction typically goes like this: You cut out all of the nodes but carefully mark all the segments so that they can be reassembled in their proper order. These strips are heat-treated, and proponents point out that you can do this in your kitchen oven. The strips are then spliced, the splices are staggered like nodes, and the rest of the construction follows as with a normal rod.

Another construction technique that has a certain following is the "spiral" rod, so called because the strips, after gluing and binding, are twisted into a spiral and locked into a clamping jig while the glue dries. This idea, apparently first explored by Fred Divine, is discussed at some length in *The Angler's Workshop,* by Letcher Lambuth. This sort of construction is credited by its adherents with increasing a rod's power, but it makes for hell's own trouble getting a straight rod, because you're essentially stuck with what you get out of the gluing clamp. (Although with today's best and most heat-resistant glues, perhaps a spiral rod could be straightened without losing its twist. A good experiment for somebody.) This has scared me away, because I (perhaps foolishly, in the eyes of some) regard straightness as pretty important. There's also some disagreement about whether spiral construction actually results in a stronger rod. I can see how it *might*, though Lambuth's idea about the spiral increasing the rod's effective diameter seems wrong. His idea of "balanced distortion" seems closer but still unconvincing. Issue 15 of *The Planing Form* contains a sort of forum on the subject. At first blush it seems to me that the spiral possibly adds another degree of resistance to that provided by tension and compression in a normal rod, transferring the tension and compression that in the normal rod is borne most heavily by opposing strips to all six strips. Whatever.

Well, that should give you something to think about. Lord knows there's a lifetime of work and challenge in simply making the best rod you possibly can without any of the above. However, if your destiny as a rod maker is a 10-foot, one-piece, five-sided, hollow-built, nodeless, spiral salmon rod, my hat's off to you. Pushing the envelope is almost always worthwhile.

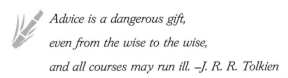

Advice is a dangerous gift,
even from the wise to the wise,
and all courses may run ill. –J. R. R. Tolkien

16. TURNING PRO

Almost all rod makers, even hobbyists making a couple of rods a year, will eventually sell some. Against almost all advice, I might add. Here is Letcher Lambuth on the subject:

> Don't try to make rods for money. There are many good reasons in support of this suggestion. Rod making for one's self and as presents for friends is a joyous and absorbing occupation; as a means of selling your time it would be a tedious business. If you give a rod, and the recipient doesn't like it, he will still appreciate your kind thought; but if you sell it to him, his opinion will likely be expressed to your embarrassment. Also, I have seen craftsmen pit their handwork against factory and machine production with disappointment as their only reward. There are, of course, exceptions: men whose love of handicraft is so sincere, whose integrity is so sound, and whose ingenuity is so great, that the world makes a place for their output and adequately rewards their skill. But these men are so rare that we may presume that there is not one of them in this company.

I don't entirely agree with Lambuth. I think that it has always been possible for the dedicated and skilled craftsman to meet or exceed the standards set by the most eminent rod companies, and there are enough of them today that bamboo rod building is a thriving cottage industry. Further, I can think of quite a few things right off the top of my head that would be more tedious ways of selling my time than making bamboo rods. He's right that making a rod and fishing with it or giving it to a friend is far more satisfying and pleasing than making one and selling it. We can't stay virtuous, however. Sooner or later you will sell a rod, probably to a friend. You want him to have the rod and consider not charging him at first, but he insists on paying and you need the money, so you compromise by not charging him enough. When the rod is done you know he's good for it. Or, if he's not, it's not exactly a surprise. I mean, he's your friend, right?

All in all, a fairly comfortable transaction. Maybe your friend shows his rod around a bit, and pretty soon you have a couple more orders, and the next thing you know, you're a small businessman. I don't have to tell you that customers can be less pleasurable to work with than friends, that you really don't make much money selling rods, and that making rods you've made before for people you don't know is less fun than making a new experimental rod for yourself. You'll find out soon enough and will come to find your own balance between fun and profit.

What we are concerned with right now is the fact that you are a small businessman—a manufacturer, actually. You buy raw materials, tools, and components, sell finished fishing rods, hand out business cards, maybe show your rods at a sportsman's show or Trout Unlimited conclave, pay taxes.

Pay taxes?

Yup. I don't mean to insult your intelligence by informing you that when you sell a rod, the difference between what it cost you to make it and how much you got for it is profit and should be reported as income on your tax returns, where it will be subject to your regular income tax *as well* as the so-called self-employment tax. And that's not all. There may be state and local sales tax for you to collect and remit, which probably means a business license, and you need to know that bamboo rods (read "fishing tackle") carry a federal excise tax under the Dingell-Jones Act to benefit wildlife. The extent to which this benefit actually accrues is sometimes debated, but that doesn't matter to the IRS. In order to comply with this excise tax, you need to obtain Form 637 and instructions from the IRS, which will get you your excise tax registration number. In order to fill *this* form out, you need to obtain an Employer Identification Number (form SS4), which is actually pretty painless but comes with the ominous knowledge that you have just been added to yet another gigantic federal computer database. Then you need to fill out forms 8837 and 720 quarterly and return them with your tax payment.

The bright side is that because your rods provide income, the necessary materials, tools, shop space, travel to shows to display your rods, and lodging and meals once you're there, all constitute expenses. My accountant disapproved heartily when I sent up a trial balloon to the effect that fishing trips could perhaps be deducted as product testing, but I suspect some tackle companies do that and pull it off. For the record, I advise keeping your expenses conservative and completely defensible, but a guy can dream, can't he? Keeping careful track of your expenses, which means keeping records and receipts, will make sure that you don't pay more than you must, but you need to be aware that the IRS expects you to make a profit in three out of five years. Two out of five years, making bamboo rods could actually save you money on your taxes, I suppose (be careful). However, if you just lose money year after year, the IRS will call your business, with some justification, a hobby.

All this sounds like a pain, and it is. It's tempting to overlook some of the details or just sell rods for cash, but that is an option only if you can pick your customers fairly carefully and are willing to play chicken with Big Brother. I'm no fan of government, but if there's one time when I want to be completely, indisputably, incontrovertibly right, it's when I have to talk to The Man about my taxes. Doing it the right way may not be delightful, but at least you can sell a rod and put the check in the bank without looking over your shoulder. Speaking of banks, having a separate checking account for your rods makes keeping track of things a lot easier and is one of the things that is expected if you are in business. Having to deal with taxes means that you must maintain a certain standard of bookkeeping, both so that you can figure your taxes properly and so that you can prove you've done so if you're audited. I'm no expert on bookkeeping, but it seems easiest in the long run to make a separate sheet or log entry for each rod that details all the materials and components that went into it. That helps track expenses and inventory.

Please realize that this is just an overview of the things I know about and does not in any way, shape, or form constitute professional tax advice. If you're not willing to do the legwork and read the various tax booklets (yawn), find a good accountant or tax consultant who gets paid to know all about this stuff.

Marketing (More or Less)

Well, you're in business. You have all the tubes hooked up to siphon off a chunk of your earnings into the vast ocean of government spending, but you try not to think about that. The question now is, What sort of business do you want to have? Are you going to make a few rods here and there (smart), or do you want to get serious about it (it's your life)? If you want to build and sell as many rods as you can, you need to think about the process a little differently than if rod making is just a hobby and you don't really care whether you sell any or not.

For me, a comforting aspect of making bamboo rods is that it's a quiet sort of subculture, that the craft is peopled mostly by independent types who prefer to work alone and accept total responsibility for their work, and that as a way to make money, it is about as far as you can get from corporate America. Just for a moment, though, let's think about this objectively. Businessmen think a great deal about marketing. You are being urged to buy stuff constantly, and advertising is only part of it. When I was in school, taking courses that purported to deal with marketing, the subject was detailed in the form of the Five P's, and that still seems as good a way to describe what happens as any.

The Five P's of marketing are Product, Price, People, Place, and Promotion. How these elements combine and interact is called a "marketing mix," and if they still teach things this way, you can bet that undergraduates across the nation are scribbling about it right now. A marketing mix defines your product, what it is, how much it costs, the sort of buyer it might appeal to, and how said product will come to the attention of said buyer. Of course, most of the people who take marketing seriously are thinking about selling lots and lots of whatever it is—breakfast cereal, for example. Still, marketing is marketing, and if you are selling ten rods a year and would like to sell twenty, what will get you there is marketing. You can market poorly and get there slowly, or you can market well and get there as quickly as your skill and product will allow.

As far as bamboo rod builders are concerned, *product* is the most important element of the marketing mix, and many builders, perhaps most, never get past this consideration. The sheer quality of your rods is a big part of this element, for if they are not good enough to put next to and compare favorably with the best rods anywhere, you will be limited in both the appeal your rods will have and how much you can charge for them. To paraphrase Steve Bodio, selling your rods is highly educational if you are interested in finding out exactly what is wrong with them. The trick is to make rods that will sell, which involves length, line weight, and action as well as cosmetics and how cool the rod tube looks. The importance of quality workmanship can't be overemphasized, because once you sell a rod and it's out there, your reputation is riding on that rod. People will be looking at that rod years from now, and you don't want them to say, apologetically, "Well, this was one of his *early* rods," when what they really mean is, "Yuck."

Also bound up in this element is the quantity of rods you can produce. If you go to a show and get orders for twenty rods (dream on), you had better be able to gear up and make them. If number twenty on your list has to wait three years for a rod, that may place a limiting factor on your ultimate success. I keep saying "may" because there are always exceptions. Some people expect their rods right away and are mightily pleased with a maker who delivers on time, whereas others figure that to get a truly desirable rod you have to wait three years. I suspect that there are more of the former than the latter, but there are makers whose rods are so desirable that they have mile-long waiting lists, and people sign up no matter how long it will take to get a rod. If your rods are good enough—and they really should be good if you want to put them on the market and look your fellow makers in the eye—people will wait, but don't abuse them. The last word on the subject comes from Daryll Whitehead: "Don't be a flake. When someone orders a rod, figure out how long at the longest it could take, add three months, and give the customer that date. Then, no matter what happens, *have the rod done by that date.* You'll get the reputation that people can depend on you, and that's worth a lot."

When we come to *price,* you're on your own. The quality of your work and the marketability of the rod have a lot to do with it, as does your reputation, how long you have been in business, and the sort of people you sell to. Some builders make relatively plain rods that sell for five hundred to seven hundred fifty dollars that are bought by people who want a new bamboo rod but are freaked out by a twelve hundred–dollar price tag. Others concentrate on making flawless, gorgeously finished rods for people who wonder what's wrong with the rod if the price is less than a grand. When you start out, you need to decide what you are comfortable asking as well as what you are likely to get. I would recommend looking at as many other rods as possible and evaluating as rationally as you can how your rods stack up, and then taking into account the fact that you have to start somewhere. I would have been embarrassed trying to sell one of my first rods for a thousand dollars because I didn't feel I had paid my dues, and I didn't sell *any* until I felt that they were competitive with rods that cost much more than the seven hundred fifty dollars I started out asking. But that's just me. I'm not going to tell you what to do.

People is generally used in reference to the folks you want to buy your rods, or, in marketing parlance, your "target market." A target market is defined in order to orient marketing materials and approaches to the segment of the population most likely to buy your product. Of course, we're talking about handmade fly rods, not a new brand of deodorant soap, so it's not a big mystery. The stereotypical bamboo rod buyer is older, well-heeled (as in attorney, dentist, and so on), and has at least several bamboo rods already. I guess that stereotype is no more inaccurate than any other, but in addition to dentists and other affluent folks, I've built rods for a machinist, a telephone lineman, and an engineer. In short, bamboo rods are bought by all sorts of people, from the guy who buys several rods a year for his collection to the guy who has scrimped and saved so he can buy the custom rod he's always wanted.

If you were thinking about doing some sort of direct mail marketing and were buying a list from one of the fly-fishing magazines, you'd probably want to concentrate on the higher income brackets. Frankly, though, if you're buying lists from major fly-fishing magazines, you've probably put a lot of thought into this already. And if you haven't, you want to put a lot more thought into it than you will pick up from this chapter. For the rest of us, People means paying attention to anyone who shows an interest in bamboo, even if he or she isn't wearing a Rolex.

Place usually means the stores or other locations where your product is sold. If you're like me, you don't have a store, and Place means getting your rods in front of people who might buy them. The opportunities for placement begin with fishing your rods and getting them in the hands of good fishermen who will use them and speak favorably of them. It's amazing how bamboo rods will attract people who are interested in them, and if you don't make many rods anyway, this exposure alone will likely be enough. If you want more exposure, you can display your rods at Trout Unlimited events (perhaps you can donate a rod or a portion of its cost for auction or raffle) and sports-men's and tackle shows, though the latter will cost some money. You can put rods on consignment in fly shops or offer them through rod lists and catalogs. I don't have a lot of experience with the latter sorts of out-lets, mostly because I already have a full-time job (for the time being), and I manage to stay busy just selling rods on my own. Dealers, naturally enough, make their living by selling stuff for more than they pay for it. Of course, you know what that means. If you really want to sell rods, though, giving up the 20 to 30 percent that a dealer takes may be worth it in the long run because the ma-jor dealers sell rods all over the world. It's one way to get your rods and name out, if that's your objective.

Which dovetails rather nicely into *pro-motion.* According to the textbooks, Promo-tion consists of advertising, which refers to exposure your rods receive for which you pay, and publicity, which refers to exposure for which you don't. If you run an ad in *Fly Rod & Reel,* that's obviously advertising, whereas if *Fly Rod & Reel* does a laudatory article on you and your rods, that's publicity. There are a few makers who have advertised rather heavily in major publications, but I re-main dubious of the value of such an invest-ment for the average maker. I think bamboo rod buyers are impressed by what they see and cast, and by the opinions of people they trust. I remember reading that Lyle Dicker-son ran an ad in *Field & Stream* and prepared a catalog, only to conclude later that "neither one brought in any business."

Advertising can be expensive, in a way, because you pay more or less according to how many people the carrier reaches, and because it takes multiple exposures for ad-vertising to have an impact. I suppose adver-tising (We're talking about print advertising, or direct mail. Unless you have a vast per-sonal fortune, bamboo rod buyers are far too widely dispersed to make broadcast advertis-ing cost-effective.) would make sense if you

are fairly well known and want to make sure people know how to contact you or if you make a conscious decision to use advertising to achieve name recognition, can afford a major initial investment, and are prepared to back it up with plenty of product. You need to decide for yourself how many rods you can make for sale, and how much money you're willing to pay, if necessary, in order to sell them. If you want to become another Payne, Winston, or Thomas & Thomas, you will need to advertise. For the maker who does something else for a living and puts out a maximum of a dozen rods a year, it's a waste of money. Better to go to a couple of shows and present your rods in person. You may not reach every bamboo fancier in, say, Denver, but those you do reach will remem-ber meeting you and handling or casting your rods.

One essential aspect of your Promotion, even if you're small, is the quality of your printed materials. I don't mean that you need a full-color glossy brochure with gold ink proclaiming yourself to be the world's greatest rod maker. What you need are sim-ple, clear, sharp materials that reflect your personality and your commitment to your craft. You'll need business cards and proba-bly some sort of brochure. I don't think brochures sell rods, but they do give poten-tial customers a feel for your business and a little added assurance that you're legit. You want to get your point across without spend-ing all of your money on printing and with-out coming across as self-inflated. A clean, distinctive logo is helpful, and if you aren't a graphic designer yourself or good friends with one, it might be worth a few bucks to pay for one. On the other hand, some of the best makers I know have no logo other than their names.

It's up to you to formulate your own marketing mix, whether you deliberately en-gineer it or simply do what comes naturally. You may not want or need to think about any of this, but you should realize that the bamboo rod market is increasingly competitive, and if you wish to make a mark, or if you harbor any thoughts of doing it for a living, it will take a determined and intelligent effort to be successful. Or plenty of luck.

Salesmanship

All of this marketing mix stuff, although helpful, is too abstract just to leave it there. Perhaps more important than all five P's put together is your own salesmanship. That word evokes nasty images for a lot of people because we've all had to fend off obnoxious salesmen, but let's forget about all that for a moment. For quite a while I worked under the impression that I didn't have to be a salesman, that if I made the best rods I could, then people would buy them, and I could just be myself—which is to say, a recluse. If somebody was going to buy a rod, he or she was going to buy a rod, period. No sense in getting all worked up about it.

This comforting idea was reinforced by the fact that, for a certain segment of the rod-buying public, this is true. However, as I started making more rods and showing them to more people, I started noticing something. Some people would cast a rod and reach for their checkbooks. Others, however, would cast rods, examine them, say that they really liked them, that they wanted such-and-such, and that they'd send me an order in a week or two. Of course, I'd never hear from them again.

This mystified me to some extent, but I figured those folks just didn't want a rod after all. God knows there are plenty of reasons not to spend a grand on a fly rod. Finally, I mentioned a particular incident to my friend Dale Darling, who, in addition to a number of other qualifications, owns fly shops in Longmont and Estes Park, Colorado (The St. Vrain Angler and Estes Angler, respectively. Good shops, and I'd say that even if I didn't know Dale.). I'd shown a few rods to a fellow who collects bamboo. He'd been happy with the rods, said lots of nice things, among them that he'd order a rod when he got back from a bonefishing trip. We talked about what he wanted, shook hands, then I got in the truck and left. Never heard from him again.

"You didn't close the sale," Dale explained in the tone one hears from a college senior telling his kid brother how to get a date. "The guy wanted a rod, but he's used to being sold and you didn't close the deal. You didn't say 'Fine, I'll go ahead and start the rod. I know you're good for it.' That would have either closed the deal or he would have had to back out, and at that point backing out would have hurt his pride.

"You're not going to sell a rod to someone who doesn't want one," Dale continued, "but lots of people who want something won't buy unless you show an interest in selling, unless you put it in their hand and say 'How would you like to pay for that?' To them, if you don't sell, that means you don't care about them or want their business."

The point of all of this is not that you need to be a shark, only that, if you reach a point where how many rods you sell matters to you, you need to pay attention. If you show rods to someone and they start talking about what they like, go with them. "Would you prefer a seven-six or a seven-nine? What kind of grip do you like on a rod like that? I think flaming makes a little better rod, but some people like the look of light rods better. Which do you like?" You don't want to come off like a used car salesman ("What a beautiful day to buy a car!") but as what you are: a craftsman who is committed to his work and who wants the customer to have exactly the right rod.

Sooner or later, unless you're lucky enough to be dealing with the sort of customer who just starts writing a check, you have to close the sale, which means obtaining a specific commitment. "Would you like to put a deposit on that, or should I start on a set of sticks and give you a call when it starts getting custom?" You don't want to get a bunch of orders from people who will back out later, but a good salesman will never ask a question that can reflexively be answered "No." Of course, a customer can say no at any time and may be turned off if you push too hard or try to close too soon. It's tricky, and the flip side of consciously selling is that you are more aware of rejection than if you just passively sat and waited for checks to drop into your lap. It's up to you, but it probably will occur to you that one nice thing about building rods purely as a hobby is that you don't have to worry about any of this.

Time

One final thought, before you get too pumped about selling rods. It was instructive for me to write down the cost of all the materials that went into a bamboo rod, to figure in the cost of my tools and shop, subtract all that from the price of a rod, subtract taxes from that, and divide the final result by the number of hours I put into a rod to determine how much I was making per hour. Before you try to depend on bamboo rods for anything other than your materials and a lit-tle walking-around money, you might consider doing the same.

The old saw that time is money is particularly true when you're self-employed, and if you really try to make money with rods, that means saving time without compromising quality. After you build a few rods, you may get a little faster at some jobs, but that probably will be offset by your finding more things to pay attention to. One thing that can save you time is machinery, but you'll have to be careful or you'll wind up spending all your time tinkering with home-made equipment that never really works.

A good first step might be to build (or have built) a machine that makes rough beveled strips. You can build one fairly easily using a router, and with proper attention paid to safety, you can cut the eighteen rough-beveled strips for a rod in about a half hour. That's a savings of at least a couple of hours per rod with no sacrifice in quality. If rod building is just a hobby, a couple of hours isn't much, but if you're making rods to sell it's money in your pocket. A full discussion of rod-making machinery would be a whole separate book, but this should get you thinking about it if you feel the need.

If wisdom were offered me
with the proviso that I should keep it shut up
and refrain from declaring it,
I should refuse. There's no delight in owning
anything unshared. —Seneca

CONCLUSION

It's my hope that if you are a newcomer to the craft you have been encouraged by this book, and that if you're an experienced builder you've found it interesting. I've tried to maintain a relaxed, companionable tone and not be too rigid because there's more than one way to do everything, and you may find a better way than mine. Still, everyone has to start somewhere, and if this book has given you that start, I'm honored.

One final thought. Bamboo rod building is a craft ultimately sustained and propagated by people, not books or tools or things. If you build a few rods, sooner or later you will have a chance to help or teach someone. I'd recommend doing so, because we're all in this together and none of us is here for very long. To put a finer point on it, someone who is determined and has the ability to build rods will succeed whether you help or not, so you might as well help and enjoy whatever comes your way as a result.

I don't want to try to make bamboo rod building into more than it is, but at its very least it affords the opportunity to make something beautiful and useful in a society that often seems propelled by ugly and useless things, as well as the opportunity to get to know some outstanding people whose paths you might otherwise never have crossed. You could do worse.

171

Appendix A: Health and environmental Concerns for the Bamboo Rod Builder

There's a lot of talk these days about Repetitive Motion Injuries, or RMIs. I may hear a bit more about them than most people because, as a musician, I have a number of colleagues who either suffer or have suffered from them. I know musicians with bad backs, tendonitis, shoulder problems, you name it. Any time you make one motion over and over, you run the risk of injuring yourself. Even at that, I wouldn't have thought much about RMIs in connection with rod building except that, a couple of summers ago, I gave myself a beauty. I got in the habit of keeping my left leg locked at the beginning of every planing stroke and rocking back on it. If I rocked back and rocked forward, I could make a single pass on a 45-inch spline without moving my feet. I wasn't really doing much else physically, but I was spending close to eight hours a day in the shop. Every time I rocked back on that back leg with my knee locked, I tugged on the hamstring. You know how they tell you not to bounce when you're trying to touch your toes? Well, there's a reason for that. As I kept tugging, the muscle got shorter and shorter until the tugging was being done on a muscle that was stretched pretty close to as far as it could go. After a while I'd wake up in the morning with a sore leg, but there was stuff to do, and the soreness went away as I limbered up and got to work.

This went on for some time until I got up one morning, couldn't straighten my leg, and locomoting presented real difficulties. When I could walk, I had a hard time pushing in the clutch on the truck to get to the chiropractor, who couldn't figure how someone who hadn't really engaged in any sports in the past month wound up with such an outrageously pulled hamstring. I spent the next few days on the couch, and the muscle took forever to heal and never has been quite the same. I now keep that leg slightly flexed, shift my foot position regularly, and take a break every half hour to stretch.

Other body parts could get hurt planing bamboo. There's a bundle of nerves in your palm that can be irritated by steady pressure (as in pushing a plane down a strip over and over). I'm a little more sensitive about my hands than I am about my legs, so when my fingers start to tingle a bit I know that's a bad sign, and I either back off or don a cycling glove with exposed fingers and a padded palm. Workbench height can make a big difference, and your back and legs can really pay if you get it wrong.

Planing bamboo can be hard work, and it's probably no coincidence that most professional rod builders (not all, of course— I'm perfectly aware of exceptions) use milling or beveling machines. Most builders undertake hand-planing rods as a hobby and spend a few hours a day on it at most. If you contemplate doing it more than that, work into it gradually. And pay attention to your body—if something starts to hurt, slow down (or better yet, stop) and figure out what it is and what's causing it. This is nothing more than common sense, but I know from experience in several different endeavors that it's possible for enthusiasm to mask pain. Anybody who has left a fly imbedded in their (insert body part) for more than a few minutes because the fish were biting knows what I mean. Still, the best way to cure an RMI is not to have it in the first place. That statement may not prevent anything, but at least I told you so.

The Environmental Rod Maker

Anyone who does anything is faced with environmental concerns. The reason that petroleum products and plastics exist is not that their inventors were evil but that they work, and there was a time when that was all that mattered. A lot of us are more or less hooked on function and feel shielded from the consequences because we only use a little bit of whatever it is (or only drive a small car or only use styrofoam cups every once in a while). The typical rod builder uses glues, varnishes, and thinners of varying degrees of toxicity, and I'm as typical as anybody. I'd hate to try to do without my favorite varnish, which is not water-based, which means I need a thinner for it. I'm also pretty attached to epoxy. So I won't tell you not to use toxic stuff, partially to avoid hypocrisy and partially because the EPA (assuming Congress doesn't gut it) will tell all of us that eventually. Formulations for varnish have been changing since the early 1970s to reflect growing awareness of environmental issues, and it won't be too many years before water-based varnishes will be all that's available. In the meantime, if you don't want to use environmentally friendly stuff, at the very least be careful. Use only as much as you absolutely need, and buy it in quantities that you will use up before it goes bad. If you use spar varnish on the wraps and polyurethane to dip, buy the smallest possible can of spar, because once you open it the clock is ticking. One day soon you'll open it up and find a gummy mass. Try to find a use for the varnish in your dipping tube before it gets thick and skins over, and be sure that your tube will seal airtight to prevent that from happening prematurely. If you use epoxy or URAC to glue, be aware that both products have a shelf life, and try either to buy in quantities where there won't be any waste or, if the stuff comes only in large quantities, to get together with other builders and divvy it up so that it all gets used.

There's a lot of bamboo waste generated by rod building, and you should try to be a little creative with that instead of just shipping it to the dump. I know one builder who gives and sells scrap and rejected cane to makers of traditional Chinese kites, which, you've got to admit, is pretty creative. I save some of mine and periodically unload it on somebody who comes along wanting to learn to build rods so he'll have something on which to practice splitting and straightening nodes and planing. Shavings go in the compost pile.

Just a couple of things to think about. I'm fairly confident that pollution from bamboo rod makers is a fairly small problem in the larger scheme of things, by which I mean that an EPA crackdown on hobbyists would be misguided because we use so little stuff and there are so many much larger problems. On the other hand, "the larger scheme of things" can be a pernicious myth that inhibits action. I believe in thinking globally and acting locally, and far too many otherwise rational people take the filth poured out by various industries as an excuse not to examine their own output. Lots of little problems add up. Do your best. And exercise your own personal equivalent of prayer for the Clean Water Act.

Appendix B: Resources for the Bamboo Rod Builder

A list of sources can be guaranteed accurate only as of press time, because businesses close, change hands, or move. However, most of these companies have been in business for quite a while, so I hope that this list will be useful for some time to come. The following isn't a comprehensive or complete list, because I'm limiting myself to companies I know about; therefore, many worthy suppliers will be excluded.

Some of these sources are included because stuff like bamboo and thousand-ring bags of cork are not typically found locally. Other things, like woodworking supplies or machine tooling, probably are available locally, and I would encourage you to patronize your neighborhood hardware store or industrial supplier before resorting to mail order. Don't get me wrong, I like mail-order outfits just fine and use them plenty. I just think it's a good idea to give your local small businesses a chance to earn your loyalty. Reel-seat and guide manufacturers are listed in case you intend to buy in sufficient quantities to qualify for wholesale prices. If you're buying retail anyway, you might as well check your local fly shop for components.

Adhesives

Brownell's
Route 2, Box 1
200 South Front Street
Montezuma, IA 50171
(515) 623-5401

Source for Acraglas Gel, though most sporting goods and gun stores carry it also. This is a gunsmith's catalog, containing bluing solutions, rubbing compounds, stains, finishes, and a variety of tools and products of interest to the builder.

GolfSmith International, Inc.
11000 North IH-35
Austin, TX 78753
(800) 456-3344

Source for shafting epoxy (Stock #909S) for ferrules. The catalog also has Black & Decker heat guns for a not unreasonable price, should you be unable to find one locally.

Nelson Paint Company
One Nelson Drive
Kingsford, MI 49801
(906) 774-5566

Source for URAC 185.

Nyatex Chemical Co.
P.O. Box 124
Howell, MI 48843
(517) 546-4046

Nyatex sells epoxy (part nos. 10E007 and 10EH008) in quarts. Two quarts is a lot of glue, but they're used to selling it in 55-gallon drums.

Wicks Aircraft Supply
410 Pine Street
Highland, IL 62249
(800) 221-9425

Source for Aerolite adhesive.

Bamboo

Charles H. Demarest
P.O. Box 238
Bloomingdale, NJ 07403
(973) 492-1414

The Demarests have been supplying Tonkin cane to rod makers in the U.S. almost since rod makers started using it. If you call, you'll probably talk to Eileen Demarest. They're lovely folks. The best way to order cane is by the bale (twenty pieces) if you can afford it or can get together with some other makers. Demarest will ship as few as three pieces (sawn in half for UPS), but the increased cost of the material and the shipping will eat you up.

Tuxedo Custom Rod
P.O. Box 1167
Stockton, CA 95201
(209) 948-6508

A fairly recent venture offering purportedly more select cane, albeit at a higher price. I haven't dealt with this company, mostly because I already have as much cane as I can store, but makers I've spoken to who have say the cane isn't bad, basically the same stuff the Demarests have, only with the really bad pieces picked out. Probably worth a try.

Cork

C&D Trading, Inc.
6451 Lyndale Avenue South
Richfield, MN 55423
(612) 574-1563
(612) 572-9876 (fax)

A very good supplier, with reasonable prices (for today). Also has 1/4-inch thick rings.

Pace
P.O. Box 5127
Fort Lauderdale, FL 33310
(954) 975-6333
(954) 975-6422 (fax)

More expensive than C&D, but good cork if you get the best grade.

Silk

Silk is available from most of the rod building suppliers listed in a separate category, but if you are willing to buy in quantity, the following manufacturers and suppliers could save you some money.

YLI Corporation (Kanagawa/Osprey)
161 West Main Street
Rock Hill, SC 29730
(803) 985-3063

Kanagawa (now called Osprey, a recent name change) is really pretty good thread for rod building: It is available in a wide variety of colors, comes in very fine sizes, and is relatively inexpensive. The main problem I have had with it lies in the application or fastness of the dyes, which can be inconsistent when using penetrating varnish. I still use it quite a bit, though, especially the finest stuff for tipping.

Utica Threads
240 Merrick Road
Lynbrook, NY 11563
(516) 887-3900

Not as fine as Kinkame, but good silk at a very reasonable price. Obtaining exactly the right color can be a challenge, because the company's sample chart uses cotton thread instead of silk.

Barbour (formerly Belding Corticelli)
P.O. Box 1520
Hendersonville, NC 28793
(800) 346-7448 (call for local distributor)

Still available at retail here and there, though not in many of the old desirable colors, and not commonly in the finer sizes.

Gudebrod, Inc.
P.O. Box 357
Pottstown, PA 19464-0357
(610) 327-4050

The only Gudebrod silks available today are too heavy for my taste, but I know quite a few makers who use them. They are of good quality and come in about a dozen colors, and are available at retail from rod building suppliers like Angler's Art.

Other Silks

The other silks most often heard of in rod building are Elephant and Phoenix. These threads, both English brands, are available from various suppliers in the U.S. Thomas & Thomas, for instance, has carried Elephant. You'll have to check around for retail sources, but I don't know of a wholesale source in the U.S. for either brand.

Ferrules

Classic Sporting Enterprises
RD 3, Box 3
Barton, VT 05822
(802) 525-3623
(802) 525-3982 (fax)

I think CSE's ferrules are the best available, period. They are available in Super Swiss (essentially the same design as the Feier-abend Super Z) and Super SD (Leonard-style, with a stepdown required for the male). They'll sell you single ferrules at retail, but you're really better off saving your nickels or getting together with other makers for a wholesale order.

Cortland Line Company, Inc.
P.O. Box 5588
Cortland, NY 13045
(607) 756-2851

Cortland sells ferrules that are very close to the Super Z design. The samples I have seen are a little rougher than those of Classic Sporting Enterprises, but a little less expensive as well. If I were to try to save money on components I'm not sure I'd start with the ferrules, but the Cortland ferrules I have seen certainly seemed usable. Cortland also sells rod tubes.

Oven Heating Element

Hi-Watt
26600 Schoenherr Road
Warren, MI 48089
(313) 772-5090

Probably the best way to get a mica-strip element is to contact *The Planing Form* and see if anyone is putting an order together. There's a substantial set-up charge, so the more units ordered at one time the better. The heaters (information courtesy Wayne Cattanach) are manufactured by Watlow in

St. Louis, Missouri, and the manufacturing code is S1J54AS1. The heaters are 54 inches long and are rated 650 watts at 120 volts. Watlow supplies local manufacturer representatives all around the country; Hi-Watt is simply the representative in Michigan. If you place an order yourself, you will need to identify your local rep. Hi-Watt will try to help, though you could save them some trouble and call around your local heating contractors yourself first.

Planing Forms

Colorado Bootstrap, Inc.
P.O. Box 440104
Aurora, CO 80044
(303) 745-1353

I've heard from several makers using Frank Armbruster's (proprietor of Colorado Bootstrap) forms. To wit, they're a good value and perfectly usable. A couple of the early versions I saw had problems, but reports are that they've been corrected. They use the push-pull mechanism with a dowel between two screws, which helps keep the price down to $350 (including shipping) as we go to press.

Jeff Wagner
6549 Kingsdale Road
Parma Heights, OH 44130
(440) 845-4415

Jeff Wagner has taken over the planing form market niche formerly held by Joe Saracione. He uses stress-relieved, surface-ground steel stock (much more expensive than cold-rolled steel), resulting in forms that look like gauge blocks and are highly accurate. The 76-inch-long forms cost $750 as of this writing, but if you want the ultimate and are able to pay for it, this is the way to go.

Woodworking Tools

Garret Wade
161 Avenue of the Americas
New York, NY 10013
(800) 221-2942

A gorgeous catalog with everything a woodworker could need. Record, Stanley, and Lie-Nielsen planes, and Hock blades. Also a source for URAC 185.

Lee Valley Tools
P.O. Box 6295, Station J
Ottowa, Ontario K2A 1T4
Canada
(800) 461-5053

The only source I have found for a 60-degree grooving router bit that actually measures 60 degrees. More expensive than U.S. sources, but good stuff and beautiful catalogs.

Woodworker's Supply
5604 Alameda Place N.E.
Albuquerque, NM 87113
(800) 645-9292

Sharpening stuff, tools, finishes. A little less expensive than Garret Wade, but not as wide a selection of hand tools and sharpening equipment. Geared more toward the power tool user. Still, a good catalog.

Woodcraft
210 Wood County Industrial Park
P.O. Box 1686
Parkesburg, WV 26102–1686
(800) 225-1153

Sort of in between Garret Wade and Woodworker's Supply in both price and selection. A good source for planes, Hock blades, sharpening stones, and jigs. Also a source of some interesting burl wood for reel seats.

Machine Tools and Tooling

Enco
5200 West Bloomingdale Avenue
Chicago, IL 60639
(800) 873-3626

An inexpensive source for measuring devices and tooling.

Grizzly Imports, Inc.
2406 Reach Road
Williamsport, PA 17701
(800) 523-4777

Supplier of tooling and imported machine tools. They sell a couple of small lathes that would work well for rod builders. Also woodworking machines, tools, and supplies, including waterstones, a Record no. 9 1/2 plane, and wood-turning spurs. The fingernail router bit (Part #C1215) is what I use for mortising reel-seat fillers.

Rod-making Tools and Supplies

Angler's Workshop
1350 Atlantic Avenue
P.O. Box 1044PF
Woodland, WA 98674
(206) 225-9445
www.anglersworkshop.com

An extensive line of rod-making components and supplies, including thread tensioners, rod-wrapping jigs, and some very nice snake guides (bronze and chrome) from England.

Bellinger Reel Seats
2017 25th Street S.E.
Salem, OR 97302-1121
(503) 371-6151

Bellinger seats are available from a variety of retail outlets as well as direct from the manufacturer. Very nice hardware, a decent schedule of quantity price breaks, and Al Bellinger is the nicest guy —a bamboo rod builder, as you may know.

Los Pinos Custom Fly Rods
3214 Matthew NE
Albuquerque, NM 87107
(505) 884-7501

Source for *the* best rod tubes. Also a retail source for guides, reel seats, and other components.

Sweet Water Bamboo Rods/
Pocono Gateway
George Maurer
361 Siegfriedale Road
Kutztown, PA 19530
(610) 756-6385

Retail source for Daryll Whitehead's new agate stripping guides (and his electric beveler), as well as forms, ferrules, guides, cork, silk, and everything else.

REC Components
72 Shaker Road
Enfield, CT 06082
(860) 749-3476

Reel seats, winding checks, nickel silver stock. Quite expensive, but very pretty.

Glenn Struble Manufacturing Co.
206 West View Drive
Roseburg, OR 97470
(503) 673-7977

Very nice stuff at a decent price. I never met Glenn, but I always heard great things about him, and the folks keeping the company going seem solid. They have a nifty little nickel silver screw-locking seat, and I use their regular nickel silver downlocker occasionally, especially on light rods that, for one reason or another, need a locking seat.

Daryll Whitehead
611 NW 48th Street
Seattle, WA 98107
(206) 781-0133

Agate stripping guides. Gorgeous. The word from Daryll is that if you just want a couple of guides, you'd better get them from George Maurer (Sweet Water Rods/Pocono Gateway, above). Daryll has plenty to do making rods and guides. If you wish to buy in quantity, however, you can contact him directly. Daryll also sells a fine beveling machine that turns raw strips into untapered triangular ones.

Thomas & Thomas
2 Avenue A
Turners Falls, MA 01376
(413) 863-9727

In addition to rods and blanks, T&T sells reel seats, silk thread, and select cork in bags of fifty rings.

Pacific Bay
540 South Jefferson Street
Placentia, CA 92870
(714) 524-1778

Widely used guides. Not terribly expensive, and a decent discount schedule is available. The feet are a little narrow for bamboo rods, but then they aren't really *for* bamboo rods.

Perfection Tip Company
1340 Cowles Street
Long Beach, CA 90813
(800) 441-2940

Perfection's price breaks aren't (as of this writing) all that great for the little guy, but they're the only ones making snake guides smaller than 1/0. They go down to 2/0 in hard chrome and down to 4/0 in stainless (which I don't recommend using because they wear so rapidly). A source for stripping guides as well. (See also Angler's Workshop for English chrome and bronzed guides.)

Miscellaneous

Edmund Scientific
101 East Gloucester Pike
Barrington, NJ 08007–1380
(800) 728-6999

A catalog primarily intended for science teachers, but a source for Kevlar thread (#F34,863), bottles and labware, magnifiers, motors, and plenty of other good stuff.

Books and Periodicals

Lindsay Publications
P.O. Box 538
Bradley, IL 60915–0538
(815) 935-5353

Metalworking books and other interesting titles.

Angler's Art
P.O. Box 148C
Plainfield, PA 17081
(800) 848-1020

New and used fly-fishing books, and especially valuable in the latter capacity if you are looking for old rod building books.

The Planing Form
Ron Barch, Editor
P.O. Box 365
Hastings, MI 49058

Rod-building newsletter, and a book consisting of back issues from the first five years is available. If you're into building and don't already subscribe to this newsletter, you should do so.

Wilderness Adventures
P.O. Box 627
Gallatin Gateway, MT 59730
(800) 925-3339

A great mail-order source for fishing and hunting books, including in-print books on rods and rod building.

Rod-Building Online

I started out intending to simply mention a couple of Internet and Web sites in the Bibliography, but the paragraph took on a life of its own. There's a ton of information out there online, and although much of it is junk designed to keep you online at fifteen cents a minute, some of it is good, and fly fishing and rod building are interests that are finding ever greater expression online. Some of the people who write letters or articles in *The Planing Form* include their e-mail addresses, and if you spend time on the fly-fishing newsgroups you'll probably strike up an e-mail correspondence with someone independent of the newsgroups.

A newsgroup is an electronic bulletin board, usually located on the part of the Internet known as Usenet. (There are private Bulletin Board Services, or BBS, but that's a different matter entirely.) Anyone who subscribes to the newsgroup (subscribing means that your online service connects you more or less directly to the newsgroup when you sign on, and you may or may not become part of that newsgroup's mailing list) can read all the messages that have been left by others as well as leave messages.

You'll find the occasional post by a rod-builder on a fly-fishing newsgroup either posing a question or answering a query about how much a bamboo rod is worth or how to refinish an old rod. If you post your own question, you'll probably get at least one response, and it could be the start of a worthwhile association. The most well established fly-fishing newsgroup as of this writing is rec.outdoors.fishing.fly, though you'll find some fly-fishing souls on alt.fishing. A newsgroup often has a number of FAQs, or Frequently Asked Questions—more or less comprehensive guides to a subject that will be posted periodically or on request. There's a good one by Bruce Conner (bconner@cybercom.net) on rod building that appears from time to time on rec.outdoors.fishing.fly and is located at www.cybercom.net/nbconner/rodNframes.html.

Another mechanism that's like a newsgroup is the mailing list, on which any message you write is simultaneously sent to everyone on the list, and once you've subscribed, any message that anyone else writes is sent to you. A mailing list is easier to set up and manage than a full-fledged Usenet account, so a smaller, more focused group is better served. Probably quite a few mailing lists dealing with fly fishing are spotted around the net. Of prime interest to us, however, is the rod-building mailing list, rodmakers@mail.wustl.edu. It seems to work pretty well. Questions are answered quickly and generously, and the group has a nice rapport.

Beyond newsgroups, rod builders on the Internet can access the World Wide Web. Not every Internet server offers Web access, and some older computers and modems may lack the speed and graphics capability to use the Web. The Web is made up of "sites" or "pages," which are individual repositories of text and graphics, often detailed and cross-indexed, often with links provided to yet more pages, which are in turn cross-indexed and linked. You need a pretty fast modem to make the Web usable because many sites have lots of graphics that take much more digital information to convey than text. Recently I signed on to Bruce Conner's Web page (http://www.cybercom.net/~bconner/rod.html) and was amazed at the richness and comprehensiveness of the site. This guy and his friends have done a lot of work. Besides lots of information up front, the site has links to a list of sources; a rod maker's directory (along with links to their pages, where they exist); a "small but growing" (means it will probably be enormous by the time you read this) repository of tapers, drawings of binders, a fine guide to building wooden planing forms, a backlog of mail sent and answered on the rodmakers@mail. wustl.edu mailing list; and tons of other stuff. I'm tremendously enthusiastic about the technology and this Web page. It's good now, but as it grows and as more builders create and link their own sites it's going to be phenomenal.

Besides rod building, which is a tiny corner of fly fishing, literally dozens of sites dealing with various aspects of the sport are available, including commercial shopping or information sites provided by manufacturers or retailers, regional fishing information, fly tying and special interest. *The Classic Chronicle* (http://www.gorp.com/bamboo.htm), which you might want anyway if you're interested in cane rods (256 Nashua Court,

Grand Junction, CO 81503), has supplied a print directory of websites in its spring 1996 newsletter, with more promised for the summer issue. *The Classic Chronicle*'s own website is pretty good too, with a variety of useful links.

If you're wondering how to get started, the easiest thing to do, assuming you have a computer and modem, is to join one of the national online services such as America Online, CompuServe, or Prodigy. These companies usually have the most user-friendly software (often preloaded on new computers), and they all cost about twenty dollars a month for unlimited service.

This is interesting stuff, but don't let your subscription to *The Planing Form* lapse. I know a few people who will see fly fishing on the Internet as simply the final clinching evidence that the sport has gone to hell. I don't necessarily disagree, but if so, it's not the Net's fault. Things just keep changing.

GLOSSARY

Arundinaria amabilis. The scientific name for the bamboo used to build fly rods, meaning "the lovely bamboo."

Binder. Any device for wrapping thread onto rod sections under pressure and tension.

Burr. A very thin flap or wire that forms on an edge being sharpened. A burr is more prominent when coarse stones are being used and less prominent when finer stones are being used. On a truly sharp edge, the burr has been removed through use of an extremely fine stone, strop, or buffing wheel, leaving an edge that is as fine as the crystalline structure of the steel will allow.

Butt. The larger, lower section of a fly rod, or the larger end of any rod section.

Check Split. A split purposely put into a bamboo culm before storage to partially relieve the stress caused by drying.

Chuck. An attachment for a lathe or drill that holds objects to be turned. A three-jaw chuck, which is about all we need for rod building, is made to center round objects. I've seen some very nice (read "expensive") six-jaw chucks for lathes and thought they would be perfect for rod building, but that's probably overkill.

Culm. From the Latin *culmus,* meaning "stalk." For our purposes, a culm is the stick of bamboo that one receives from the importer in either 12- or 6-foot lengths.

Cork. Used to denote both the grip of a rod and the material of which it is normally made. The best cork is grown in Portugal and is the bark of the tree. Rings used for fly rod grips are specie cut (pits traveling crosswise through the cylinder), which is what you normally see in wine corks; and specie cut (pits traveling lengthwise through the cylinder), which is what you see in the rings for fly-rod grips. The best cork has the fewest pits and is very firm and dense.

Diaphragms. The internal membranes that, together with the nodes, divide the bamboo stalk into segments.

Enamel. The smooth outer covering of bamboo. It is very hard and tough, containing quite a bit of silica, but has no strength and is therefore removed when building a rod.

Epoxy. A relatively modern adhesive consisting of separate resin and hardener components. Available in many different formulations and brands.

Face Ring. The cork ring on the grip nearest the blank, which therefore has its end grain exposed.

Ferrule. The metal joint, consisting of male and female parts, that connects the separate parts of a multiple-piece fly rod.

Flaming. Heat-treating and darkening the bamboo for a rod by direct application of a flame.

Froe. A splitting tool that looks like the letter L, with the upright stem being the handle and the horizontal foot being the blade. It's usually used for splitting shingles, but some rod builders use it for splitting bamboo culms in half.

Gouge. A wood chisel with a U-shaped cross section used in rod building to chip out the diaphragms inside the tube.

Grower Mark. Chinese characters scratched or carved into the enamel of a bamboo culm. These characters are used by the sharecroppers who grow and harvest the bamboo to mark the edges of their plots. They've been doing this for hundreds of years, so it seems that the ruination of good bamboo that these marks cause will just have to be borne.

Heat Treating. The application of heat, either by oven or by direct flame, to the bamboo in order to remove moisture and toughen the fibers. This may be done to the whole culm or to rough-beveled strips.

Hollow-Built. A rod in which the pithy center of the section is removed in an effort to increase power by removing weight.

Inertia. The property of matter expressed by Newton's first law, namely, that an object at rest will remain at rest, and an object in motion will remain in motion in the same straight line unless acted upon by an external force. It is inertia that gives a fly line the weight to bend a fly rod when opposed by the motion of your arm.

Lathe. A stationary machine for spinning objects, normally with the aim of producing something round, such as a cylinder or a hole.

Lignin. *Merriam Webster's* defines lignin as "an amorphous polymeric substance related to cellulose that together with cellulose forms the woody cell walls of plants and the cementing material between them." It's this cementing material that makes lignin of interest to us, binding together as it does the long cellulose fibers that give bamboo its unique properties.

Medium-Action Rod. It's bad form to use other terms that need defining in a definition, but a medium-action rod is in between a tip-action rod and a parabolic rod. Defining rod action is slippery enough as it is, but there are a bunch of rods I've cast, all different, that would qualify as medium-action. Such a broad category might be considered useless, but if it's not a tip-action rod and it's not parabolic, I guess that tells you something.

Node. The bane of the rod builder's existence. The short raised area of interlaced fibers between the long segments of bamboo—crooked, fractious, capable of being straightened with heat and some degree of difficulty.

Parabolic. A type of rod action that bends fairly evenly over its entire length.

Pith. The white inner portion of the bamboo. This portion has no strength and carries very few power fibers, so its presence in the finished bamboo rod is to be minimized as a general rule.

Planing Form. Twin bars of metal or wood that are fastened together in a fixed or adjustable relationship with a 30-degree bevel on the inside edge of each, and that together form a 60-degree groove that holds the spline for planing.

Power Fibers. The very fine, tough cellulose fibers just under the enamel in the bamboo plant. These fibers are very strong and tightly packed together and are responsible for most of the plant's elasticity.

Reel Seat. The device that secures the reel to the rod. Placed below the grip on a fly rod, this device may be any one of several configurations. The main division is between sliding-band and locking varieties, in which the immobile cap is either concealed under the grip or affixed to the end of the seat, respectively.

Rough Beveling. The task of transforming the rectangular strips (once the nodes have been straightened) into triangular strips that can be bound together for heat treating. This is accomplished either by hand, using a plane and wooden rough planing forms, or by machine.

Serrations. The thin tabs where the ferrule meets the blank. Also the cuts that form the tabs, as in "serrated ferrule."

Silk. Silk thread traditionally used to bind guides to the rod. As opposed to nylon, which performs well and is easy to use but looks funky, or other threads (cotton, rayon, and so on), which are unsuitable.

Snake Guide. A guide made of a single piece of wire shaped into a spiral loop.

Spine. The plane in which a rod section most resists bending.

Spline. One of the tapered triangular strips that make up a split-cane rod. This may be arbitrary, but let's say a strip becomes a spline when it is first beveled into a triangle. Of course, splines can be and often are referred to as strips during any stage of the rod-building process, but the raw square or rectangular strips of bamboo are almost never referred to as splines.

Staggering. The process of displacing adjacent strips prior to trimming them to length, so that no two adjacent strips have adjacent nodes. This is done for both structural and cosmetic reasons, and there are several common permutations.

Stress Curve. A set of numbers that describes the action of a rod in terms of the amount of bending force (stress) sustained by the rod at various points along its length during casting.

Stripping Guide. The first guide after the grip on the butt section, so called because one reaches up to this guide to strip in line. The most common stripping guide on bamboo rods is the Carbaloy boat-style guide. The coolest stripping guides have agate or agateen inserts, but they cost eight to ten times what the plain Carbaloy

ones do. The modern stripping guides with stamped frames and ceramic inserts probably are superior, functionally, to the old wire frames and metal with agate rings, but they look like hell and the difference in performance is slight enough that you should go with beauty.

Swell. A marked increase in diameter over a relatively short distance. The only place this is likely to occur on a fly rod is directly in front of the grip. This is referred to as a "swelled butt." A true swell, such as one might see on Thomas & Thomas rods, is difficult to achieve with planing forms simply because the bars don't like to bend that much over a short distance. A moderate swell is achievable, you just don't want to strip the threads on your adjustment screws.

Taper. A set of numbers that describes the measurements taken at regular intervals on a fly rod. These numbers, in turn, express the rod's action. Tapers may be expressed in 5- or 6-inch intervals; the former is more common in my experience, but makers who learned from the Crompton-Kreider (see Kreider in the Bibliography) school use the latter.

Tip. The thinnest, uppermost section of a fly rod. Also, the thinner end of any section; when one refers to the tip of the butt section, one means the end that carries the ferrule, as opposed to the end that carries the reel seat and grip.

Tip-Action Rod. A rod that flexes mainly in the upper one-third of its length. The shortness of the flexing length gives such a rod a "fast" action relative to its length, but the stresses imposed by such an action can make for a short-lived bamboo rod.

Tip Impact Factor. A unit used by Everett Garrison in his method of calculating rod tapers via the stress curve. Also called the "dynamic tip impact factor," this is a unit of weight consisting of the weight of the length of line the rod is designed to cast multiplied by four to approximate the inertia (and correspondingly greater weight) generated by casting. This is the load presented to the tip of the rod during casting, and how this weight is transferred down the rod is what Garrison's math is all about.

Tip-Top. The guide at the very tip of the rod, which, for fly rods, consists of a tube that fits over the tip and a pear shaped loop of wire soldered into the tube.

Welt. The reinforcing decorative ring or band at the mouth of the female ferrule.

Winding Check. A narrow band of metal that fits right against the front of the grip, serving to provide a small bit of decoration and balancing the reel seat aesthetically.

SELECTED BIBLIOGRAPHY

This bibliography is intended to give you a few leads to books that you may want (or need) to track down, not to list every rod-building book in existence. There's tons of information out there tucked away in old magazines or anthologies, and an exhaustive treatment would be beyond the scope of this book. For the record, there is no such thing as a bad book about rod building or bamboo rods; some are just more helpful than others. The books and publications listed below are those I have found useful and that you may be able to obtain. Many of them are either out of print or soon will be, but if there are enough book-buying rod builders out there, perhaps some of them will be reprinted.

Rod-Building Books

Cattanach, Wayne. *Handcrafting Bamboo Fly Rods.* Casnovia, Mich.: Wayne Cattanach, 1992.

A good book widely available today that offers start-to-finish instruction on building a bamboo rod. If you've ever attempted Garrison's math with a pencil and calculator, you will agree that the included Hexrod computer program, though primitive by today's standards for software fit and finish, is worth forty dollars by itself. The package includes a

variety of Wayne's tapers, instructions for building equipment, and an additional computer program for guide spacing. It's a highly useful book that gets right to the point. If the book you are holding is your first rod-building book, acquiring copies of the Garrison and Carmichael *A Master's Guide* and Wayne's *Handcrafting Bamboo Fly Rods* should be your next priorities.

Frazer, Perry. *Amateur Rodbuilding.* New York, New York: Outings Publishing, 1914.

One of my favorite books of its generation, and the source of the idea for using a 60-degree steel gauge to shave out the groove in planing forms. A small book and naturally overtaken by modern tools and adhesives to some extent, it nonetheless reads quite well and provides real insight into the craft. Long out of print, of course, but still occasionally obtainable and less expensive than many similar books. Highly deserving of a modern inexpensive reprint.

Garrison, Everett, with Hoagy B. Carmichael. *A Master's Guide to Building a Bamboo Fly Rod.* New York, N.Y.: Winchester Press, 1985.

This book is *the* source. It represents an act of devotion by Carmichael, who wrote the book and did all the work but remains virtually transparent as he details the methods and temperament of one of bamboo rod building's most lauded and influential craftsmen. The book has drifted in and out of print over the years and of this writing was recently reprinted in a limited edition of two thousand copies by Meadowbrook Press, all of which sold in a matter of weeks. Some of those undoubtedly were bought by booksellers who intend to sell them later at higher prices, so you may still be able to buy a new one, though probably not at the initial price of sixty dollars. Although the Martha's Glen first edition is all but unobtainable, copies of the more numerous edition by Winchester Press/Nick Lyons Books turn up for sale every once in a while. Many makers own copies, public libraries may be able to obtain a copy through interlibrary loan if they don't have it, and some Trout Unlimited chapter libraries may have it. In other words, it should be possible for a determined person to either obtain a copy or get a look at one. Doing so is highly recommended, because this is a pivotal rod-building how-to book. It is the first book to explain many aspects of the craft in detail with clear photos and illustrations, the first to put forth a mathematical tool for designing rod tapers from scratch, and the first, really, to discuss rod building in a precise and analytical manner. I just finished rereading the chapter titled Theory of the Six-Strip Rod. Brilliant.

Herter, George Leonard, and Jacques P. Herter. *Secret Fresh and Salt Water Fishing Tricks of the World's Fifty Best Professional Fishermen, Plus the Professional Secrets of Fishing Rods and How Fishing Rods are Made.* 10th ed. N.p.: Herters, 1961.

The dedication reads "To my wife Berthe E. Herter—No one else would ever love and care for a person with such fixed habits and strong opinions as myself." Such dedications usually are self-effacing, but the book tends to convince the reader that there may be something to this one. Obviously a fascinating person; despite some faults, the book is pithy and informative, and well worth having if you are fortunate enough to find a copy. There's a very good section on cane, an interesting section on rod design, and a section devoted to "Secrets of Professional Fishermen," most of which consist of sophisticated chumming. A couple are fabulously disgusting. Allow me to quote one of my favorites, "Using Snakes and Birds to Catch Trout:"

> Take two or three dead snakes and wire their tails together. Hang them up from a branch or stick over a pool in a trout stream. If you can not find snakes to kill shoot some black birds and wire their feet together and hang them up over a pool, they work just as well. Blow flies will soon lay their eggs in the snakes or birds and the eggs will turn into maggots. The maggots will start dropping off into the water and the trout will collect to feed on them. Go up toward the pool after about three days and quietly drop an imitation maggot into the pool on a light leader and small hook. You will catch any trout in the area. Do not get close enough to the pool so that the trout can see you.

Sounds like it would work, though one can't help wondering why the use of an imitation maggot was specified. Seriously, though, although there are many fine nuggets of information in this book, reading it is like pawing through a dusty attic: The items found are more often interesting than useful. Most of the tools and materials recommended were offered for sale by Herter's, and the fact that many are obsolete is overtaken by the fact that all are unavailable. Much space is devoted to debunking what the authors clearly viewed as false and pernicious ideas and methods. This gives the book a flavor that is either attractively opinionated and pugnacious or unattractively querulous, take your pick.

Holden, George Parker. *Idyl of the Split Bamboo.* Lyon, Miss.: Derrydale Press, 1993.

Holden was the mentor of Everett Garrison and influenced many other rod makers of that generation. *Idyl of the Split Bamboo* contains little information that cannot be obtained from more easily obtainable books, and many of the methods were rendered obsolete by Garrison, but it is a classic and a good read. Contains an appendix on growing silkworms and drawing one's own gut leaders that I found considerably more fascinating than the rod-building discussion. Available as of this writing only in astronomically expensive old editions or as part of the Derrydale Press Fly Fisherman's Gold limited edition series. If you can find it, by all means read it.

Kirkfield, Stuart. *The Fine Bamboo Fly Rod: A Master's Secrets of Restoration and Repair.* Harrisburg, Pa.: Stackpole Books, 1986.

Out of print, but some copies still are probably floating around. Not really a rod-building book, but some parts are of interest to the rod builder, who will sooner or later wind up having to refinish or repair an old rod. The section on removing ferrules is helpful, and the section on oxidizing ferrules is interesting (in an historical sense), dealing as it does with the old pre-EPA arsenic solution. Good luck obtaining arsenic trioxide, if you're actually mad enough to try it.

Kreider, Claude M. *The Bamboo Rod.* Grand Junction, Colo.: Centennial Publications, 1992.

A valuable little book that filled the gap for many builders between Holden and Garrison. It is still useful today, particularly for builders who wish to make do with a minimum of equipment. Heat treating using a steel pipe and blowtorch are discussed, as well as binding by hand and seating ferrules without a lathe. Interesting discussions of hollow-building and ammonia toning (darkening) are included as well. Glues have progressed a bit since this book was written, and it discusses planing in terms of nonadjustable Herter's forms, but it is well worth having and reading, particularly because it is currently available in an inexpensive reprint by Centennial Publications. Includes a variety of tapers, including bait-casting rods, though they are all given on 6-inch centers and are mostly large rods. The book's most interesting feature is its treatment of the five-strip rod and its construction. The fact that the equipment it refers to was primarily made by Herter's and has been unavailable for years limits its usefulness as a primary guide but in no way decreases its interest as an ancillary text.

Lambuth, Letcher. *The Angler's Workshop.* Seattle: Champoeg Press, 1979.

A fine book, currently out of print but deserving of a persistent search. Foreword by Roderick Haig-Brown. Lambuth covers the topic thoroughly, and although some of his tools, methods, and measurements have since been replaced by more effective ones, he includes an interesting comparative method of rod design, a comprehensive chapter on bamboo, and several projects for the angler in addition to fly rods. Lambuth was most well known for the spiral construction of his fly rods, meaning that the bound-together strips were twisted into a spiral when they were glued. Although he did not originate the method, his seems to be the only book to deal with it comprehensively. If you are interested in spiral rods, Lambuth is the source.

McClane, A. J., ed. *McClane's Standard Fishing Encyclopedia and International Angling Guide.* New York, N.Y.: Holt, Rinehart and Winston, 1965.

An interesting book in any number of ways, but particularly notable here because among its many entries are one on rod building and another on Tonkin cane. The rod-building section was written by Claude Kreider and Louis Feierabend and is both fairly complete and necessarily abbreviated. It may be viewed as a synopsis of Kreider's book but has merits of its own as well, including a drawing of a single-string binder that is slightly different from Garrison's.

Periodicals

The Planing Form. Ron Barch, Editor.

A lively forum of rod builders from around the world. Lots of tapers, articles on restoration, how to build equipment, ads selling rod-building stuff, and much more. A fine resource. The newsletter's first five years are also collected and available in book form.

Biographical, Appreciation

Keane, Martin J. *Classic Rods and Rodmakers.* Ashley Falls, Mass.: Classic Publishing Company, 1976.

Classic Rods is of definite interest to the rod builder: There are pictures of a couple of machines, including Powell's saw and the Winston binder, a picture of Jim Payne pressing nodes, and many other tantalizing glimpses. For the most part, though, it is a paean to the romance and myth of the legendary craftsman. There are no small fish here: Payne, Powell, Edwards, Leonard, Garrison, Dickerson, Howells, all big names and big reputations. A great deal of history and lore is well covered, and the collector will find the book indispensable. Lavishly and selectively illustrated. A good section on rod care and use that I would like to make required reading for all customers. Even if the book does lean more toward worship than evaluation, it is sincere and eloquent, and I wouldn't change it.

Spurr, Dick. *Classic Bamboo Rodmakers, Past and Present.* Grand Junction, Colo.: Centennial Publications, 1992.

A series of profiles on rod makers past and present. All biographies are one page long, give or take an inch or two, which means that some of them are longer than they need to be and some barely cover the most prominent facts. An interesting book, though, that digs well past the Garrisons and Paynes into contemporary full-time makers as well as the more prominent fifteen- or twenty-rods-a-year craftsmen.

Spurr, Dick, and Michael Sinclair. *Colorado Classic Cane: A History of the Colorado Bamboo Rodmakers.* Grand Junction, Colo.: Centennial Publications, 1991.

A very interesting book. I'm partial to Grangers, myself, and if they were still making rods, I'm not sure half the rod makers today could stay in business. Fine history, many illustrations, photos, excerpts from old catalogs. If you enjoy bamboo rods, you'll want to have this book.

Spurr, Dick and Gloria Jordan. *Wes Jordan: Profile of a Rodmaker.* Grand Junction, Colo.: Centennial Publications, 1992.

Another nice piece of historical work by Dick Spurr, and a good read. Jordan's rod building was a very different activity from what you or I will probably ever undertake. Where we might think in terms of dozens of rods, Jordan was thinking in thousands. Jordan's ideas on bamboo are very interesting and are laid out in some length, as are his ideas on impregnation and several other topics of immediate interest to the rod maker. Still, the most valuable contribution of this book is its history, its portrait of a man who was vital and central to our craft.

Stein, Gerald S., and James W. Schaaf. *Dickerson: The Man and His Rods.* Grand Junction, Colo.: Centennial Publications, 1991.

Every rod maker should have this book. Dickerson was the prototypical ingenious Yankee who made everything himself, and the narrative, photos, and documents are fascinating. The book provides a unique insight into the life of a legendary craftsman who made rods for a living. This includes hard info on what he did and how he did it, as well as a peripheral but distinct vision of how difficult it must have been to make ends meet. Both authors obviously are affectionate toward their subject, and, although they are not transparent, they certainly have their hearts in the right place. Highly recommended.

Miscellaneous

Classic Chronicle, The. Spring 1996 issue. Grand Junction, Colo.

Colvin, Fred H. *Running an Engine Lathe.* Bradley, Ill.: Lindsay Publications, 1987.

If you've never run a lathe before, it's an excellent idea to read up on it first. Lindsay Publications is a good source for quite a few books on machine tools. Many of their books are reprints of manuals that predate dirt, but they're inexpensive and still quite useful. The Colvin book is one of several that Lindsay offers.

Gierach, John. *Trout Bum.* Boulder, Colo.: Pruett Publishing Company, 1986.

Just in case there's anybody out there who *hasn't* discovered Gierach, he writes very well about fishing and other things. He fishes a lot, and because he does so almost exclusively with bamboo rods, they show up in his work with some frequency. It's my personal theory that his writing has had something to do with the resurgence bamboo rods have enjoyed, both in building and using. I suppose I *might* have eventually stumbled across a rod-building book somewhere, but if it weren't for the Cane Rods chapter in *Trout Bum,* I'm not sure it would ever have occurred to me that a bamboo rod was something that one person could build in his garage. There's also a nice chapter on bam-

boo in a later book, *Even Brook Trout Get the Blues.* All Gierach's books are good, but if you read *Trout Bum* you'll get the rest with no further urging from me.

Marden, Luis. "Bamboo, the Giant Grass." *National Geographic,* October 1980.

A fascinating, in-depth look at the raw material of our craft. Well worth a trip to the library or some time spent scrounging through the ubiquitous stack of *National Geographic*s at the thrift store.

Marinaro, Vincent. *In the Ring of the Rise.* New York, N.Y.: Crown Publishers, 1976.

Marinaro thought pretty deeply about a lot of things having to do with fly fishing, and he wasn't shy about putting forth his conclusions. He was a rod builder, and this book includes a chapter on rod action that I found to be quite interesting. His theories on rod design result from what I can only call a unique perspective, and I sure wish the tapers to some of his rods were available. Among other things, he states that the business about balancing the rod with a reel of correct weight is buncombe, that what you want is the lightest reel possible no matter how heavy the rod. Read the book, he's got a point. Available in a reprint from Lyons & Burford.

Mason, Jerry, ed. *The American Sportsman Treasury.* New York, N.Y.: Alfred A. Knopf, 1971.

Out of print, I'm sure. Sigh. Includes a fine piece on bamboo rods by Leonard M. Wright Jr. titled "The Ultimate Fly Rod." Many other good essays as well by some of our finest authors, including one on whitetail hunting by Lee Wulff.

Middleton, Harry. *The Earth is Enough.* Boulder, Colo.: Pruett Publishing Company, 1996.

There are bamboo rods in this book, and Middleton discusses them with an aficionado's reverence, but that's far from the only reason to read it. Harry, who died in 1993, was a talented writer who just had more bad luck than he could take. *The Earth is Enough* is his first and best book, and if you have any love of angling literature, or just literature in general, you should read it. I think the romance that attaches to bamboo rods provides as good a reason to build them as any, and that even the most prosaic "I-just-build-fishin'-poles-so-leave-me-alone-with-your-poetry-crap" curmudgeon is secretly warmed by the thought that his work will outlive him. And if we do get lost in the details and lose that thought, books like *The Earth is Enough* bring it back to life.

Muir, John. *How to Keep Your Volkswagen Alive*. 14th ed. Santa Fe, N. Mex.: John Muir Publications, 1990.

You're right, nothing about bamboo rods in here, but an awfully good book anyway. Easily the clearest, most encouraging how-to book I've ever read, and even though I've never owned a Volkswagen, I read it cover to cover. It's a common malady to look at machines as just things, mere items to be used, discarded, and replaced with new and better things, as though the raw materials and the work that went into them mean nothing beyond our own convenience. That's wrong, of course, but it's the cornerstone of our society. If consumerism is a poison, Muir's book is an antidote.

Quammen, David. "Reluctant Provider." *Outside*, June 1995.

Quammen's Natural Acts column in *Outside* is the prime reason I subscribe (or buy the thing at the store when my subscription lapses), and it seemed propitious that his piece in the last issue that came out before this book was due at the publisher's happened to deal with bamboo, specifically its reproductive strategy. The topic of reproductive strategy has its own special pertinence during the month of June, but that's another story. It's a good article, but then they all are.

The Winston Company Catalogue. Annual, available at Winston dealers nationwide.

A very nice catalog—the best rod catalog, in my opinion—full of interesting photos and text. Of particular interest to the rod builder is the discussion of bamboo rods, the description and diagrams of "Fluted Hollow Construction," the section on bamboo rod care, and the casting primer.